UNDERSTANDING
EUGÈNE IONESCO

UNDERSTANDING MODERN EUROPEAN AND LATIN AMERICAN LITERATURE

James Hardin, *Series Editor*

ADVISORY BOARD

EUGÈNE
IONESCO

NANCY LANE

UNIVERSITY OF SOUTH CAROLINA PRESS

Library of Congress Cataloging-in-Publication Data

Lane, Nancy, 1947–
    Understanding Eugène Ionesco / Nancy Lane.
        p.   cm. — (Understanding modern European and Latin American
    literature)
    Includes bibliographical references and index.
    ISBN 0–87249–981–2
    1. Ionesco, Eugène—Criticism and interpretation.   I. Title.
    II. Series.
    PQ2617.06Z743   1993
    842'.914—dc20   93–42291

For Kay McFarland

CONTENTS

EDITOR'S PREFACE

*U*nderstanding *Modern European and Latin American Literature* has been planned as a series of guides for undergraduate and graduate students and nonacademic readers. Like the volumes in its companion series, *Understanding Contemporary American Literature,* these books provide introductions to the lives and writings of prominent modern authors and explicate their most important works.

Modern literature makes special demands, and this is particularly true of foreign literature, in which the reader must contend not only with unfamiliar, often arcane artistic conventions and philosophical concepts, but also with the handicap of reading the literature in translation. It is a truism that the nuances of one language can be rendered in another only imperfectly (and this problem is especially acute in fiction), and the fact that the works of European and Latin American writers are situated in a historical and cultural setting quite different from our own can be as great a hindrance to the understanding of these works as the linguistic barrier. For this reason, the UMELL series emphasizes the sociological and historical backgrounds of the writers treated. The peculiar philosophical and cultural traditions of a given culture may be particularly important for an understanding of certain authors, and these are taken up in the introductory chapter and also in the discussion of those works to which this information is relevant. Beyond this, the books treat the specifically literary aspects of the author under discussion and attempt to explain the complexities of contemporary literature lucidly. The books are conceived as introductions to the authors covered, not as comprehensive analyses. They do not provide detailed summaries of plot because they are meant to be used in conjunction with the books they treat, not as a substitute for study of the original works. The purpose of the books is to provide information and judicious literary assessment of the major works in the most compact, readable form. It is our hope that the UMELL series will help to increase knowledge and understanding of European and Latin American cultures and will serve to make the literature of those cultures more accessible.

J.H.

CHRONOLOGY

1909	Born on 26 November in Slatina, Romania. Son of Eugen Ionescu and Thérèse Ipcar (see chapter 1, note 2).
1911	Sister Marilina born; family moves to Paris.
1912 (1913?)	Brother Mircea born; he dies of meningitis at eighteen months.
1916	Father deserts family, returns to Romania.
1917(?)	Father marries Hélène Buruiana (nicknamed Lola).
1917–1919	Sojourns at La Chapelle-Anthenaise with sister.
1920–1922	Lives in Paris with mother and grandparents; discovers literature and writes first plays.
1922	Returns to Bucharest to live with father and stepmother.
1926	Leaves father's home.
1928	Finishes secondary school (Lycée Saint-Sava).
1929	Enrolls in Bucharest University.
1930	Publishes first article in magazine *Zodiac*.
1931	Publishes *Elegii pentru fiinte mici* (Elegies for Minuscule Beings, a volume of poetry).
1932–1935	Contributes to *Azi, Viata literara,* and other literary magazines; military service.
1934	Receives degree (Capacitate) from University of Bucharest; publishes first book, *Nu* (No) (essays).

1936	Marries Rodica Burileanu; death of mother.
1936–1938	Works as French teacher in Cernavada, then at orthodox seminaries; becomes literary critic for magazine *Facla*.
1939	Leaves Romania and arrives in Paris with wife.
1940–1941	Brief return to Romania; efforts to return to France.
1942–1944	Lives in Marseille during war; premature birth of daughter Marie-France (26 August 1944), in Vichy.
1945	Returns to Paris, rue Claude Terrasse.
1945–1950	Works as proofreader, translator, and free-lance writer; death of father (1948).
1950	Premiere of *The Bald Soprano* (written 1948).
1951	Premiere of *The Lesson* (written 1950).
1952	Premiere of *The Chairs* (written 1951).
1953	Premiere of *Victims of Duty* (written 1952).
1954	Premiere of *Amédée, or How to Get Rid of it* (written 1953).
1955	Premiere of *Jack, or The Submission* (written 1950); premiere (in Swedish) of *The New Tenant* (written 1953).
1956	Premiere of *Improvisation, or The Shepherd's Chameleon* (written 1955).
1957	French premiere of *The New Tenant;* premiere of *The Future is in Eggs* (written 1951).
1958	London Controversy.
1959	World premiere of *Rhinoceros* (in German) (written 1958); premiere of *The Killer* (written 1957).
1960	French premiere of *Rhinoceros*.
1961	Writes scenario *Anger* for Sylvain Dhomme's segment of 1962 film *Les Sept péchés capitaux;* named "Chevalier des arts et lettres."

1962	Premiere of *Exit the King* (written 1962); *Notes et Contre-notes* (*Notes and Counter Notes*); *La Photo du colonel* (*The Colonel's Photograph*); world premiere (in German, at Dusseldorf) of *A Stroll in the Air.*
1963	French premiere of *A Stroll in the Air* at Odéon (national theater).
1964	World premiere of *Hunger and Thirst* at Dusseldorf (30 December).
1966	French premiere of *Hunger and Thirst* at Comédie française (28 February); acclaimed reprise of *Exit the King,* directed by Jacques Mauclair.
1967	*Journal en miettes* (*Fragments of a Journal*).
1968	*Présent passé. Passé présent* (*Present Past Past Present*).
1969	*Découvertes;* receives two literary prizes (Grand Prix littéraire Prince Pierre de Monaco, Grand Prix National du théâtre).
1970	World premiere (in German) of *The Killing Game* at Dusseldorf; French premiere of same play; *La Vase* (*The Mire*), film for German television. Ionesco elected to Académie française; receives Austrian State Prize for European literature; awarded Legion of Honor.
1971	Received into Académie française; awarded honorary doctorate, New York University; broadcast of *The Mire.*
1972	Premiere of *Macbett.*
1973	*Le Solitaire* (*The Hermit*). Premiere of *A Hell of a Mess!;* receives Jerusalem Prize.
1974	Receives International Writers' Prize.
1975	Premiere of *Man With Bags;* awarded honorary doctorate, University of Tel Aviv.
1977	*Antidotes.*

1978	International Colloquium at Cerisy-la-Salle devoted to Ionesco.
1979	*Un Homme en question;* acclaimed reprise of *Exit the King,* directed by Jorge Lavelli.
1980	Artist in residence at University of Southern California; participates in seminar on his work. Premiere of *Journeys Among the Dead* in New York.
1981	*Le Noir et le blanc* (drawings and essay; a limited edition of two hundred copies, reprinted by Gallimard in 1985 as *Le Blanc et le noir*); beginning in this year, Ionesco's paintings, drawings, and prints are exhibited around the world.
1982	*Hugoliade* (translated from Romanian).
1985	Receives Ingersoll Prize.
1986	*Non* (translated from Romanian).
1987	*La Quête intermittente.*
1988	Premiere of opera *Maximilien Kolbe.*
1989	Receives a Molière (prize awarded by Antenne 2 television network and the Association professionelle et artistique du théâtre).

A NOTE ON CITATIONS AND TRANSLATIONS

Page references are given in the text for all citations. For works by Ionesco, most references are to published American translations for most plays and for other works, abbreviated in the text as follows:

> *NCN = Notes and Counter Notes*
> *FJ = Fragments of a Journal*
> *PP = Present Past Past Present*

Some citations are given in my translation of the original French; this is the case for works not widely available in English, including the novel *Le Solitaire* (*The Hermit*) and the plays *Macbett, L'Homme aux valises* (*Man With Bags*), and *Voyages chez les morts* (*Journeys Among the Dead*), as well as the book that appeared in Romanian as *Nu* and in French as *Non* (No). For these works, as well as for other writings whose abbreviations are listed below, the page references are to the French editions (for the plays in this category, page references are to the Pléiade edition of 1991).

> *ENT = Entre la Vie et le rêve* (the revised and expanded edition of 1972; the earlier 1966 edition of Claude Bonnefoy's interviews appears in English as *Conversations with Eugène Ionesco*)
> *DEC = Découvertes*
> *Homme = Un Homme en question*
> *Anti = Antidotes*
> *Quête = La Quête intermittente*

Complete publication information for all editions used is given in the bibliography. For the English language translations of the plays, the American translation precedes the British one; there are differences between the two.

UNDERSTANDING
EUGÈNE IONESCO

CHAPTER ONE

Introduction

Eugène Ionesco's life, like his work, can best be understood as the product of conflicts, contradictions, and dichotomies.[1] He was born on 26 November 1909 in Slatina, Romania.[2] His Romanian father, Eugen Ionescu, was a lifelong civil servant (working in law and law enforcement). Ionesco's memoirs portray his father as somewhat cruel and despotic in his private life and as unprincipled and opportunistic in his public life, readily changing political hue in order to adapt to whatever regime was in power in Romania. His mother (née Thérèse Ipcar) was French,[3] and the family moved to Paris in 1911, the year his younger sister Marilina was born. Thus Ionesco's first language—his mother tongue—was French. A brother, Mircea, was born in 1912 or 1913, only to die of meningitis eighteen months later; this event was Ionesco's first encounter with death, and he has been haunted by mortality ever since.

The first years in Paris were difficult; the family moved often, and Ionesco's parents fought constantly. In 1916 Ionesco's father returned to Romania, supposedly to serve in the military. In fact, he pursued the study of law, divorced his wife on grounds of desertion, and remarried, all without Mme Ionesco's knowledge; she thought him dead in the war. She went to work in a factory, putting Eugène briefly into a children's home at Longjumeau (near Paris), where he suffered from being separated from her.

Ionesco and his sister spent the years 1917–19 as boarding students in La Chapelle-Anthenaise, a small village in the Mayenne, about 130 miles southwest of Paris. These years were the happiest of Ionesco's childhood, an Edenic period evoked repeatedly both in his memoirs and in his work. On the old farm named Le Moulin, Ionesco enjoyed a feeling of extraordinary well-being, both sheltered from harm and free to roam.[4] Upon his return to live with his mother and grandparents, around the age of eleven, the unhappy young boy felt that the streets of Paris had become a prison, and he found some consolation for the first time in literature. Inspired by Flaubert's "A Simple Heart," he began to write himself. His first efforts included an apocalyptic film scenario in which a group of young boys demolish a house (Ionesco's film scenario, *Anger,* produced in 1962, takes up the same subject), a "patriotic play," some poetry and a journal.

In 1922 Mme Ionesco took the two children to Romania, since Ionesco's father had been awarded custody of them. Their stepmother Hélène sent Ionesco's sister back to her mother after a month, but Ionesco remained. He was something of an outcast in his new family, taking his meals alone in his room. Furthermore, he had to learn a new language, and this experience has left its traces in his work in the form of a certain hostility to and estrangement from language itself.

Ionesco's difficult relationship with his father during this period marked the beginning of a lifelong attitude of revolt against all forms of authority. Coupled with resentment of his father's mistreatment of his mother was his resentment at finding himself in a strange land. In a volume of memoirs originally published in 1968, Ionesco specifically rejects the idea of a "fatherland" in favor of his "mother country": "My country, for my part, was France, simply because I lived there with my mother when I was a child, during my first years in school, and because my country could be no other country than the one in which my mother lived" (*PP* 16). Moreover, he soon discovered that his father was a brutal bigot: shortly after arriving in Bucharest, he witnessed a scene in which his father beat an elderly Jewish tenant who had been living in a small house behind his.[5]

Ionesco left his father's house in 1926, finished secondary school in 1928, and enrolled in Bucharest University in 1929; he supported himself by giving French lessons. He began to publish his own work in Romanian: an article in the magazine

Zodiac in 1930, a volume of poetry entitled *Elegii pentru fiinte mici* (Elegies for Minuscule Beings) in 1931, and, in 1934, a series of essays entitled *Nu* (No), in which he first attacked and then rehabilitated famous Romanian writers, thereby showing how fickle and unfounded literary criticism can be. (His animus against certain critics continues to this day.) During this period he also finished his military service and wrote for several literary magazines. In 1934 he received his degree in literature from the University of Bucharest. He married Rodica Burileanu, a philosophy student, on 12 July 1936; three months later his mother died.

For the next two years, he worked as a French teacher, became the literary critic for the magazine *Facla,* and enjoyed a growing reputation as a critic of promise. Alarmed by the rising tide of fascism around him, he determined to get back to France, and when the opportunity arose to study in Paris with a grant from the French Institute of Bucharest, he seized it. He was to write a doctoral thesis entitled "Sin and Death in French Poetry Since Baudelaire," but he has acknowledged that the thesis was largely a pretext to allow him to return to France, and he never finished it. It was around this time that he had his last meeting with his father, who died a little more than ten years later.

Ionesco and his wife arrived in Paris in 1939, only to leave again for Romania in 1940, fearing the German occupation. They immediately regretted this decision and began nearly two years of desperate efforts to obtain the passports and visas necessary to return again to France. They were finally successful and spent the years 1942–44 in Marseille before settling in Paris in 1945. Their only child, Marie-France, was born (prematurely) on 26 August 1944. (The four "Tales for Children Less Than Three Years Old" published in *Present Past Past Present* reveal a father with all the whimsical, mordant humor and linguistic ingenuity that we find in the early plays.)

Ionesco was making a living as a proofreader and free-lance writer when his long career as a playwright was launched with the 1950 production of *La Cantatrice chauve* (*The Bald Soprano*), a play he had written shortly after the war. Because he was over forty when his first play was produced, he has sometimes been characterized as a late-blooming novice playwright, a character-ization he vigorously rejects.[6] The play (or rather anti-play), in-spired in part by Ionesco's efforts to learn English, was initially turned down by the publisher Bernard Grasset and the Comédie française, among others. Nicolas Bataille, just beginning his ca-reer at the age of twenty-one, finally produced it at the tiny Théâtre des Noctambules on 11 May. It closed after a short run to small audiences, but Ionesco's name had become known to a few critics and directors, and he soon emerged as one of the lead-ing avant-garde playwrights of the early 1950s, along with Samuel Beckett and Arthur Adamov. (Revived on a double bill with *The Lesson* in 1957, *The Bald Soprano* is still playing today at the Théâtre de la Huchette in Paris.)

Ionesco began to write plays at a furious pace, and every season saw at least one Ionesco piece produced in the small experimental theaters of Paris. The early plays are largely one-act pieces or short sketches: *La Leçon* (*The Lesson,* pre-miered in 1951), *Les Chaises* (*The Chairs,* premiered in 1952), *Victimes du devoir* (*Victims of Duty,* premiered in 1953), *Jacques, ou la soumission* (*Jack, or The Submission,* premiered in 1955). At the same time, Ionesco began to publish short stories, all of which were subsequently rewritten for the stage or screen. Ionesco's first three-act play (*Amédée,* based on the story "Oriflamme") was produced in 1954, and by the mid-1950s he had become known to the English-speaking theater world with the London productions of *The Lesson* (1955), *The Bald So-prano* (1956), and *The New Tenant* (1956). In January 1958, Tony Richard-son's double bill of *The Chairs* and *The Lesson* introduced New York's theatergoers to the avant-garde French playwright.

With *Tueur sans gages* (*The Killer,* written in 1957, pre-miered in 1959) and *Rhinoceros* (written in 1958, premiered in 1959), Ionesco's career entered a new phase. These plays were the first two of four whose main character is named Bérenger, the other two being *Le Roi se meurt* (*Exit the King,* written and premiered in 1962) and *Le Piéton de l'air* (*A Stroll in the Air,* written and premiered in 1962). The plays of the Bérenger cycle are longer, more classically structured, more literary than the early works. When *Rhinoceros* had its French

4

premiere on 22 January 1960 at the Odéon-Théâtre de France, a national theater subsidized by the government, the avant-garde iconoclast of ten years earlier officially entered the ranks of the modern classics. Ionesco's status as a revered contemporary master was confirmed when *La Soif et la faim (Hunger and Thirst)* had its French premiere at the Comédie française on 28 February 1966. He was elected to the Académie française in 1970 and received on 25 February 1971.

Critics have been sharply divided about the merits of Ionesco's work: both French and British critics of the left at first defended and praised the innovative absurdist (Martin Esslin's term, made popular by his influential study *The Theatre of the Absurd*), while conservative critics dismissed his work as meaningless trash. Soon, however, some critics of the left turned against him, denouncing in his theater an empty formalism and a refusal to grapple with socioeconomic reality, preferring Brechtian, committed, or Marxist theater practice. With Ionesco's increasing popularity and new, more lyrical and accessible style, other former champions from the left accused him of selling out to the establishment, while some of the conservative critics who had failed to understand his earlier work now lamented his loss of invention and experimentation. Ionesco has always been quick to respond, both in the press and in the theater: his play *L'Impromptu de l'Alma (Improvisation,* premiered in 1956) was a scathing satiric attack on both bourgeois and left-wing critics, and in 1958 he became embroiled in what came to be known as the London Controversy, an extended exchange of open letters with Kenneth Tynan, Philip Toynbee, Orson Welles, and others. Beginning with his *Notes and Counter Notes* (1962), he has published six volumes of memoirs and essays in which he expresses at length his animosity toward every kind of dogma and ideology (particularly those of the left) and his profound belief in the freedom of the individual.

After Ionesco's induction into the Académie, he seemed to be searching for a new style in *Jeux de massacre (The Killing Game,* premiered in 1970), based in part on Daniel Defoe's *Journal of the Plague Years* and Antonin Artaud's writings on the plague; and *Macbett* (1972), adapted from Shakespeare.

Since then his work has become increasingly personal and introspective. He has written a novel (*Le Solitaire* [*The Hermit*], 1973) and three plays: *Ce Formidable Bordel!* (*A Hell of a Mess!*, premiered in 1973), based on *Le Solitaire; L'Homme aux valises* (*Man With Bags,* 1975); and *Voyages chez les morts* (*Journeys Among the Dead,* 1980). Each work is primarily a transcription of Ionesco's own dreams, fears, and obsessions as set forth over the years in his published journals, with a protagonist who is clearly the author's alter ego. Encouraged by his friends, Ionesco has also published some of his drawings in *Découvertes* (1969) and *Le Noir et le blanc* (1981), and he continues to publish fervent political essays and reviews in the French press. He has received many literary prizes, honorary degrees, and decorations.[7] He lives today with his wife in Paris.

The first place to look for a guide to understanding Eugène Ionesco is in his own writing; there are few writers who have commented as extensively on their own work as he. A critic himself before he became well-known as a playwright, he has continued to be a prolific writer of essays. He has published several volumes of his journals and memoirs and has granted many interviews in which he talks at length not only about his work but about intimate details of his personal life. Certain themes surface again and again: his struggle with language; his lifelong obsession with the fundamental issues of meaning, time, death, and religion; his hatred of dogma and antipathy toward authority; his fervent defense of the individual's right to freedom. Just as in his work, in these interviews impish wit and congenial warmth exist side by side with pessimism and despair.

The value of Ionesco's theater lies not so much in its recurring themes, however; they are not original or compelling in themselves. Ionesco's theater entertains audiences because of his ability to create some memorable and explosive theatrical experiences. Driven to write for the theater, he has said, because he found it unreal, contrived, and unconvincing, he set out to demolish it. Thus his early plays are anti-plays, iconoclastic attacks on the conventions of mainstream, boulevard theater. Designed to make audiences uncomfortable, they are original, explosive, outrageous.

The Bald Soprano, The Lesson, and *The Chairs* have remained fresh—funny, disturbing, and moving by turn—to this day.

The paradox of Ionesco's career is that his iconoclasm brought him early recognition and popularity among the cultural elite of Paris in the 1950s, and his anti-theater became a "new theater" with unconventional conventions of its own. From the late 1950s on, Ionesco sought with increasing difficulty, and with uneven success, to remain innovative. *Rhinoceros* and *Exit the King* stand out among his mature work as powerful theater, having already entered the repertoire of twentieth-century classics. In much of his later work Ionesco returns again and again to the themes that recur in his earlier plays, however, obsessively reworking the issues that haunt his personal life.

The Struggle with Language

Since Ionesco's first language was French, his first encounters with literature, around the age of twelve, were in French. Forced to learn Romanian when he was taken to live with his father at age thirteen, he clung to French and suffered from the separation: "And yes, then I felt torn apart, I felt exiled" (*ENT* 23). He learned Romanian quickly, however, and published his first works in that language, only to have to relearn how to write French when he returned to France seventeen years later. This wrenching experience of having to learn and relearn languages is perhaps one reason why estrangement from and fascination with language hold a central place in his work. It was, in fact, his efforts to learn English that led him to write his first play (or so the story goes).

Conscious that "he who speaks is not *in* his language" (*PP* 141), Ionesco has often felt alienated from or hostile to the spoken language, not because he lacks facility in it (on the contrary, he is an engaging, witty conversationalist) but because he mistrusts it. For Ionesco it is far too easy to be carried away by words and to become lost in them: "The hardest thing is to avoid being taken in, that is, to avoid being carried away—to speak words and not to allow words to speak you" (*DEC* 97–98). His career represents in a certain sense his lifelong struggle against words: "The *logos* once meant action as well; it has become paralysis. What's a word? Whatever is not lived with ardent intensity. . . . Words no longer demonstrate: they chatter. Words are literary. They are escape. They stop silence from speaking. . . . Words wear out thought, they impair it" (*FJ* 73). "How," he has written, "with the aid of words, can I express everything that words hide? How can I express what is inexpressible?" (*PP* 168). He sometimes feels that he is "the victim of words, . . . dragged along, carried away by the flood of words" (*PP* 169). Certainly, such is the case in Ionesco's theater, especially the early works.

Ionesco himself labeled his first play a "tragedy of language" (*NCN* 179). The tragedy of language is its inability to express, a theme to which Ionesco repeatedly returns in his plays, journals, and essays. Finding realistic or bourgeois theater inauthentic and inadequate as an art form, he set about in his first plays to undermine and dismantle the spoken language. In these plays, one might say that the characters do not use language so much as language uses them, carrying them off on a wild torrent of language gone mad. *The Bald Soprano* ends in the chaos of disintegrated meaning, with the Smiths and the Martins shouting disconnected sounds and syllables at each other; it is language that brutalizes and kills the young student in *The Lesson;* and language is what ultimately beats Jack into submission in *Jack, or The Submission.* Ionesco was aiming, he said, to "break the neck of pompous verbiage on the stage" (*ENT* 187). "My first plays, *The Bald Soprano* for example, were quite simply about the astonishment I felt at being confronted with this world and these people who talk without saying anything, or whose words are incomprehensible to me. Language is incomprehensible because people don't talk about the most important thing" (*Homme* 21). The early plays are for this reason a parody of theater and theatrical language—*The Bald Soprano* is subtitled "anti-play," *Amédée* is subtitled "pseudodrama." Speaking of *The Bald Soprano* and *Jack, or The Submission* in 1955, Ionesco called these plays "a kind of parody or caricature of boulevard theatre, boulevard theatre going bad, gone mad. In *The Bald Soprano* the characters spoke a language made of the most threadbare everyday clichés, so commonplace that banality acquired a certain strangeness. . . . *Jack* is primarily a family drama or a parody of family drama. . . . Both the language and behavior of the characters is noble and distinguished. But this language gets dislocated and disintegrates" (*NCN* 194–95).

The deconstruction of everyday language in these early plays is explosive and outrageous—at times exceedingly funny and at other times menacing and disquieting. The shocking language and scathing, daring humor of these plays are reminiscent of Alfred Jarry's violent farce *Ubu Roi* (1896), that turning point in the history of avant-garde theater much admired by Ionesco. The premiere of *The Bald Soprano* in 1950 produced, in fact, the same sort of bombshell effect on the Parisian theater scene that *Ubu Roi* had had some fifty years earlier. Daring neologisms, deformed clichés, nonsensical associations of sounds, outrageous puns, and crude, sometimes scatological humor characterize the work of both authors. Even as Ionesco's work has become less violent, more poetic, or more accessible, his language remains rich in humor, invention, and mordant wit.

Paradoxically, it is through language itself that many of Ionesco's characters try to recover the lost paradise that preceded language, or to "express the inexpressible." As the Old Woman in *The Chairs* says, "It's by talking that we find ideas, words, and even ourselves, in our own words, and the city too, the garden—maybe we can find everything and we won't be orphans any more" (139). Choubert in *Victims of Duty,* Amédée in the play of the same name, Bérenger in *The Killer,* and Jean in *Hunger and Thirst* use poetic language to try to find "the garden, everything," but their quest always ends in failure. These characters' struggles with language parallel Ionesco's efforts to transcend the limits of language in his own theater.

Faced with widespread misunderstanding of his first plays, Ionesco soon felt a certain need to explain himself, and his career entered a second phase or second style. No longer able to write comedies, he began to write "gloomier dramas": "the more amusing my writing appeared the more my unhappiness increased. . . . I found a certain satisfaction in writing about misery and anguish; how can one talk of anything different when one is aware that one's going to die?" (*FJ* 104). Beginning as early as *The Chairs* (1952), the language of the plays becomes more coherent and literary until, in *The Killer* and *Exit the King,* for example, Ionesco later found that the language was "too discursive and too clear." "Those plays," Ionesco continues, "were understood too soon, too quickly, and they no longer hold any mystery. They are now easily explained in schools and universities" (*ENT* 171). Reflecting in a 1978 interview on this evolution to a more accessible style, Ionesco again expressed misgivings: "I should have continued with the inextricable, the incomprehensible. I think that it is only insofar as people are faced with the incomprehensible that they approach a possible understanding" (*Homme* 21).

After *Hunger and Thirst* (1966), which had been commissioned for the Comédie française, Ionesco's struggle with language—or at least with writing—reached a point of crisis. In treatment for depression in 1967, he wrote, "I shall write no more dramas henceforward. I shall only write to amuse myself. I really ought not to write any more at all, but I have to make up plays and stories since I am a professional author, since that's my function. But really it's all worth very little. Literature is something derivative. . . . I shan't write any more . . . except to construct objects, little make-believe worlds" (*FJ* 100). In one sense, Ionesco did stop writing dramas after this period, if we define drama as an original structured fiction invented for the stage. *The Killing Game* (1970), *Macbett* (1972) and *A Hell of a Mess!* (1973), all adaptations, mark a transition and a search for a new style; and his two most recent plays (*Man With Bags,* 1975, and *Journeys Among the Dead,* 1980) consist almost exclusively of Ionesco's dreams and memories, many of which had already appeared in his journals, essays, and interviews. With this new, third phase of his career, Ionesco has sought to find a more hermetic, allusive language that would be capable of translating his dreams into scenic terms. Speaking about *Man With Bags,* Ionesco said, "The audience was perhaps a bit confused because it's a rather hermetic play, made of images and silences much more so than words. These images, these silences are intended to be a clear break with the wordiness of *Exit the King, A Hell of a Mess* or the end of *The Killer*" (*ENT* 170).

Ionesco's struggle with language ends in an impasse. In his personal life, the impasse leads to his conversion to a very mystical Catholicism, in which God becomes the interlocutor who doesn't need words: "There is no need for words; they only confuse us. We are all alike, all the billions of human beings on earth" (*Quête* 30). This silencing of the word has led to his abandoning theater in favor of painting: "Literature, that used to excite me so (that interested me above all else), is of no interest to me today. . . . Colors, and nothing but colors, are the only language that I can speak. . ." (*Quête* 12–13). The irony, of course, is that, even after giving up the struggle, Ionesco remains trapped in language; he cannot stop talking and writing about the inadequacy of "the word."

The Language of Images

As a young student of literature, Ionesco had admired the Italian philosopher and aesthetician Benedetto Croce (1866–1952) and retained from his writing a fundamental distinction between two kinds of thought: logical, discursive thought and aesthetic, intuitive thought (*ENT* 21). As he became a more and more successful playwright, he searched increasingly for a means of dramatic expression that would come closer to revealing "what words hide." Distinguishing his own theater from a purely "literary" kind of theater (that of Vauthier or Audiberti, for example), he tried "to create a different kind of theater and to find for it a poetic tone that is not in the spoken language but in the language of images" (*ENT* 187).

In the early plays, Ionesco was trying to "strangle the shoddy eloquence on the stage" (*ENT* 187). Looking back toward *The Bald Soprano* in 1987, he wrote, "I might even say that language explodes into the silence of incomprehension, bursts it open, shatters it in order to be reconstituted differently. A purer language that went right to the limit, right up to the edge of silence" (*Quête* 30). The "purer language" here is inextricably linked to theatrical performance. Nicolas Bataille's production of *The Bald Soprano* was a revelation to Ionesco, who had never seen a play produced before (*NCN* 59). Because the signifying system of a theatrical production encompasses much more than

11

words, a play always expresses what words hide. Having set out to demolish theater because of its inadequacy as a medium of expression, Ionesco had discovered the ability of scenic writing (or the language of images) to dislocate the real and reveal the strangeness of the world.

Most of Ionesco's most expressive and successful use of *mise en scène* and specifically theatrical scenic language dates from the plays of the 1950s (from *Jack* through *The New Tenant*). At the end of *The Chairs,* for example, the mute poetry of the stage full of empty chairs is a moving image of the ontological void evoked in the play. Similarly, the stage in *The New Tenant* is gradually invaded by piles of furniture that bury the single human actor, so that the final image in the play is an eerily silent vision of humanity displaced by the products of our own materialism. Other objects proliferate out of control during this period: in *Amédée,* a corpse dressed in formal wear grows to enormous size and displaces the human characters before turning into a brightly colored balloon; the newly-married couple in *The Future is in Eggs* are literally buried under thousands of eggs. Likewise, characters may be distorted physically by means of masks, a visual correlative of their inability to articulate any coherent message: Roberta, the lovely bride-to-be of *Jack,* wears a mask with three noses, and the long-awaited Orator in *The Chairs* is costumed to resemble a large puppet. Lighting is an important means of expression as early as *The Chairs,* in which the quality of the lighting creates disquieting effects, shading as it does from murky green to brilliance and back to darkness at the end.

With the more personal and humanized style of the late works, the language becomes more and more dominant as a means of expression, and the plays are sometimes poetic and lyrical, sometimes (as Ionesco said), too discursive and clear. Even in the most discursive (or "popular") plays of the Bérenger cycle, however, the final image on stage may have an emotional impact that makes the play particularly memorable: *The Killer* ends in near darkness, with Bérenger on his knees in wordless submission to death; the strange music and shadowy images of rhinoceros heads on the wall behind an illogically defiant Bérenger in *Rhinoceros* leave a haunting impression; and the slow dissolve into darkness at the end of *Exit the King* is profoundly moving. Less successful are other scenic effects that rely more heavily on elaborate special effects, as in *A Stroll in the Air* or *Hunger and Thirst.*

Ionesco is not the only playwright to confront the inadequacy of words as a means of theatrical expression, of course. Like Ionesco, Samuel Beckett struggled throughout his career with the problem of language and expression; unlike Ionesco, however, he was able to find a way out of the impasse. Like his characters from Didi and Gogo in *Waiting for Godot* to Mouth in *Not I,* Beckett was always acutely conscious of the double impossibility of meaning anything and of stopping the flow of expression. Where Ionesco's theater became perhaps too garrulous, Beckett's became more and more reticent, yet expressive. This is because Beckett, unlike Ionesco, sought to move away from representation toward presentation. Beckett was able to refine a purely theatrical "parole," in Antonin Artaud's sense of the word. Artaud called for a specifically scenic language that is immediate rather than mimetic, a concrete poetry of space that would be capable of expressing without signifying, presenting without representing. All of Beckett's later work in the theater exploits the expressive power of this kind of "concrete language"; the impact of his late works is profoundly visceral. Even in Ionesco's late dream plays, in which he was searching earnestly for a way of translating dream imagery directly onto the stage, the level of meaning is as verbal and intellectual as a psychoanalytic session. Ionesco himself has recognized that he might have pursued a different course. Speaking to an interviewer in 1978, he said, "I should have remained more profoundly enigmatic and accepted the risk that the critics and spectators would understand nothing. Beckett was more successful in this regard" (*Homme* 21).

Dreams, the Unconscious, and Surrealism

Ionesco's is a very personal work that draws heavily on his dreams. As he told Claude Bonnefoy in 1977, "Dreams are drama itself. . . . I believe that dreams are lucid thought, more lucid than conscious thought, imaged thought, and, at the same time, that they are already theater." (*ENT* 12). Some plays originated with a single image from a dream: *Amédée* began with a dream of a corpse lying in the hallway of a house Ionesco lived in, and a recurring dream of flying was the source of *A Stroll in the Air.* Other plays (*Jack, Exit the King,* and *Hunger and Thirst,* for example) contain transcriptions of dreams that Ionesco had shortly before or during their composition. As he told Bonnefoy, however, he transcribed remembered dream material in these plays in a fashion too articulate to convey the "incoherent coherence" of dreams, and his last two plays (*Man With Bags* and *Journeys Among the Dead*) represent his attempt to present his dreams unaltered, "without cheating" (*ENT* 73). He has elaborated a personal dramatic vocabulary in which the traces of the unconscious revealed in dreams through myths, Jungian archetypes, and symbols play an important role.[8] For him, however, "the great, auspicious symbols that arise from the depths of the psyche" have a meaning that is the opposite of the one generally ascribed to them. Thus the father figure in Ionesco's work is a monster and tyrant; fire is a symbol of death rather than purification; the earth is a symbol of death; the interiors of houses are tombs, not shelters; water is a symbol for anguish and decomposition (*FJ* 133–34).

Ionesco has long been engaged in exploring the unconscious, although he prefers Jung to Freud, he says, because Jung allows for a spiritual dimension lacking in Freud (*FJ* 60). One of his plays (*Victims of Duty*) is, in fact, an explicit depiction of the protagonist's descent into his past and his unconscious. He has affirmed on several occasions that all of his plays "have their origin in two fundamental states of consciousness": evanescence, transparency, and light versus heaviness, opacity, and darkness (*NCN* 162). When Claude Bonnefoy suggested that there is a basic opposition in Ionesco's theater between light, air, and weightlessness on the one hand and thickness and heaviness (usually associated with water or sinking into mud) on the other, Ionesco readily agreed: "I feel either very heavy or very light, or much too heavy or much too light. Lightness is euphoric evanescence that can become tragic or painful when accompanied by anguish. When there is no anguish, it is ease of being" (*ENT* 36). In Jungian terms, says Ionesco, this split between two states of consciousness makes what he writes neurotic, an expression of the lack of integration and balance between earth and sky. His feeling that the earth and sky were perfectly integrated at La Chapelle-Anthenaise was, in fact, one reason that he found such happiness there (*ENT* 15).

Like the surrealists, Ionesco seeks to lower the barrier that separates dreaming from waking life, the conscious from the unconscious, thereby achieving a new manner of being that might approximate that state of grace for which he and his characters long. As defined by André Breton in the *First Manifesto of Surrealism* (1924), surrealism is "pure psychic automatism" whose goal is to allow access to "pure thought," unencumbered by any constraints imposed by reason, morals, or aesthetic considerations. Automatic writing (transcribing whatever happens to flow from one's pen in free association) is one way of exploring this privileged state, and another is the recording of dreams. These surrealist practices are closely related to the free association techniques of psychoanalysis, a field of great interest to both Breton and Ionesco. Breton was one of the first French intellectuals to discover and appreciate Freud. Ionesco expressed his admiration for Breton and for the surrealist project on the occasion of Breton's death in 1966: "This theoretician of the irrational enlarged, deepened, increased reason; irrationality thus appeared to be something like the hidden face of reason that consciousness could explore and integrate . . . he wanted poetry to be life, he wanted us to live in a poetic state of grace, of spiritual tension, of lucid ecstasy that would multiply the powers of the mind ten times over . . ." (*PP* 148–49). Although he cannot properly be called a surrealist playwright, Ionesco's debt to surrealism is clear; it may be found in the startling juxtaposition of words reminiscent of automatic writing, in disquieting nightmarish images that come straight from the playwright's dreams, and in the refusal of many of the protagonists (Jack, Amédée, Jean, or the narrator of *The Hermit,* for example) to accept living in any way other than a "poetic state of grace."

Character

One reason that Ionesco's early work was controversial was that the characters in the plays were so strange. They were either mechanized automata seemingly devoid of any psychological content (as in *The Bald Soprano*), grotesque, vampirish monsters (as in *The Lesson* or *Jack,* for example), or possibly deranged fools (the old couple in *The Chairs*). Certainly, just as he had sought to demolish language in a savage assault on the conventions of boulevard theater, Ionesco set out to destroy the conventional notion of the dramatic character. In conventional realistic theater, dramatic characters are understood to be like human beings, complete with a past, desires, fears, motives for action, and so forth. They are presumed to have a certain character or psychology that will precipitate or explain their actions, and they are expected to use language in ways consistent with norms existing in the real world. The characters in Ionesco's early plays meet almost none of these expectations. Their behavior is not logical and neither is their language: they appear constantly to contradict themselves and each other, and their actions may be either inexplicable or at least inconsistent with what they say. These characters are deliberately dehumanized to such an extent that the boundaries between the realm of the human and that of the nonhuman are quite often blurred. It is not always the case, for example, that a human actor appears to perform the role of a character: the clock in *The Bald Soprano* seems to participate in the action on the same level that the other characters do, and a large number of unseen characters crowd the stage in *The Chairs,* performed by the mass of empty chairs and some sound and lighting effects. Human actors who do appear may be made up or costumed so as to appear as unreal as possible (the Orator in *The Chairs* and Roberta in *Jack,* for example). Objects appear to be endowed with a life of their own, from the growing corpse of *Amédée* to the mountains of furniture in *The New Tenant;* these characters are either at the mercy of the material world around them or even seemingly indistinguishable from it.

This systematic dehumanization of the dramatic character in Ionesco's early theater did not translate a belief that human beings are mechanized automata: on the contrary, the mechanization of these characters functions to denounce the depersonalization of humankind that Ionesco sees as perhaps the principal evil of contemporary society. As he said to Claude Bonnefoy, "I think I tried to put into my plays a denunciation of mechanization and emptiness. . . . if my characters are puppets, they are suffering puppets. Caricature is criticism" (*ENT* 179). The meaningless chatter, grotesquely illogical behavior, and gratuitous cruelty and violence of many of these early characters are therefore absurd in both a comic and a pathetic (Ionesco would say tragic) sense: "I tried to show characters in search of a life, in search of an essential reality. They suffer from being cut off from themselves. That's what absurdity is— that people are separated from their roots and are seeking them desperately" (*ENT* 180).

The early characters could not feel ill at ease in their environment since they lacked any consciousness whatsoever of their situation. As Ionesco's work evolved away from pure parody or anti-theater and entered its second phase, however, he turned away from caricature and mechanization and began to create humanized protagonists who were increasingly articulate about their painful search for an essential reality. As early as *Victims of Duty,* and especially in the Bérenger plays, the main characters are more coherent, humanized incarnations of Ionesco's personal anxieties and obsessions. As he has said, "I destroyed the character in my first plays. I then reintroduced him by incarnating, by giving a human face to my phantasms" (*Homme* 178). The four Bérengers are all ordinary men, four versions of Everyman with distinctly Ionesco-like diction and desires. Each is an individual struggling to discover or maintain his own identity in the face of obstacles posed by society, by his own mortality, or by the senseless suffering inherent in the human condition; each seeks to find a way out of the incomprehensible situation in which he finds himself; each pursues an unattainable ideal of happiness.

Even in the plays of this second phase, however, the characters' grasp on a stable human identity is tenuous at best. They move in a nightmarish environment that refuses to remain passively inanimate and clearly separate from them, so that their attempts to affirm their individuality and humanity are constantly opposed by a hostile and menacingly vivified world: an invisible killer (who may or may not be human) stalks the

Radiant City in *The Killer,* Bérenger watches in horror as his friends and colleagues are metamorphosed into beasts in *Rhinoceros,* and King Bérenger sees the cataclysmic decay of the world around him signal his own imminent demise.

In the last two plays, the characters once again lack coherence and are replaced by hermetic and shadowy images wandering through dreamscapes. The protagonists of *Man With Bags* and *Journeys Among the Dead* are surrealistic projections of Ionesco's autobiographical phantasms, and their identity is as slippery and mysterious as that of any character in a dream.

The Role of Women

The authorial presence and the point of view in Ionesco's work are always male. The protagonists in all of his work after *The Bald Soprano* (in which no character can be said to be the protagonist) are male.[9] All of these characters are involved in ambivalent relationships with women, however, so that female characters play a central, if secondary, role. Some of the female characters are stock types commonly found in traditional French theater. The impertinent maid who appears so often in Molière as the voice of common sense, for example, may perform the same function in Ionesco's theater, as in *The Lesson, Improvisation,* and even to some extent *The Bald Soprano.* The lovely young ingenue, object of the protagonist's desire, is another recurring character (in *The Lesson, Rhinoceros,* and *The Killer,* for example). Most often, however, the female character is the protagonist's wife, a maternal figure who may be the nurturing, supportive "good mother" (as in *The Chairs*) or the demanding, authoritarian "bad mother" (Mother Peep in *The Killer* or the mother figures in *Jack*). This dichotomous nature is most clearly portrayed in *Exit the King,* in which the King's young wife, Marie, is sexually alluring and steadfast in her refusal to accept Bérenger's death, while his older wife, Marguerite, is the voice of authority whose job it is to make Bérenger face his agony and accept his death. This play ends with Bérenger symbolically reentering the womb as he dies; here, as throughout Ionesco's work, women are closely linked to life and death.

Critics are divided as to whether the women in Ionesco's theater are the source of man's fall from grace[10] or the "only authentic form of salvation."[11] What is clear is that they are the object (if never the subject) of highly fraught desire that is often Oedipal in nature. Women tend to be strongly associated with guilt, either through marital infidelity (as in *Amédée*) or filial neglect (in *The Chairs* or *Man With Bags*), and their relationship to the protagonist is usually conflictual. If the male protagonists are visionary, artistic idealists who long to escape the confines of earth and time, women are often practical figures who condemn the male characters' search for an Edenic state of grace as impractical and tie them to earth (as in *Victims of Duty, Amédée, A Stroll in the Air,* and *Hunger and Thirst*). Ionesco has written of his own ambivalence toward women, feelings arising from having witnessed at a very early age his father's brutality toward his mother. "Ever since," he wrote in the mid 1940s, "I have pitied all women, rightly or wrongly. I have taken my father's guilt upon myself. Being afraid of making women suffer, of persecuting them, I have allowed myself to be persecuted by them. It is they who have made me suffer. I have made women suffer. . . . But each time that I have made a woman suffer . . . I have suffered from her suffering" (*PP* 21).

The Problem of Existence

At the heart of Ionesco's work is a fundamental contradiction between astonishment and anguish, between joy and despair. As the narrator of Ionesco's only novel (*The Hermit*) says, "Joy is suddenly realizing in a way that could be called supernatural that the world is there and that we are in the world, that we exist, that I exist" (111); "There's *that,* especially, there's that, the astonishment that I exist and that things exist" (102). The almost miraculous, gratuitous fact of existence is unveiled only rarely, however, during epiphanies of euphoric joy—for both Ionesco and his characters. Described repeatedly in Ionesco's memoirs and works (for example, *The Killer, Hunger and Thirst, The Hermit, A Stroll in the Air*), these moments of intense joy are most often triggered by a certain quality of light and are characterized by feelings of weightlessness, calm, and plenitude. During these moments, the world's strangeness (that is, the impossibility of accounting for existence in any rational way) is an overpowering revelation, and most of Ionesco's work attempts to convey this feeling of discovery and surprise. These moments of joy can never last, though, because time and habit inevitably make a mockery of joy and plunge Ionesco and his characters into despair. For Ionesco, time is a cancer leading to death, and habit is "a gray cover that hides the virginity of the world" (*ENT* 32).

The inevitability of death is a constant source of anguish, an unacceptable negation of man's "astonishment at being": "The meaning of our existence is that we are here in a state of astonishment and that we are made for death" (*ENT* 160). Ionesco discovered time and death simultaneously. This twin discovery makes existence unbearable, and yet we cling desperately to it; Ionesco's central paradox is to be "conscious of the fact that human existence is unbearable, . . . intolerable, and nonetheless [to] cling desperately to it, knowing and complaining that one is going to lose what is unbearable. . . . Torn to pieces between the horror of living and the horror of dying" (*PP* 81). Always at least implicit in his work, the theme of anguish in the face of death moves to the foreground in *Exit the King* and remains there for the rest of his career.

What keeps many of Ionesco's characters going is a vision of paradise accompanied by a quest to regain a lost state of grace. The garden of Eden to which Ionesco and many of his characters would like to return is timeless and resembles nothing so much as La Chapelle-Anthenaise, the lost paradise where he spent the happiest years of his childhood: "At La Chapelle-Anthenaise time did not exist. I lived in the present. Living was grace, the joy of living" (*ENT* 14). From the Old Man in *The Chairs* onward, characters seek in vain to achieve this state of grace; as the narrator of *The Hermit* puts it, "I can't live except in a state of grace. But who lives in a state of grace? And yet not to live in a state of grace is unacceptable. For me, there's no middle ground between grace and shit" (101). Despite the Judeo-Christian symbolism that appears so often (the Edenic garden, the Fall from grace, Jacob's ladder, and the like), the universe of Ionesco's theater is godless: however ardently these characters may long for grace or the explanation of existence that a God might furnish, each quest ends in failure or silence. As Ionesco wrote in 1967, "I have always tried to believe in God. I'm not naive enough, not subtle enough" (*PP* 40). For much of his life Ionesco rejected institutionalized religion, but he is quite attracted to mysticism and gnosticism, and his work after about 1960 bears clear traces of his interest in mystical experience, Zen Buddhism, myth, and parapsychology. Attracted by its mystical quality, Ionesco has come to embrace Catholicism as he has grown older, and he attends mass regularly.

Ionesco is a resolute essentialist for whom existentialism is an anathema. For him, what is important is *being*: "To be, to exist without being existentialists, for to be an existentialist is to be the prisoner of logomachies, shut up in words while being escapes us" (*PP* 149). In this respect his thought parallels that of Albert Camus, whom he admires and who, like Ionesco, valued humanism and the individual and opposed any theory (Marxism or existentialism, for example) or institution (such as political parties and bureaucracies) that would make of the individual life an abstraction.

The Individual, Authority and Freedom

Ionesco's ambivalence toward religion parallels the deeply divided feelings he has had about his father and about authority figures in general. Not yet seven years old when his father abandoned the family to return to Romania, Ionesco did not see him again until he was nearly thirteen; it would be surprising if this absence had not had some effect on his subsequent development.

His earliest written memories of his father describe a large, usually silent, not unfeeling man who favored his eldest son. One episode from this period stands out, however—a very violent argument during which his mother threatened to commit suicide. Ionesco traces his visceral hatred of all authority to this incident, for it instilled in him a deep revulsion for his father's power and authority. Speaking of his father in the early

21

1940s (several years after seeing him for the last time but a few years before his death), Ionesco wrote, "Everything that I have done was done more or less against him. . . . Everything that represented authority seemed to me, and is, unjust. . . . I know that every sort of justice is unjust and that every sort of authority is arbitrary, even if this arbitrariness rests on a faith or an ideology whose myths it is easy to show up for what they are" (*PP* 16–17). Ionesco's attitude of revolt against all forms of authority extended to his professors at the University of Bucharest and played a role in his opposition to the rise of fascism in Romania.

Ionesco values the individual and his freedom above all else and views society, especially bureaucratic mass societies, as an enemy. He deplores the dehumanization of modern society, in which the individual is identified with his function, and he is an ardent anticommunist because he considers all communist regimes to be totalitarian governments that deny individual freedom. His theater is peopled with many grotesque authority figures, from the Professor in *The Lesson* and the parents in *Jack* to Mother Peep in *The Killer* and the former friends turned rhinoceros in *Rhinoceros;* and his heroes tend to be ordinary men, often minor functionaries (as in *The Hermit, Rhinoceros, The Killer*) who are threatened by a faceless, senseless society. Individuals like Jack or the Bérenger in *Rhinoceros* are obstinate rebels who desire to affirm their own identity in the face of monstrous tyrants or anonymous, frightening mass movements.

Humor

Ionesco made his reputation as a writer of comedies, and his early plays are indeed quite funny. His humor ranges from the juvenile to the sophisticated, from the gentle to the cruel: slapstick, farce, and physical comedy, nonsensical silliness, linguistically inventive puns and wordplay, and hilarious parody and pastiche sometimes coexist in the same play.

Farce in Ionesco's theater carries on a long French tradition that runs from medieval farces through Molière to Jarry's *Ubu Roi.* The broad, scatological humor, trickery, and slapstick (pratfalls, beatings, and so forth) characteristic of farce are found throughout Ionesco's early work. This sort of humor may reflect the cruelty and violence that Ionesco associates with a dehumanized, mechanized world (as in *Jack,* for example, or in the violent ending of *The Bald Soprano*), or it may be a clear throwback to French tradition (as in *Improvisation,* a self-conscious tribute to Molière). The characters in Ionesco's early plays are often puppet-like, grotesque and violent, strongly reminiscent of guignol (Punch and Judy shows) and of Jarry's notorious Père Ubu. Like Jarry, Ionesco was aiming to "go all-out for caricature and the grotesque" in these plays, mounting a frontal assault on the audience: "No drawing-room comedies, but farce, the extreme exaggeration of parody. Humor, yes, but using the methods of burlesque. Comic effects that are firm, broad and outrageous. . . . Everything raised to paroxysm, where the source of tragedy lies. A theatre of violence: violently comic, violently dramatic" (*NCN* 26). Another, less violent form of farce—the bedroom farce—is parodied in several early works; *The Bald Soprano* and *Jack,* for example, exaggerate, deform, and generally ridicule the convoluted plots and romantic entanglements of boulevard comedies. In *The Chairs,* a "tragic farce," and in many of his later, more serious plays, Ionesco uses the physical humor of farce to prevent his play from lapsing into pathos and sentimentality.

Like Flaubert (whom he so admires), Ionesco is a connoisseur of the cliché, and much of the humor in his work derives from his ability to expose the emptiness and banality of the threadbare clichés that people use to avoid saying anything important. Clichés are most often distorted, as when the characters in *The Bald Soprano* conclude, for example, that "he who sells an ox today, will have an egg tomorrow," or "Take a circle, caress it, and it will turn vicious." Clichés also have their dark side, as in *Jack,* where they function primarily as a bludgeon used by society to subdue individual liberty.

Ionesco's wit and linguistic inventiveness extend beyond the lampooning of clichés to encompass every kind of wordplay, including puns and silly nonsense rhymes. One particularly frequent kind of wordplay is the use of lists that begin logically but quickly degenerate into free association driven sometimes by the sound of the word: "Yogurt is excellent for the stomach, the kidneys, the appendicitis, and apotheosis" (*The Bald Soprano*); "The papacy, the papayas, and the papers?" (*The Chairs*). Ionesco is also a master of parody, as in *Improvisation,* in which he turns his scathing wit against theater critics of both the right and the left, mocking their pompous jargon; even he does not escape mockery, as the character named Ionesco himself succumbs to the lure of pomposity at the end of the play, only to be chastised by his cleaning lady.

Another frequent source of humor is incongruity between the words the characters speak and their actions or appearance, a sort of humor commonly found in burlesque or vaudeville. Much of the dialogue in *The Chairs,* for example, is comic because the childish or highly charged romantic language of the old couple is at odds with their extremely decrepit appearance; moreover, the old couple perform feats of strength and agility that clash in comic fashion with their appearance. Likewise, the ravishing young beauty in *Jack* turns out to have three noses when her veil is lifted.

The humor that runs through Ionesco's work—especially in the plays written before 1968—is, like that of his famous contemporary Beckett, largely a product of despair: "For my part, I have never understood the difference people make between the comic and the tragic. As the 'comic' is an intuitive perception of the absurd, it seems to me more hopeless than the 'tragic'" (*NCN* 27). "We are comic. That's the way we should look at ourselves. Only humour, bland or black or cruel, only humour can give us back serenity" (*FJ* 100).

Notes

1. The best sources of information about Ionesco's life are Emmanuel Jacquart's detailed chronology published in the Pléiade edition of Ionesco's complete theater, the interviews Claude Bonnefoy conducted with him, and his own published journals: *Present Past Past Present, Fragments of a Journal, Un Homme en question, Antidotes,* and *La Quête intermittente.*

2. Until 1990, 1912 was the published, universally accepted birth date. This erroneous date was invented—either by Ionesco himself

(according to Jacquart) or by Jacques Lemarchand (according to Hubert)—at the time of the premiere of *The Bald Soprano* (1950) in order to make Ionesco a "young" playwright (that is, under forty years old). (Marie-Claude Hubert gives the correct birth date in her book on Ionesco but fails to change the dates for other events in Ionesco's life, which leads to some anomalies and contradictions in the biographical information in her otherwise excellent book.)

3. She was one of twelve children of Jean and Anne Ipcar. They lived in Romania because Jean was an engineer employed by the Romanian national railroad. She and Eugen Ionescu were married in Bucharest in 1906 or 1907.

4. Reminiscing about this period with Claude Bonnefoy, Ionesco said, "It was a perfect nest, a shelter. . . . I can remember one very happy, bright morning going to church dressed in my best clothes. I can still see the blue sky, and, in the sky, the church's spire. I can hear the church bells. There was the sky and there was the earth, the perfect union of sky and earth. I think that some psychoanalysts—the Jungians—say that we suffer from feeling within ourselves the separation of the sky from the earth" (*ENT* 15). "The countryside was both open space and a nest for me" (16).

5. Shortly after World War II, Ionesco wrote, "Everything that I have done was done more or less against him. I published pamphlets against his fatherland (the word fatherland is unbearable because it means the country of the father . . .). He wanted me to become a bourgeois, a magistrate, a soldier, a chemical engineer. I was horrified by prosecuting attorneys; I couldn't set eyes on an officer, a captain shod in boots, without giving way to fits of anger and despair. Everything that represented authority seemed to me, and is, unjust" (*PP* 16–17).

6. In a letter written in 1979 to his friend Monique Lovinesco, he says, "You say that I didn't have a very good idea about whether I had written a play or not when I wrote *The Bald Soprano*. I was sure in any case that I had written an anti-play. I was neither naive nor a novice at the time. Besides, I had behind me an entire literary past: dozens and dozens of articles published in Romanian journals, a slim volume of bad poetry and above all a book entitled *No* in which I tried to blow up critics. I wanted to repeat a similar experiment by blowing up theater" (*Homme* 178).

7. He was named "Chevalier des arts et lettres" in 1961; in 1966 he was awarded the grand prize for theater by the French Society of Writers in recognition of his entire corpus; in 1969 he received two lucrative literary prizes—the Pierre de Monaco prize of 30,000 francs, given annually to a French writer for lifetime achievement; and the

National Theater Prize of 20,000 francs, given by the Ministry of Cultural Affairs to authors who have contributed significantly to the art of the drama. In 1970 he was elected to Jean Paulhan's seat in the Académie française, and he also received the Austrian State Prize for European literature. Other prizes he has won include the Jerusalem Prize (1973), the International Writers Prize (1974), and the Ingersoll Prize (1985), and he has been awarded several honorary degrees.

8. For an extended discussion of the significance of certain archetypal dreams for Ionesco, see *ENT* 33–38.

9. Ionesco differs markedly in this regard from his famous contemporary Samuel Beckett, who wrote many powerful principal roles for female characters.

10. See, for example, Philippe Sénart, *Ionesco:* "Symbol of death, of matter, of gravity, Woman . . . is the Enemy of Dream, liberating and uplifting. She refuses hope. She is always blaming man for being lazy and cowardly but, when he takes off in pursuit of a dream, she cries . . . : 'Don't try flying higher, it's not worth it'" (107–8).

11. Robert Frickx, *Ionesco* 122.

CHAPTER TWO

Theater of the Absurd:
The Bald Soprano and *The Lesson*

"Theater of the absurd" is a term that has come to refer to much of the avant-garde theater of the 1950s. Coined by Martin Esslin in his seminal study first published in 1961, it is most often applied to plays by Ionesco, Samuel Beckett, Arthur Adamov, Jean Genet, and Harold Pinter. As Esslin and his successors most often use the term, it describes a kind of theater in which illogical language and lack of conventional plot and character reflect postwar angst and an ontological void. Characteristics of this kind of theater include nonlinear structure, characters who are devoid both of a past and of what might be termed psychological content, and a vivified and stylized decor. Ionesco's earliest plays are among the most noteworthy and influential of absurdist theater.

The Bald Soprano

The circumstances surrounding the composition of *La Cantatrice chauve* (*The Bald Soprano*) and its subsequent production are so well-known that they have assumed almost legendary status.[1] According to Ionesco's frequently cited, whimsical account of 1958, he set out in 1948 to learn English by means of the "Assimil" method, using a text called *L'Anglais sans peine* (English Made Easy). In copying the platitudinous dialogues between Mr. and Mrs. Smith and their friends the Martins, Ionesco claims, he was suddenly struck by the strangeness of surprising truths (for example, there are seven days in a week, the ceiling is above us and the floor is below) and decided to communicate these eternal verities to others. He discovered that he was writing a play, or rather a parody of a play; after all, the dialogues that inspired him were already theater. Soon, however, the language taken from his textbook began to disintegrate and run wild until it was devoid of meaning: the days of the week became Tuesday, Thursday, and Tuesday, for example. A fifth character (a fireman) appeared on his own, and the play ended in chaos.

This early version makes Ionesco's debut as a playwright sound almost like an accident, an unintended consequence of his efforts to learn English. (Such an explanation is consistent with his impish humor and his fondness for putting people on.) Other accounts of the play's genesis are less ingenuous regarding the author's motives. Writing in the late seventies, Ionesco is clearer about his intent to write a parody of boulevard theater—the French equivalent of popular Broadway shows.[2] No literary novice, he had already published many articles, a collection of poetry, and, most importantly, a series of essays (*Nu*) in which he tried to demolish literary criticism by unveiling its arbitrary, petty, fickle nature. Ionesco had never liked theater, he said; he was bothered by both its lack of innocence and its clumsy falseness.[3] He therefore set out deliberately to write an anti-play, a parody of the kind of salon comedy he particularly despised. While his English lessons doubtless played a key role in the composition of *The Bald Soprano,* then, it would be a mistake to take at face value Ionesco's assertion that he became a playwright more or less by accident, because he failed to learn English.[4] Ionesco entertained his friends by reading the manuscript at home and approached several important figures in the Parisian theater and literary world (the publisher Bernard Grasset and Pierre-André Touchard, director of the prestigious Comédie française, among them) with hopes of having his as yet untitled play (it was called "Anti-play") produced. He met with no success until a mutual friend, Monique Lovinesco, showed the manuscript to Nicolas Bataille, an actor-director who had just founded an experimental theater company. Bataille found the piece hilariously funny and decided to produce it; the young company was fortunate enough to receive a free thirty-day run at the tiny Théâtre des Noctambules, albeit at the unpopular hour of 6:30.

In the manuscript that made Bataille laugh, the curtain rises on a "middle-class English interior, with English armchairs," on an "English evening." After the "English clock strikes seventeen English strokes" (the introductory stage directions are often read aloud when the play is produced), Mr. and Mrs. Smith engage in what might be a typical after-dinner conversation were it not for its increasingly nonsensical character. The platitudes and clichés of Ionesco's English lessons reappear, sometimes unaltered, more often deformed. Mary, the maid, enters to tell them that their dinner guests, the Martins, have arrived, and they leave to change clothes, they say. Mr. and Mrs. Martin appear to be total strangers, but in the ensuing conversation they discover an amazing series of coincidences, leading them to conclude that they must be husband and wife. As they fall into each other's arms in a parody of a classic recognition scene from melodrama, Mary enters and informs the audience that they are mistaken: they both have a daughter with one red eye and one white eye, but Donald's daughter has a red left eye and a white right eye, while Elizabeth's daughter has a white left eye and a red right eye.

The Smiths reenter (in the same clothes), and the two couples have just begun to exchange fractured pleasantries when the doorbell rings several times, precipitating an argument about whether there is always someone there or never anyone there when a doorbell rings. The Fire Chief enters, looking for some fires to extinguish. Disappointed at finding none, he stays while everyone takes a turn telling anecdotes. When Mary enters, demanding to tell a story herself, there is a second recognition scene; it turns out that Mary and the Fire Chief are long-lost lovers. Mary is carried away (literally and figuratively) reciting a poem about fires, the Fire Chief leaves, and the play culminates in a violent quarrel in which the Smiths and the Martins hurl disjointed clichés, words, and finally just sounds at each other.

The play as we know it today owes a great deal—including its title—to the work of Bataille and his company. Ionesco had proposed the title "L'Anglais sans peine," but Bataille rejected it because of possible confusion with another play, Tristan Bernard's *L'Anglais tel qu'on le parle* (English as it is Spoken).

Bataille proposed "Il pleut des chats et des chiens" (a literal translation of "It's raining cats and dogs," not a French idiom); Ionesco rejected that title and offered "Big Ben Follies," "An Hour of English," and "The English Hour," none of which was satisfactory to Bataille. The present title is the result of a slip of the tongue of Henry-Jacques Huet, who played the Fire Chief. While rehearsing his long, absurd anecdote "The Headcold," he inadvertently said "cantatrice chauve" (bald singer) instead of "institutrice blonde" (blond schoolteacher). Ionesco liked the sound and asked that the play be named *La Cantatrice chauve,* a proposal that was accepted after brief hesitation. (Ionesco then inserted one cryptic line for the Fire Chief to say at his exit, which is the only mention of any bald soprano in the play itself.)[5] The style of staging and acting the play was also a product of collaboration between the author and the company. In early rehearsals they played the piece as a broad farce, but this style satisfied no one. It was then decided to adopt a serious, even tragic style (inspired by Ibsen), which clashed with the absurd dialogue and situations. In subsequent performances, the style of the acting became closer to melodrama, which is how it is played today in Paris.[6] The Belle Epoque costumes (a gift from the movie director Claude Autant-Lara) and conventional middle-class interior further added to the play's jarring effect by leading the audience to expect a play in the realistic style and immediately flouting these expectations. Ionesco's original ending called for enraged (planted) spectators to invade the stage, causing the theater's director to summon the police, who then would shoot the rebellious spectators and order the audience to leave the theater. The company rejected this idea as well as an alternative proposal that called for the author to appear and insult the audience. As finally performed, the play ended with a repetition of the beginning dialogue between the Smiths; subsequently, the Martins were substituted for the Smiths. Ionesco's original ending, with its aggressive assault on the audience, would have made *The Bald Soprano* truly anti-theatrical and disruptive, as were Jarry's *Ubu Roi* and the outrageously provocative Dada manifestations of the early 1920s. Ionesco has said (*NCN* 184) that he had originally envisioned a more violent, burlesque production, in the style of the Marx brothers.[7]

The Bald Soprano opened on 11 May 1950; it played to nearly empty houses, and the little critical attention it attracted was mostly unfavorable. Ionesco had discovered the theater, however, and it was the production of this play, he says, that inspired him to write his second play, *The Lesson* (*Homme* 182). *The Bald Soprano* was revived on a double bill with *The Lesson* in October 1952 and ran for nearly seven months. In 1957 it was again revived at the Théâtre de la Huchette, where it is still playing.

A Tragedy of Language

In an important essay dating from 1958, Ionesco says that he became dizzy and nauseated while writing his first play and imagined when he was done that he had written "something like the tragedy of language" (*NCN* 179). *The Bald Soprano,* he said in a 1978 interview, was about the astonishment he felt when confronted with a world in which people talk without saying anything, or at least anything comprehensible to him, because they don't talk about "the most important thing" (death, metaphysics, the unbearable condition of human existence) (*Homme* 21). Awakened by the stock phrases and clichés of his English textbook to the emptiness of what passes for conversation, he set out to expose the mechanical, threadbare automatisms that have replaced "meaningful" language: "My plan was to empty words of their content, to designify language, to abolish it. . . . I was trying to find the most worn-out clichés, I was trying to express ontological absence, the void; I was trying, in other words, to express the inexpressible" (*Homme* 186–7).

The dislocation of everyday language in the play is progressive, passing through several phases. At the beginning of the play, the language is remarkable primarily for its sheer inanity. In a series of non sequiturs that might remind American audiences of Edith Bunker from the television show "All in the Family," Mrs. Smith appears to be telling her husband a variety of things he most likely already knows very well— that their name is Smith and they live in London, that they have a son and have two daughters named Helen and Peggy, that they had fish and potatoes for dinner, and so forth; the only response she receives is an occasional click of the tongue from Mr. Smith, who is reading the paper. At this point the language is empty of meaning not so much at the level of the word or the sentence but rather at the level of the entire context of the pseudoconversation. Mrs. Smith's monologue ridicules from the start the language of those who "talk without saying anything": like the dialogues in Ionesco's English textbook, her speech is pointlessly precise in stating the obvious (the children drank "English water" with their dinner, for example) and is strewn with maxims both straight ("We must teach the children sobriety and moderation") and distorted ("Yogurt is excellent for the stomach, the kidneys, appendicitis, and apotheosis").

The second stage in Ionesco's assault on language encompasses most of the rest of the play; it begins when Mr. Smith starts to speak and continues until the departure of the Fire Chief (scene 10). As soon as the monologue becomes dialogue, it is apparent that the logic governing the world of this play has nothing to do with that of spectator's world. In this part of the play, the forms of polite conversation are left largely intact, but their content is skewed and zany, much like the rapid-fire dialogue found in the movies of the Marx Brothers. A dizzying variety of techniques are used to effect this disruption of logical discourse; they include the following:

1. Pseudoexplanations. When Mr. Smith asks why the patient died and the doctor didn't, his wife answers, "Because the operation was successful in the doctor's case and it was not in Parker's" (10).

2. False analogies. Mr. Smith says that "a conscientious doctor must die with his patient if they can't get well together," comparing the doctor to a sea captain who goes down with his ship. When his wife objects that one cannot compare a patient with a ship, he says, "Why not? A ship has its diseases too; moreover, your doctor is as hale as a ship; that's why he should have perished at the same time as his patient like the captain [the French version has "doctor"] and his ship" (11). The Fire Chief complains that "pro-

duction is down" in fires, and you can't import them as you can sugar because the tariffs are too high (28).

3. Flat contradictions. Mrs. Smith describes in great detail in her opening monologue what they had for dinner, and then, when Mary announces that the Martins, their dinner guests, are waiting, she declares that she and her husband have been waiting for the Martins and have had nothing to eat all day (14). She then tells the Martins that she didn't know they were coming, while Mr. Smith says that they had been waiting for them for four hours (20). Describing Bobby Watson (widow, wife, and fiancée of the deceased and living Bobby Watson), Mr. Smith says that she has regular features but isn't pretty because she's too fat, and that, while her features are irregular, she is quite pretty although she's a little too thin. After exclaiming that the widowed Bobby Watson is lucky to have no children, Mrs. Smith wonders who will take care of the children (12).

4. Specious reasoning. Mrs. Smith asserts that "experience teaches us that when one hears the doorbell ring it is because there is never anyone there" (23). In one of the anecdotes, a calf is obliged to give birth to a cow as a result of having eaten too much ground glass (30).

5. Surprise at the obvious. Mr. Smith wonders why the newspaper always prints the ages of the deceased and never the ages of the newborn babies (11). Mrs. Martin amazes everyone with her story of having seen a man tying his shoelaces, and her husband tops her by saying that he saw a man sitting quietly reading a newspaper, whereupon Mr. Smith exclaims, "Perhaps it was the same man!" (22).

6. Unreliability of proper names. The three days of the week when there is no competition in business are Tuesday, Thursday, and Tuesday (13). "Bobby Watson" refers to all members (whatever the gender or age) of one family, and since Bobby and his wife had the same name, it was impossible to tell them apart (12).

7. Aphasia. The Fire Chief tells of the young woman who was asphyxiated when she left the gas on because she thought it was her comb (28).

8. Contradiction between word and gesture. The Fire Chief says he can't sit down but will take off his hat while he sits down without taking off his hat (27).

Logical distortions are not the only means of "designifying" language in this part of the play. The emptiness of aphorisms and clichés continues to be foregrounded, for example, and social amenities (talking about the weather, telling pointless jokes and meaningless fables, and so on) are parodied.

The third stage in the demolition of language takes place in the final scene (immediately following the Fire Chief's exit). Now even the outward forms of conversation and dialogue are abandoned as the four remaining characters begin to hurl unconnected aphorisms and pseudoaphorisms at and past each other: "One must always think of everything"; "An Englishman's home is truly his castle"; "He who sells an ox today, will have an egg tomorrow"; "I can buy a pocketknife for my brother but you can't buy Ireland for your grandfather" (38). Phrases from Ionesco's English textbook reappear, some in English in the original: "Edward is a clerck [sic]; his sister Nancy is a typist, and his brother William a shop-assistant" (38); "Charity begins at home" (39). By this stage of the play, language has been emptied even of the appearance of being a means for conveying meaning or intentions from one character to another; rather, the characters are traversed by a flood of words and sentences that have lost their power to designate referents outside themselves. From the point when Mr. Smith exclaims, "To hell with polishing!" (39) words, phrases, and unconnected sounds, spoken in an increasingly hostile tone, circulate freely among the now undifferentiated characters until the play reaches its climax in a cacophony of violence. The sense of the individual utterances collapses as free association of sounds generates the text. This constant play between sound and sense makes the end of the play essentially untranslatable, although Donald Allen does an admirable job of trying to find English equivalents in exchanges like "Don't ruche my

brooch!—Don't smooch the brooch!" ("Touche pas ma babouche!—Bouge pas la babouche!") or "Groom the goose, don't
goose the groom—Groom the bridegroom, groom the bridegroom" ("Touche la mouche, mouche pas la touche") (40). Con-
tributing to the abolition of language in the final scene are
the frenzied pace of the speech, the repetition of sounds, and
the sheer accumulation of words.[8]

What Ionesco is attacking in this tragedy of language is not
just certain types of clichéd social interchange but language
itself. Despite a later, much more coherent style, his fundamental attitude toward language ranges from distrust to down-
right hostility. Twenty years after writing *The Bald Soprano,*
he expressed this hostility in the following terms: "Words no
longer demonstrate: they chatter. Words are literary. They are
an escape. They stop silence from speaking. . . . Words wear
out thought, they impair it" (*FJ* 73).

Humor

Ionesco claims to have been surprised that his play elicited
laughter from the audience when it was first performed.[9] Freud
and Bergson both have much to say about the dark side of
laughter as a release mechanism for pent-up cruelty and hostility, an effect of grafting the mechanical onto the human, and
the comic in Ionesco is definitely tinged with black. The comic
is tragic and the tragic is comic, he has often said,[10] and it is
true that the overall effect of his "tragedy of language" is most
disquieting. Humor (as distinct from the comic) is nevertheless far from absent. The play is in fact exceedingly funny, with
much of the humor coming from devices as old as theater itself: parody, punning, and wordplay; sudden ruptures in the
level of discourse; scatological, sexual, and physical humor.

In addition to the humor arising from the paralogical discourse and the play between sound and sense outlined above,
there are several other kinds of verbal humor in the play, not
all of which are translatable. They include the following:

    1. Puns. After Mary recites her poem in which ev-
erything (including the fire) catches fire, for example,

the Martins exclaim, "That sent chills up my spine. . . . And yet there's a certain warmth in those lines." The Fire Chief then says that he has to leave to put out a "straw fire [a flash in the pan] and a little heartburn" (37) on the other side of town.

2. Unexpected juxtaposition of nouns and adjectives. Mrs. Smith plans to buy a large vat of "*native* [folkloric] Romanian yoghurt" (10); the fox jumps into a valley full of "*chicken* honey" in Mr. Smith's anecdote (31) (emphasis added).

3. Inappropriate levels of discourse. During the stiffly formal introductions of the Martins and the Smiths, Mrs. Smith says of her husband, "Il s'emmerde" (translated as "He's wet his pants" [20]), a vulgar expression that connotes boredom while incorporating a scatological reference. Hovering over the Fire Chief, Mr. Martin and Mr. Smith coo, "Oh, the sweet child!" (30).

4. Scatological and sexual references. The Fire Chief recognizes Mary as the girl who "put out his first fires," while she exclaims that she's "his little firehose" (35). Mary announces that she bought a chamber pot in town (15). Mrs. Smith comments that eating the fish made her go to the bathroom (9).

5. Intrusion of English into the French version of the play. This device, not apparent in the English translation, includes many phrases and some complete sentences in English as well as instances of English structures wrongly imposed upon French: Mr. Martin says that he was on the train "d'une demie après huit le matin," for example, whereas the French structure is "de huit heures et demie."

Finally, physical humor plays a role here, albeit a lesser one than it does in subsequent plays. Mary is pushed offstage against her will as she shouts her incendiary poem; characters are called upon to show their teeth and grimace; and actions occasionally directly contradict words (as in the scene in which the Fire Chief sits down without removing his hat, after saying that he cannot stay but will remove his hat; or when Mrs. Smith, dressed in ordinary clothes, says that they've put on formal attire to receive their unexpected guests).

Anti-Theater

Ionesco's fondness for burlesque and slapstick reflects his childhood love of guignol. He describes in his seminal essay "Experience of the Theater" what it was that attracted him to this kind of puppet theater: "It was the very image of the world that appeared to me, strange and improbable but truer than true, in the profoundly simplified form of caricature, as though to stress the grotesque and brutal nature of the truth" (*NCN* 20). By way of contrast, Ionesco detested "legitimate" theater, finding it unconvincing and inauthentic, and he set out to "blow it up" with his first anti-play (just as he had attacked literary criticism when he wrote the literary criticism in *Nu*) (*Homme* 178). More than just a parody of boulevard theater, *The Bald Soprano* was an experiment in abstract theater, designed to unveil and thereby denounce the emptiness of traditional dramatic forms (*NCN* 181–82).

Just as the dialogue in most of the play parodies ordinary language by adopting and then violating its outward forms, so does the form of the play parody boulevard theater by adopting some of its conventions. (It is also the only one of his plays in which Ionesco respects—in the French version—the traditional division of the text into scenes that change with the entrance or exit of a character.) These conventions include the use of stereotyped characters (the saucy maid, the randy Fire Chief, the bourgeois English couple), hackneyed situations (two recognition scenes, the unexpected arrival of dinner guests), and traditional dramatic techniques (Mrs. Smith's laborious exposition, Mary's asides to the audience). The antics going on are, in fact, all the more disorienting just because the outward form looks familiar. As the action mounts and hurtles toward its frenzied climax, the play resembles nothing so much as guignol, with the characters using sound instead of clubs to beat each other; by the play's end, the demolition of boulevard theater is complete.

According to Ionesco, theater makes a mistake when it tries to hide its own theatricality (the "strings" that make it work) and present itself as some sort of realistic portrait of the world. On the contrary, to be effective, theater must not "conceal the devices of the theatre, but rather make them still more evident, deliberately obvious"; "Drama lies in extreme exaggeration of the feelings, an exaggeration that dislocates flat everyday reality" (*NCN* 26). While he set out to demolish theater, then, what Ionesco discovered when his first play was produced was the possibility for a new kind of theater, one that would exploit its own artificial status *as theater* rather than attempting to present yet another worn-out version of stale reality. What had begun as anti-theater had become metatheater.11 Although he did revert to more literary, more classical forms and language later in his career, Ionesco (like several of his contemporaries in what Martin Esslin called the Theater of the Absurd) went on to question and experiment with theatrical form itself in his early plays.

Characters as Automata

The characters in *The Bald Soprano* are radically different from those that theater audiences were accustomed to seeing. At one level they are certainly parodies of stock characters from boulevard theater, as previously noted, but they lose even that degree of coherence as the play progresses. They lack any discernible motivations, rationality, or internal life; rather, they are like puppets from guignol, automata as mechanical as the clock that chimes in at will on the dialogue throughout the play. Ionesco described them in his notes as "characters without character. Puppets. Faceless creatures" (*NCN* 181).

They appear to suffer from total amnesia: the Martins have no recollection of having seen each other before, and the Smiths directly contradict themselves and each other without noticing it. Every remark disappears without a trace, allowing for no continuity of personality; indeed, these characters can have no personality because they are not integrated subjects.[12] Undifferentiated from each other and indistinguishable

38

from their surroundings, they are traversed by language, which uses them rather than the other way around. They are vehicles for unveiling the automatisms of language and behavior that mask the metaphysical void of a world in which the mechanical has replaced the human and the personal, where there is nothing to say (*NCN* 180). As such, they are, as Ionesco has said, "suffering marionettes" (*ENT* 179).

Social Satire

Like Gustave Flaubert, whom he so admired as young man, Ionesco has a great horror of bourgeois pettiness, vacuity, and stupidity, especially as they are exemplified in the cliché. On one level, then, *The Bald Soprano* is a satire of stuffy, class-conscious bourgeois society: the Smiths are quite smug and self-satisfied with their one hundred percent "English" existence, they treat their maid contemptuously, and they exhibit a certain amount of xenophobia. As Ionesco has repeatedly emphasized, however, his play does not satirize any particular bourgeois society but rather a certain kind of mindless conformism that can be found in every society and every social class (*NCN* 180). The object of the satire is all those who accept and repeat slogans and received ideas, of whom the Smiths and the Martins are grotesque caricatures, pushed to the extreme.

At a deeper level, however, Ionesco's critique is aimed at the very necessity for the individual to live in society at all. This critique, which is elaborated as Ionesco's career continues, is founded on two basic points. The first is Ionesco's absolute devotion and commitment to the individual and his deeply rooted distrust of any group that might require the individual to sacrifice personal freedom. The second objection to society is metaphysical: all social concerns are a form of Pascalian divertissement, diversions that tempt us to avoid thinking about or talking about the only things that "really matter"—the meaning of existence and the inevitability of death. Viewed from this perspective, the mindless chatter and frenzied actions of *The Bald Soprano* presage the gloominess and despair that emerge more clearly as Ionesco's work evolves.

The Lesson

After a short stint as an actor in Akakia Viala's adaptation of Dostoevsky's *The Possessed,* Ionesco wrote *La Leçon* (*The Lesson*), his second play, in three weeks in August 1950. Marcel Cuvelier produced it, selling all his furniture to raise the money (*Homme* 188), and it premiered on 20 February 1951 at the Théâtre de la Poche, another small experimental theater.[13]

Like *The Bald Soprano, The Lesson* is a one-act play. After the curtain rises on an empty stage, the doorbell rings and the Maid shows in an attractive young woman of about eighteen who has come to be tutored for her "total doctorate." The Professor enters to begin the lesson; he is a small, older man who is at first quite timid and polite, deferential to and supportive of the lively, well-mannered young girl. He congratulates her effusively, for example, for knowing the four seasons almost by heart. They move on to arithmetic, despite some veiled warnings from the Maid about its dangers, and it soon becomes apparent that the Pupil has no understanding whatsoever of subtraction—although she can count all the way to sixteen. The Professor's frustration mounts as his increasingly hilarious attempts to explain simple arithmetic are met with the Pupil's absolute lack of understanding of the difference, say, between units, numbers, figures, and sticks. When he asks how she can ever expect to do simple calculations like 3,755,998,251 x 5,162,303,508, she instantly gives him the correct answer; knowing that she will never be able to rely on her reason, she has memorized, she says, all possible answers to all possible multiplication problems. The lesson then moves on to the field of linguistics, over the strong objections of the Maid, who warns that "philology leads to the worst." As he lectures on the remarkable identity of all "Neo-Spanishe" languages, the Professor's demeanor grows progressively more menacing and lewd, while the Pupil becomes depressed and begins to suffer from a terrible toothache. The lesson ends in a paroxysm of violence, as the Professor rapes and murders his pupil with an invisible knife. When the Maid enters to admonish him and help him clean up, we learn that this has been the fortieth murder and that this happens every day. As the curtain falls, we hear the doorbell ring, and the Maid enters to receive yet another Pupil—his forty-first victim.

Language and Logic

The Lesson might also be called a tragedy of language. In this play, as in *The Bald Soprano,* it is language that drives the action, becoming finally a weapon with which the Professor rapes and murders his Pupil, in much the same way as words become weapons at the end of *The Bald Soprano.* Although syntax and morphology remain intact in *The Lesson,* the logic behind the language is as skewed as in the earlier play, effectively distorting meaning and turning language into nonsense. Nonsense, as Claude Abastado has pointed out in his brilliant essay "Logique de la Toupie" (The Logic of the Top) is not a lack of meaning but rather "an excess of meaning, too much meaning, an anarchic gift of meaning that takes us, like Alice, through the looking-glass" (159).[14]

"Through the looking-glass" is an apt description of the internal logic (or antilogic) of *The Lesson.* As in *The Bald Soprano,* tautologies, false syllogisms, identity of opposites, and fractured truisms permeate the language. When the Professor tries to get the Pupil to subtract three from four by asking how many units separate the two numbers, for example, it is pseudological reasoning that leads her to answer, "There aren't any units, Professor, between three and four. Four comes immediately after three; there is nothing at all between three and four!" (54). As the Professor says when the Pupil fails to understand why one cannot subtract figures from numbers and units and sticks, "That's the way it is, Miss. It can't be explained. This is only comprehensible through internal mathematical reasoning. Either you have it or you don't" (58). Principles of identity are violated here as in *The Bald Soprano.* The Professor cites the example of his former comrade who had a serious speech impediment: he always said "f" instead of "f" and so pronounced "filly" instead of "filly," and so forth. Fortunately for him, however, no one ever noticed it, "thanks to the hats he wore" (64–65). Similarly, the Professor concludes that all the words of all the Neo-Spanishe languages are always the same: "In any case, you always have the same signification, the same composition, the same sound structure . . . for all conceivable words, in all languages" (66).

Language and Power

If logic is turned on its head, however, language itself is not demolished ("designified") as it was it *The Bald Soprano.* On the contrary, language is a powerful tool that the Professor uses to establish his dominance over the Pupil before raping and killing her with the word knife. Furthermore, language does not traverse undifferentiated characters as it did in the earlier play; each of the characters of *The Lesson* is a distinct entity with its own language. At the beginning, the Pupil is bright, self-confident, eager, and the Professor is obsequious, supportive, and overly polite, congratulating her effusively for knowing three of the four seasons by heart, and using expressions such as "Excuse me," "If you don't mind," and "I'm only your humble servant." During the arithmetic lesson, frustrated by the Pupil's failure to understand subtraction, the Professor becomes more aggressive and verbose and the Pupil correspondingly subdued and muted. As he moves into the field of linguistics, the Professor's language and behavior both become overbearing and oppressive, while the Pupil is reduced first to simple "Yes, Sir" and "No, Sir" and then is forced to repeat the Professor's words ("The roses of my grandmother are as yellow as my grandfather, who was Asiatic" [66–67]) despite the awful pain she is experiencing. As Richard Schechner argues persuasively in his article *"The Bald Soprano* and *The Lesson:* An Inquiry into Play Structure," the play is a ritualized language game in which possession of language equals power: "When the Pupil has it, the Professor is a timid old man; when he gets it, she is helplessly gripped by a numbing pain; when Marie disarms the Professor, he becomes a whining baby" (29). Clearly, it is the characters (specifically, the Professor) who use language in this play, rather than language that uses the characters.

The Professor is the first of a number of grotesque authority figures to appear in Ionesco's theater. He is a pompous, stupid bully who will pick only weak and defenseless victims (much like Ionesco's father or the mindless Nazis whom Ionesco so despised during his youth in Romania: in the text, Ionesco even suggests that Marie put an armband with a swastika on the Professor before they carry the Pupil's body offstage). In this context the victim is a young, attractive woman; the power the Professor abuses is very clearly sexual; and language is the medium through which this power is exercised.

Beginning with the small gleam, quickly repressed, that appears in his eye when the Pupil announces that she is "at his disposal" (50), the Professor's sexual excitement mounts with each succeeding stage of the lesson. The accelerated rhythm and his logorrhea fuel his lust and make him impervious to Marie's warnings about the dangers of continuing. He uses his language both to bludgeon the Pupil into submission and to mesmerize her, forcing her to repeat the word knife in the climactic rape scene. His power over her is such that, when the pain from his "knife" invades every part of her body, she designates each body part (shoulders, breasts, arms, thighs) with both word and gesture, in a kind of a trance. (Ionesco's stage directions call for her to appear "weeping, desperate, at the same time both exasperated and in a trance" [74]). His back to the audience, the Professor delivers the two mighty blows of his invisible knife that complete the rape and murder of the Pupil, who is left sprawled in an obscene posture in the chair. Physically exhausted, the Professor shudders with pleasure, utters a vulgar insult, and slowly comes to his senses, realizing what he has done.

Like all bullies, the Professor is a coward at heart. With the sexual energy that had been fueled by language spent, he loses his dominant position and reverts to the timidity that had characterized him at the beginning of the play. Panic-stricken, he calls out for Marie to help him, just as a child would call his mother. Marie is now in the dominant position, and she scolds him: "And today makes it the fortieth time! . . . And every day it's the same thing! Every day! You should be ashamed, at your age . . . you're going to make yourself sick!" (76).

When he makes a desperate, ineffectual attempt to use his "knife" on Marie, she slaps him and shakes him exactly as she would a child. Sniveling, the Professor says that he's sorry, and Marie forgives him, saying "I can't help feeling sorry for you! Ah! you're a good boy in spite of everything! I'll try to fix this. But don't start it again" (77).

The Role of Women

As the preceding discussion indicates, the Professor is (on one level, at least) a contemptible, fearful tyrant, the target of satire directed at an authority (father) figure. At the same time, however, his relationships with the two women in the play establish a pattern that will continue to characterize Ionesco's protagonists—even those with whom the audience is called upon to empathize. The typical Ionesco protagonist is highly conflicted; he both desires and fears women. On the one hand, women represent erotic pleasure: the Pupil is the first of several beautiful young women who will be objects of desire in later plays (*Rhinoceros, Exit the King,* and *The Killer,* for example). On the other hand, these young women are generally unattainable, and this state of affairs leads to sadness and frustration for the hero.[15]

Viewed from an Oedipal perspective, the Professor's desire for and hostility toward the Pupil can be read as a result of the child's sexual desire for his mother and his rage at being denied access to her body. The great majority of women who appear in Ionesco's theater are, in fact, mother figures who form a couple with the protagonist, either as spouse or as maid. These women can be nurturing and protective, as is Marie when she plays the part of "good mother," helping the childlike Professor clean up and cover up after his crime. It is she who makes it possible for him to begin his cycle anew after each murder, taking care of the details and watching out for his health. On the other hand, women are also domineering, smothering, "bad mother" figures who stand in the way of the hero's infantile desires for gratification and are thus hated and feared. Marie plays this role as well, admonishing the Professor about the dangers of continuing the lesson and reprimanding him when he once again succumbs to his desire. She is the one who holds the real power, as the end of the play reveals; she punishes the Professor soundly when he makes his one ineffectual attempt to attack her. Unable to revenge himself upon her, he will of course murder his next Pupil instead.

The Professor's misogyny is a grotesque, exaggerated version of what will be a characteristic attitude of Ionesco's later protagonists toward women. In general, they find that they both need women for the security and support they offer and resent them for the power they have to withhold gratification or to deprive the protagonists of freedom. (Perhaps the clearest example of this profound ambivalence is the two wives in *Exit the King,* one young and adoring, the other older and authoritarian.)

A Comic Drama

The Bald Soprano lived up to its subtitle, "Anti-play," by parodying dramatic conventions. *The Lesson,* on the other hand, is subtitled "Comic Drama"; it has a clear, linear plot, recognizable characters, and a coherent temporal structure. As in *The Bald Soprano,* the end of *The Lesson* repeats the beginning, but the repetition is not gratuitous; the Pupil ringing at the end of *The Lesson* is the forty-first one, not the fortieth one all over again. In other words, time has advanced in *The Lesson* as it could not in *The Bald Soprano.*

In *The Bald Soprano,* the words and the action are equally incoherent, spinning off into a wild and funny tragedy of language, while in *The Lesson* Ionesco wanted to graft burlesque acting onto a dramatic text: "Push burlesque to its extreme limits, then, with a flick of the finger, an imperceptible transition, and you are back in tragedy. It is a conjuring trick. The public should not notice the passage from burlesque to tragedy. . . . That is what I tried in *The Lesson*" (*NCN* 182). While both plays abound in verbal and physical humor, then, *The Lesson* is disquieting in a way that the earlier play is not. Both plays climax in paroxysms of violence, but the only victim in *The Bald Soprano* is language: the characters are puppets who get up, like Punch and Judy, and start all over again. With the greater humanization of the characters in Ionesco's second play, the comedy takes on a more menacing, darker tone that will continue to color the bitter satire of several later plays, including *Jacques, ou la soumission (Jack, or The Submission)* and *L'Avenir est dans les oeufs (The Future is in Eggs)*.

Notes

1. The best account of the play's genesis and first performance is given by Ruby Cohn in her excellent *From* Desire *to* Godot 88–99. See *NCN* 175–85 for an early (1959) account; see Ionesco's 1979 letter to Monique Lovinesco (published in *Un Homme en question* 177–82) for a revised and corrected version of the play's beginnings.

2. For Ionesco's own early (1955) appraisal of various interpretations of his intentions in writing *The Bald Soprano,* see *NCN* 165–66 ("I Have Often Been Asked"). When asked by Bonnefoy twenty years later why he had given the play the subtitle "anti-play," Ionesco confessed, "I must have known exactly what that meant when I wrote the play, but now I've forgotten" (*ENT* 58).

3. In the essay "Experience of the Theatre," first published in 1958, Ionesco speculates that he may have started writing for the theater because he hated it: "A theatrical performance had no magic for me. Everything seemed rather ridiculous, rather painful. . . . For me it was a kind of vulgar trick, transparent, inconceivable" (*NCN* 15). In the same essay, he goes on to say that the experience of seeing the Bataille company rehearse and perform *The Bald Soprano* changed his mind: "And so it was only when I had written something for the theatre, quite by chance and with the intention of holding it up to ridicule, that I began to love it, to rediscover it in myself, to understand it, to be fascinated by it: and then I knew what I had to do" (*NCN* 25). Speaking with Bonnefoy, however, Ionesco maintained that he had been less than sincere in the earlier essay: "Well, yes, I said I loved the theater, but that wasn't exactly true. The truth is that I've never loved it. I'll tell you frankly that if I said in 'Experience of the Theatre' that at a certain time I discovered theater and began to love it, it was a concession I made for the drama critics who defended me and the actors who performed my works" (*ENT* 59).

4. "In fact it was because I failed to learn English that I became a dramatist" (*NCN* 175).

5. See Ionesco's letter to Lovinesco (*Homme* 179–80) for these details.

6. In the same letter to Lovinesco, Ionesco credits the public with

having shaped the production: "Today, the play is no longer performed dramatically at the Huchette, but almost in the manner of boulevard theater. It's the public that created this production" (*Homme* 180).

7. See Alexandre Rainof's development of this point in "Ionesco and the Film of the Twenties and Thirties from Groucho to Harpo," published in Lamont and Friedman, *The Two Faces of Ionesco* 65–74.

8. Commenting on the disintegration of language in the play, Ionesco wrote, "For me, what had happened was a kind of collapse of reality. The words had turned into sounding shells devoid of meaning . . ." (*NCN* 179). Acceleration, repetition, and accumulation—not just of words but also of actions and objects—are important devices in all of Ionesco's work, particularly in the early period.

9. "When it was acted, I was almost surprised to hear the laughter of the audience, who took it all (and still take it) quite happily, considering it a comedy all right, even a sort of joke" (*NCN* 179).

10. Rosette Lamont expands convincingly on this point in her seminal essay "Eugene Ionesco and the Metaphysical Farce": "It has often been said that in the twentieth century tragedy is as dead as our gods. This may be so, yet the tragic apprehension of life in art must survive. . . . On the other hand comedy, once considered a low, popular form of entertainment, is assuming in our times some of the Dionysian character of the drama. . . . The two genres, comedy and tragedy, tend to flower in the same epoch, since fear, tension, sympathy, pity can bring about a comic explosion, a liberation through laughter, as well as a purgation through pity and terror. Laughter liberates us, yet it dissolves at the same time any pre-established harmony, any pact between man and nature, between the justice of God and that of society" (177–78).

11. See Lionel Abel's *Metatheatre* and David Grossvogel's *The Self-conscious Stage in Modern French Drama*.

12. Tookey, Woolridge, and Tookey's "Pseudo-Psychotic Language in Experimental Theater" provides a fascinating description of the similarity between the formal thought disorders symptomatic of schizophrenia and manic-depressive psychosis and the dissociative language of plays by Ionesco (especially *The Bald Soprano*) and other contemporary playwrights.

13. See Cohn's *From* Desire *to* Godot (122–33) for an excellent discussion of the play's themes and early history.

14. Claude Abastado, "Logique de la toupie," in Ionesco and Vernois, eds., *Ionesco: Situations et perspectives:* 157–76.

15. Although the Professor is the only one to murder the object of his desire, the other young women do come to a bad end—Dany is murdered by The Killer, Marie disappears, and Daisy becomes a rhinoceros.

CHAPTER THREE

Guilt and Proliferation:
The Chairs, Victims of Duty, and *Amédée*

The three plays written between 1951 and 1953 mark a movement away from the nonsense of Ionesco's first works toward the more personalized, coherent plays of the later 1950s and 1960s. As he wrote in response to a written questionnaire in 1956, "In the end I realized I did not really want to write 'anti-theatre' but 'theatre'" (*NCN* 131). In these plays decor takes on a more significant role than in the earlier plays, especially in the form of nightmarish proliferation of matter; the characters begin to acquire some psychological depth; the figure of the writer/artist becomes a target for satire; and exploration of the complex dynamics of the couple is pursued in depth. These plays do not, however, represent a total break with the earlier style. The remarkable play of language continues, along with satire of bourgeois society, fear and hatred of authority, and experimentation with dramatic form. The short play *Jacques, ou la soumission* (*Jack, or The Submission*) represents a transition from the earliest style to the more complex themes and structure of the later plays.

Although it was not premiered until 15 October 1955 (at the Théâtre de la Huchette, directed by Robert Postec, on a double bill with *Le Tableau*), *Jack, or The Submission* was written in 1950, immediately after *The Bald Soprano*. It is a nightmarish one-act play that has much in common with the two absurdist plays discussed in the previous chapter, as Ionesco emphasizes in his written first night preview: "Like *The Bald Soprano*, *Jack* is a kind of parody or caricature of boulevard theatre, boulevard theatre going bad, gone mad. . . . Both the language and behavior of the characters is noble and distinguished. But this language gets dislocated and disintegrates" (*NCN* 194–95). Just as *The Bald Soprano* was an anti-play parodying drawing room comedy, *Jack* parodies family drama: the insufferably overbearing and repressive parents and in-laws-to-be of the title character succeed (after much browbeating) in forcing the rebellious young man to admit that he likes hashbrown potatoes and to marry Roberta II, who has the three noses that Jack requires in a wife.[1] Once again, a stuffily Victorian bourgeois interior establishes (in an unsuspecting audience) expectations regarding dramatic conventions that are rudely contradicted.

The characters here do speak somewhat more coherently than the automata of *The Bald Soprano,* but the logic in the world of this play is as skewed as ever: the triviality of the issue at hand (whether or not Jack likes hashbrown potatoes) is totally at odds, for example, with the violence and rage that Jack's refusal to submit unleashes. The imagery here, both scenic and verbal, is the most surrealistic of Ionesco's early plays. Roberta wears three noses and is described as having everything a man could want in a woman—"green pimples on her beige skin, red breasts on a mauve background, an illuminated navel, a tongue the color of tomato sauce, pan-browned square shoulders, and all the meat needed to merit the highest commendation" (91–92). Language in Roberta's world has lost the power to refer or signify: "In the cellar of my castle, everything is cat . . ." "All we need to designate things is one single word: cat" (109).

Much darker in tone than *The Bald Soprano, Jack* is somewhat less successful as anti-theater, primarily because Ionesco had yet to work out specifically theatrical correlatives for the obsessive themes (repressive family structures, guilt, virulent hatred of authority, psychoanalytic dream material) that run through this piece. All of these themes would be elaborated in the plays to follow.

The Chairs

Les Chaises, farce tragique (The Chairs, Tragic Farce) was written in 1951 and premiered (on a double bill with Jean

49

Tardieu's *Les Amants du métro*) at the Théâtre du Nouveau-Lancry on 22 April 1952 in a production directed by Sylvain Dhomme. The reviews were generally unfavorable, and the play closed after the minimum thirty-day run.[2] A revival directed by Jacques Mauclair in 1956 enjoyed a much more favorable critical reception, however, including an enthusiastic review by the prominent playwright Jean Anouilh that appeared on the front page of the conservative *Figaro;* according to Ruby Cohn, this review "made the fortune of the play—and of the playwright" (*From* Desire *to* Godot 131).

The curtain rises to reveal a circular, dimly lit, nearly empty room. A very old man (the stage directions indicate his age to be ninety-five) is leaning out a window; he tells his equally ancient wife Semiramis that he is looking at the boats on the water. She pulls him back into the room and they sit together (he on her lap) in one of the two chairs on the stage, reminiscing about their past and entertaining each other with stories and private jokes. The Old Man reveals that he has invited a large group of people to come to their tower that evening to hear the message he has been working on for years and that he has engaged a professional orator to deliver that message to the assembled guests. Hearing the sound of a boat arriving outside and the ringing of the doorbell, the old couple exit to greet their first guest. The offstage dialogue indicates that they are welcoming an attractive woman, but when they reenter, the guest can be seen and heard only by the old couple. The Old Man goes to get a chair for the guest, and they converse briefly until the second guest (the Colonel, also unseen by the audience) arrives. The Colonel is seated next to the Lady on another chair brought in from the wings, and it soon becomes apparent from the old couple's reactions that he is making unseemly sexual advances toward her. Two more unseen guests soon arrive—Belle, whom the Old Man had courted when they were young, and her husband the Photo-engraver. While the Old Man declares anew his undying love for Belle and laments the loss of their chance for happiness together, Semiramis engages in openly lewd behavior with Belle's husband. The three couples (the Old Man and Belle, Semiramis and the Photo-engraver, the Lady and the Colonel) continue to converse while engaging in amorous byplay until they are interrupted by the arrival of the next group of guests. From this point on, the guests arrive at a faster and faster tempo, with the Old Man answering the doorbell and the Old Woman bringing in more and more chairs until the stage is filled to overflowing with chairs and unseen characters. The crowd becomes so dense that the old couple are separated and forced to stand on chairs near windows on opposite sides of the room in order to see each other. With a great crash and a flood of intense light, the Emperor arrives; overcome with emotion, the Old Man addresses the crowd, speaking about his life and the importance of the message that the Orator will deliver. The Orator does finally arrive; his entrance is something of a shock, since he is visible to the spectators as well as to the old couple. Feeling that their life is complete now that the message will be delivered, the old couple jump simultaneously from the two windows, shouting, "Long live the Emperor," and we hear the sound of their bodies hitting the water below. The Orator turns out to be hearing- and speech-impaired, however; unable to make himself understood, he exits. The play ends with the stage full of empty chairs, the main door open onto darkness, and the uneasy sounds of the invisible crowd audible for the first time as the curtain falls very slowly.

The Presence of Absence

The Chairs is arguably Ionesco's finest dramatic work in that it exploits the concrete language of the stage to express absence and emptiness in specifically theatrical terms. Ionesco has said that the origin of the play was a single image of a room being filled up by empty chairs. "When I wrote *The Chairs,* I first had the image of chairs, then of someone carrying chairs onto the empty stage at top speed. I had this initial image, but I had no idea at all of what it meant" (*ENT* 71). Upon reflection, he says, he realized that the meaning or theme of the play was "total absence," "nothingness" (and not, as some critics saw it, the failure of the old couple): "The chairs arriving at top speed, and faster and faster, constituted the central image, expressing for me the ontological void, a kind of whirlwind of emptiness. On to this initial image, this primary obsession was grafted a story of two old people who are themselves on the edge of nothingness. . . . But their story is meant only to support the fundamental initial image that gives the play its meaning" (*ENT* 81–82). Viewed from this perspective, the central scene in the play is the long sequence during which the Old Woman carries an astonishing number of chairs onstage (twenty in the space of one minute and thirty-five seconds in the 1952 production, according to Jacques Lemarchand [Cohn, *From* Desire *to* Godot 128]) while the Old Man greets the huge mass of invisible guests. Ionesco makes clear in a note to the French text that it is essential that a very large number of empty chairs ("at least forty, more if possible") be used: "The stage is invaded by these chairs, this crowd of absent presences."[3] Asked about the significance of the chairs, Ionesco told an interviewer, "They express the proliferation of material things. The obtrusive presence of objects expresses spiritual absence" (*NCN* 132). Since "absence can be created only in opposition to what is present," "what is needed is plenty of gesture, almost pantomime, light, sound, moving objects, doors that open and close and open again, in order to create this emptiness, so that it grows and devours everything" (*NCN* 189).

While the first plays had exposed the emptiness and vacuity of language through dizzying proliferation of sound and sense, *The Chairs* goes a step further by representing the ontological void through proliferation of matter. The chairs invade the stage in a mounting crescendo that takes on a rhythm and volition of its own, such that the human characters are overwhelmed and eventually expelled by their sheer mass and density. Yet it is this very proliferation that signifies futility and absence; as Serge Dubrovsky says, "That uncontrollable growth and geometrical progression of objects, for the most part of human fabrication, that finally drive man out, convey both the futility of man's attempt to give himself through boundless material production the fullness of being which he lacks, and the inevitable ultimate triumph of object over subject. Things are like the nightmare of consciousness."[4] This sort of proliferation of matter will be a prominent feature of the plays of this period and will continue, although to a lesser degree, throughout Ionesco's career.

More importantly than through their sheer numbers, however, the chairs signify the presence of absence through their participation in the representation of the "blank" characters in the play. It is clear from the outset that the many guests are not the product of the old couple's senile hallucinations. They are present onstage, performed by the sound effects accompanying their entrance, the conversations that the old couple have with them, the intensification of the light as more and more guests arrive, the large number of chairs, and finally the sounds of the end of the play. The first guest's arrival is a coup de théâtre, since she is invisible and inaudible to the play's spectators. With the subsequent arrivals, however, the presence of the guests is established and the ground rules governing their representation (symbolized by the "empty" chairs that fill the stage) are validated. The status of the guests as absent presences (culminating in the fanfares and blaze of light that greet the Emperor) is naturalized to such a degree that the arrival of the Orator is a shock for the old couple as well as the audience:

> The Old Woman: It's really he, he exists. In flesh and blood.
> The Old Man: He exists. It's really he. This is not a dream! (154)

The fact that he is performed by a human (or perhaps a puppetlike) actor makes him appear even less real than the blank characters: as the stage directions accompanying this scene note, "just as the invisible people must be as real as possible, the Orator must appear unreal" (154).[5] Furthermore, the stage directions indicate he is to behave like a robot as he signs autographs for the invisible crowd. This second coup de théâtre focuses the full attention of all the spectators (those onstage as well as those offstage) on the message the Orator is to deliver, so that his inability to transmit it becomes all the more devastating and poignant.

It is only at the end of the play, after all three human actors have left the stage, that the full impact of the palpable presence of nothingness is felt. As Ionesco wrote in a letter to the play's first director, "The very last scene, after the disappearance of the old couple and the Orator's departure, must be very long: the sound of murmuring, of wind and water, should be heard for a very long time, as though coming from nothing, coming from the void. . . . The tightly-packed crowd of non-existent beings should acquire an entirely objective existence of their own" (*NCN* 189–90).

Space

The Chairs is Ionesco's first play in which spatial structures play a significant role. In the earlier plays the setting was some recognizable interior, such as a living room or study, and the onstage (scenic) space encompassed almost the entire world of the play (the dramatic space). In *The Chairs,* on the other hand, spatial relationships (scenic space versus dramatic space, inside versus outside, up versus down) become very important, reflecting Ionesco's growing recognition of the specifically theatrical, as opposed to literary, resources of the stage. The stage directions describe in detail a circular room with a double door upstage center, two windows on opposite sides of the stage, and seven smaller doors on either side of the main door. This circular interior suggests security, like the womb: at one point the Old Man says, "Sometimes I awaken in the midst of absolute silence. It's a perfect circle. There's nothing lacking" (145).[6] It is a personal space where the old couple can play their private games and a sheltered space where the Old Man has been able to work on his message. Inside the room, the Old Man enjoys the undivided attention of his wife/mother who mirrors his image and desires. This is a privileged space where their private language allows them to communicate perfectly with each other in much the same way that an infant can communicate with its mother. At the same time, however, the room is a claustrated space that smothers the Old Man: he complains that he is suffocating, and he is leaning out the window for a breath of fresh air and a glimpse of boats on the water when the play begins.

The space outside the room can be divided into the immediate offstage scenic space (the water outside, the boats, and so forth, directly linked to the onstage scenic space by the chairs and characters that enter the stage as well as by sound and

lighting effects) and the dramatic (or fictional) space compris-
ing the larger world of the play, evoked only in the dialogue.
The immediate exterior space is a powerful presence in this
play (in marked contrast to the situation in earlier works), at
once menacing and inviting. For the Old Man, the space outside the room is associated with poetic beauty (shimmering
sunlight) and the possibility of escape (the boats). Furthermore,
recognition, vindication, and validation can come to him only
from the public domain outside; both the professional Orator
and the guests who will hear his message must be brought in
from the outside world. The outside also represents the threat
of extinction. Semiramis (here the smothering mother) fears
the world outside: the Old Man wants to see the sunlight on
the water, while his wife can see only the darkness of night.
She wants to shut out the mosquitoes and the smell of the stag-
nant water that can come in through open windows, and the
sight of the vast expanse of water surrounding their tower only
makes her dizzy. For her, it is the water outside the room, not
the closed space inside, that is associated with suffocation
through drowning.

As breaches in the barrier separating inside from outside,
windows and doors are highly charged. The Old Woman pulls
her husband back in through the open window in the beginning, prefiguring the double suicide leap at the end. The main
double door in the center of the wall remains closed until the
entrance of the Emperor, when it bursts open with a great blaze
of light; it remains open for the rest of the play, but the light
turns to darkness with the death of the old couple. The way
the many side doors (the stage directions call for seven of them)
function undermines any possibility of identifying certain doors
with rooms where chairs are stored and others with outside
entrances. When the guests begin to arrive in large numbers,
the Old Man rushes to door after door to admit them, while
the Old Woman exits and enters with more chairs at an equally
furious pace, never entering through the same door through
which she has exited. The immediate offstage space thus becomes an undifferentiated "outside" that serves first to define,
through opposition, what "inside" means; the outside then destroys inside by invading it. At the end of the play, the barrier

that had both protected and imprisoned the old couple is effectively destroyed as the main double door and the two windows stand wide open. Like holes in a ship's hull, the doors and windows in the wall have allowed the old couple's secure, private interior space to be filled to overflowing, expelling them into the darkness outside. Viewed from the perspective of spatial structures, then, the climactic double suicide leap is the result of a reversal of the initial situation, in which inside was private, closed, and secure, and outside was public, open, and vertiginous.

The immediate offstage space is inscribed in the same temporal frame as the onstage scenic space, linked to it through the sounds of the boats arriving and the doorbell, through the accumulation of chairs (and guests) brought in from the wings, and through the lighting—watery green at first (like the water outside), brightening as more and more guests arrive, reaching its greatest intensity with the arrival of the Emperor, and fading into gloomy darkness with the death of the old couple. This confirmation of the concrete existence of the space in the wings belies any reading of the play that would make all the invisible guests hallucinations of a senile old couple. By contrast, the exterior *dramatic* space evoked in the dialogue between the old couple is clearly unreal, logically impossible. Its temporal relationship to the action that unfolds on stage is unstable, situated in a past that has the quality of myth rather than history. "Before," says the Old Man, "it stayed light outside until nine, ten, even until midnight" (113). The word Paris at first designates a village the Old Man walked into one day; the Old Woman maintains that the place never existed, but her husband answers that it was a city of light that burned out four hundred thousand years ago (116). The garden evoked on two occasions in the punning story is the Garden of Eden to which the old couple was denied entry (this is the first appearance of the topos of the lost paradise that recurs a number of times in Ionesco's work). Logically impossible and discontinuous with the spatiotemporal frame of the action that unfolds on stage, the exterior dramatic space of the play is evoked solely through conversation between the old couple; the internal contradictions in the conversations serve to undermine any independent reality that might be ascribed to this exterior world.[7] This external world is thus totally private, underscoring the ontological autonomy of the hermetically closed world of the play, "sharpening the apprehension of the theatrical as such" (Champigny 158). Such emphasis on the ontological discontinuity between the world of the play and the world outside is characteristic of modern metatheater, which attacks the conventions of dramatic realism according to which the audience is presumed to be looking through the "missing fourth wall" at a scene that is endeavoring to mask its own theatricality by imitating the world of the audience.

While the horizontal axis (inside versus outside) dominates, the vertical axis (up versus down) also has a role in the play's spatial structures, reflecting Ionesco's well-known and frequently cited statement that his theater reflects a tension between the twin poles of lightness (associated with movement upward) and heaviness (falling downward).[8] This dichotomy becomes more important in later plays, but it is already significant here. The old couple live up in a tower, for example, their physical position separating them from the world below just as their advanced age separates them from their past. The Old Man enjoys this view from above, while the Old Woman finds it dizzying and frightening; height represents adventure for the Old Man and danger for his wife, echoing the conflict previously discussed between inside and outside. Moreover, during the course of the play, they must leave the plane they occupied in the first scene (with the Old Man sitting on his wife's lap), forced first to stand and then to perch on chairs to see each other. The old couple reach their highest point in space precisely at the moment of their greatest triumph, with the dual arrivals of the Emperor and the Orator. Unable to maintain this precarious position, they fall to their death below, reestablishing equilibrium.

The couple's final farewell emphasizes the spatial component of their relationship; the Old Man regrets that they are separated from each other at this supreme moment by the pitiless crowd and that their cadavers will fall far apart, destined to rot in "aquatic solitude" rather than "within the selfsame skin, within the same sepulchre" (158). Separated in space, they look to the dimension of time for consolation: "Let us be united in time and in eternity, even if we are not together in space, as we were in adversity: let us die at the same moment" (158). They die confident of their place in history—"At least, they'll name a street after us" (158)—but the subsequent failure of the Orator to transmit the Old Man's message effectively forecloses this possibility. Despite their conviction that they will leave a trace—"We will leave traces, since we are people and not cities" (158)—they vanish from time as completely as from space, leaving no traces in either dimension.

Language

The old couple pass their time entertaining each other (and us) with stories that are full of highly inventive and very funny wordplay. Much of it is untranslatable punning, as in the Old Man's long story that begins, in the French version, "Alors on a ri . . ." and plays on associations both of sound and sense with the string "On a ri" (we laughed), "Òn arri . . . va" (we arrived) and "riz" (rice). (This is the passage that begins with the Old Woman's request that the Old Man tell *the* story: "Then at last we arrived . . ." [115–17].) Fanciful lists occur frequently, generated and organized by poetic rather than prosaic principles. Some lists play on associations of sound: "The papacy, the papayas, and the papers?" (121); "My pet, my orphan, dworfan, worfan, morphan, orphan" (118); "In order to make crepes de Chine? A leaf of beef, an hour of flour" (133). When the Photo-engraver offers a gift to the Old Woman, she wonders, "Is it a flower, sir? or a cradle? a pear tree? or a crow" (131). (In the French version, the relation of "cradle" to "crow" is more noticeable than in English because of the rhyme between "berceau" [cradle] and "corbeau" [crow].) The guest list includes such disparate entities as "the presidents, the police, the merchants, the buildings, the pen holders, the chromosomes" (121), and the Old Woman tells her husband that he could have been "head admiral, head cabinetmaker, head orchestra conductor" (119).

As in the earlier plays, clichés abound in *The Chairs*, exposing the automatic nature of most everyday speech. Also as in earlier works, here the cliché may be deformed to produce a comic effect ("Those days have flown away as fast as a train. Time has left the marks of his wheels on our skin" [132]), and famous lines of French poetry appear in incongruous contexts: "Where are the snows of yester year?" (from François Villon) (132); "I no longer want to gather rosebuds" (134) (a reference to Ronsard's exhortation to "gather rosebuds while you may"). The rhetoric of the Old Man's speeches to the Colonel, the Emperor, and the Orator parodies the pompous discourse of public speakers in general, and the Old Woman's crooning to the Old Man is another comically incongruous register of language, given the extreme old age of the protagonists.

The language of *The Chairs* is full of what might be termed nonsense. When the old couple reminisce about the past or refer to the world outside, for example, they often contradict themselves or each other: they have and don't have a son; the Old Man was an ungrateful son who abandoned his mother to die in a ditch, yet he was a model son who held his dying parents in his arms; the Old Woman both has and has not met the Colonel before. Many years ago, says the Old Man, they visited a place called Paris; when his wife objects that no such place ever existed, he insists that it did, since it collapsed four hundred thousand years ago. The Old Man says he loved Belle a hundred years ago, when the moon was still a living star.

All of these contradictions, illogicalities, clichés, puns, and other playful uses of language do not mean that the play is about the failure of language to communicate (although such an interpretation is a tempting one, given the failure of the Orator at the end of the play). On the contrary, the old couple communicate perfectly well with each other and with their guests. What the play does foreground is the gestural (disengaged, poetic) as opposed to the designative (engaged, practical) function of language.[9] By undermining language's designative function, the play draws attention to its own theatricality, that is, to the ontological discontinuity between its world and ours. Failure to recognize this feature of the play's language has led critics to interpret the play as a work of science fiction or to view the old couple as "the sole survivors of a world-destroying flood" suffering from a "senile loss of memory."[10] Rather than designating a preexisting reality, the language in this play calls its own world into being: as the Old Woman says, "It's in speaking that ideas come to us, words, and then we, in our own words, we find perhaps everything, the city too, the garden, and then we are orphans no longer" (120–21). Freed to a large degree from referential constraints, language becomes a game in which poetic and playful functions are foregrounded. Unlike that of the earlier plays, in which the characters are grotesque automata traversed or even used by language, the language in this play is organized around several recurring themes—the passage of time, romantic love, maternal and filial love, for example—and it has a definite lyrical quality in certain places. Furthermore, while the characters are indeed grotesque (the play is a farce, after all), they have a psychological consistency and depth lacking heretofore in Ionesco's theater.

A Tragic Farce

The Chairs is first of all a farce; as Ionesco wrote in a letter to Sylvain Dhomme, "everything should be exaggerated, excessive, painful, childish, a caricature, without finesse" (*NCN* 187). Humor abounds in the language, as the discussion above indicates. The physical humor (slapstick) characteristic of farce is also prominent in the play: the Old Man imitates the month of February by scratching his head à la Stan Laurel; the Old Woman suddenly lifts her skirts, exposes her chest, and thrusts her hips forward in lewd fashion when she meets the Photo-engraver; the Old Man cries and whines like a baby while seated in his wife's lap; and the scene in which the multitude of guests and chairs arrive is an extended sight gag reminiscent of the Keystone Cops. All of these farcical elements serve to underline the grotesque nature of the old couple and their situation, thereby preventing the play from lapsing into pathos and sentimentality.[11] At the same time, the laughter the play elicits is painful, as the humor is undercut by the themes of failure and loss and by the sense of absence and futility that the ending is designed to convey. As Ionesco wrote in "Experience of the Theatre," "it seems to me that the comic is tragic, and that the tragedy of man is pure derision." In *The Chairs,* he tried to "confront comedy and tragedy in order to link them in a new dramatic synthesis" or to "sink tragedy in comedy" (*NCN* 27).

The Couple

A central theme of the play is the ambivalent nature of love. The relationship between the old couple is clearly Oedipal: when the Old Man cries for his lost mother, the Old Woman rocks him on her knees and says, "I am your wife, I'm the one who is your mamma now" (118); later, the Old Man explains to Belle, "My worthy helpmeet, Semiramis, has taken the place of my mother" (133). In a speech suppressed in performance, the Old Man tells the Emperor that his wife replaced both his father and his mother. As the good mother, the Old Woman is nurturing and supportive, and the Old Man is grateful: "O my faithful helpmeet! . . . you who have believed in me, unfailingly, during a whole century, who have never left me, never" (158). At the same time, however, the love the old couple feel for each other is permeated with guilt. This ambivalence is already inscribed in the Old Woman's name, Semiramis. A legendary queen from Assyrian mythology who founded Babylon and Nineveh, the original Semiramis had her husband Ninus assassinated and gave up her throne to her son Ninias; she was thus the exact opposite of the self-effacing helpmeet the Old Woman appears to be. Furthermore, in Voltaire's play *Sémiramis,* the queen falls in love with her son, who kills her.

The guilt associated with this relationship is reflected in the two conflicting sets of narratives regarding 1) the Old Man's treatment of his own parents and 2) the old couple's son. (The fact that the old couple contradict each other on both of these matters does not mean that one is lying and the other telling the truth; rather, the language thematizes the ambivalence and guilt that lie at the heart of their relationship.) According to his own narrative, the Old Man was a cruel and ungrateful son who abandoned his mother to die in a ditch; this neglect has been for him a source of guilt. Read psychoanalytically, such guilt is both the sublimation of the son's resentment of the mother's smothering love and his guilt about the forbidden sexual desire he feels for her. He tells the guests that he regrets that he and his wife have no children; he would have loved to have a son, as would his wife—"and my poor Semiramis is so maternal, too" (134). Yet he already occupies the son's place with his wife, thereby making any offspring of their union a symbol of transgression. Absent from the Old Man's story (except in a passage that was suppressed for performance) is any mention of his father. In this context, the Emperor takes the place of the absent father. It is to him that the Old Man looks for approval and validation: "I might have been something, if I could have been sure of the support of Your Majesty . . . I have no other support . . . if you hadn't come, everything would have been too late . . . you are, Sire, my last recourse . . ." (150). In the Old Woman's narrative, they had a son who left them (just as the Old Man abandoned his mother) at the age of seven; that the Old Woman feels guilty for driving this son away is revealed when she says that their son left because he accused his parents of murdering all the birds. According to her, the Old Man was a model son whose parents died in his arms; she thus idealizes the husband who is also her own son.

Guilt effectively blocks open expression of sexual desire between the old couple. Because sexual relations between mother and son are taboo, the old couple's desires are deflected onto Belle and the Photo-engraver. The Old Man regrets the passage of time and laments the loss of a chance for mythic romantic love, evoking Tristan and Isolde, while the Old Woman displays lewd erotic behavior. (As is often the case in Ionesco, the man is the creative, romantic artist, while the woman is associated with down-to-earth reality and the physical.)

Authority and Society

The social satire and hostility toward authority that appeared in the earlier plays are not absent in *The Chairs*. The Colonel and the Emperor appear as authority figures, standing in for the Old Man's absent father. In the first case, the Colonel loses stature when he makes unseemly sexual advances toward the first guest. If the Old Man is overjoyed that the Emperor finally arrives to recognize and support him, he is also quite bitter that this support and recognition have been withheld so long by the society that the Emperor represents. His speech to the Emperor is a long litany of the disappointments and indignities that he has had to endure.

Ambivalence toward authority is also reflected in the comic lists of titles that the Old Woman uses to remind her husband and the guests of what the Old Man might have become. Though he is only head janitor, he might well have become head president, head king, head doctor, head sailor, head cabinetmaker, head journalist, head actor, and so on. Similarly, the guest list is an irreverent jumble of professions, buildings, penholders, and chromosomes, all of whom can be reduced to "intellectuals and proprietors": as the Old Woman says, "the intellectuals and the proprietors will take the place of papas and mammas" (122).

The Old Man has been laboring for years on a "message" that will save society, he says, but that message is never delivered. The futility of the final scene exposes not just the theme of absence but also the failure of the individual in the face of society's indifference.

Victims of Duty

Victimes du devoir (*Victims of Duty*) was the first of five plays (the others were *Amédée, Rhinoceros, The Killer, A Stroll in the Air*) that Ionesco adapted from short stories in a collection he later published entitled *La Photo du Colonel* (*The Colonel's Photograph*). Both the story and the play were written in 1952, and the play was premiered in February 1953 at the Théâtre du Quartier latin in a production directed by Jacques Mauclair. This play represents a clear break with the early, absurdist style. Compared to the earliest works, *Victims* is much more cerebral, verbal, and personalized; it is also less daring and innovative theatrically, perhaps because it was adapted from a prose narrative. (In general, it is in those works conceived directly for the theater—*The Chairs* or *Exit the King,* for example—that Ionesco makes most effective use of the specifically theatrical, concrete language of the stage.) With this play Ionesco has abandoned anti-theater in favor of a "new kind of theater." The play is certainly not lacking in innovations and powerful stage images, however. Its dramatic innovations include Ionesco's first forays into metatheater as well as his first attempts to transpose his own dreams onto the stage. The pantomimed journey that Choubert makes through his unconscious, the multiple roles played by the detective and Madeleine, and the final tableau (in which all of the characters are forcing bread down Choubert's throat) are all significant experiments with dramatic form.

The setting is once again a typical middle-class interior; the play begins with a conversation between Choubert and his wife Madeleine in which they discuss the contemporary state of affairs and of the theater. While platitudes and clichés are copious (as in earlier plays), the conversation is coherent, and these characters seem closer to "normal" than those in any previous play. When a very young and timid police detective knocks on their door, they gladly invite him in; he is looking for the previous tenant of their apartment—Mallot "with a 't.'" Once he is admitted, his demeanor immediately becomes authoritarian, then tyrannical, as he forces Choubert to undertake a grueling search for the mysterious Mallot. A suddenly seductive and erotic Madeleine becomes the detective's accomplice.

From this point on, the play becomes a dream-like psychodrama in which Choubert first descends literally and figuratively into the mud of his own past, encountering his parents (played by the detective and Madeleine) along the way. After he acts out part of his quest on a small stage for the detective and Madeleine, they urge him to climb out of the past and continue his pursuit of Mallot. His ascension accelerates too quickly, however, and they must use all their physical force to prevent him from flying away. The detective then assumes the role of doctor whose job it is to fatten up the infantile Choubert. At this point, two more characters suddenly appear. One is a woman who sits quietly eating peanuts until the end of the play; the other is Nicolas d'Eu, a poet and friend of Choubert, who enters from the rear of the stage. While he and the detective discuss contemporary theater, Madeleine carries hundreds of coffee cups onto the stage, just as the Old Woman carried chairs in *The Chairs,* and the detective cruelly forces Choubert to stuff himself with huge quantities of bread in order to "block up the holes in his memory." When Nicolas finally notices how his friend is being tortured, he turns on the detective and stabs him, despite Choubert's protestations that he is just fine and Madeleine's pleas for mercy. The detective dies in melodramatic fashion, proclaiming that he is just a "victim of duty." In order that this sacrifice not be in vain, Nicolas, Madeleine, and the silent woman immediately take the detective's place, forcing Choubert to resume stuffing himself with bread. As the curtain falls, all the characters are screaming, "Chew, swallow!" at each other; all are self-proclaimed victims of duty.

Metatheater

Victims of Duty is the first of Ionesco's plays to expose and address directly the subject of theater itself; in other words, it is the first of several self-conscious or metatheatrical plays (*Improvisation* and *Exit the King* are the most metatheatrical of Ionesco's works). We learn early on that Choubert is obsessed; he passionately wishes to know whether anything new can be done in the theater. In terms that echo Ionesco's own critique of bourgeois theater, Choubert reproaches contemporary theater for failing to go beyond the outmoded formulas of thrillers: "All the plays that have ever been written, from Ancient Greece to the present day, have never really been anything but thrillers. Drama's always been realistic and there's always been a detective about. Every play's an investigation brought to a successful conclusion. There's a riddle and it's solved in the final scene. Sometimes earlier. You seek, then you find. Might as well give the game away at the start" (119). Choubert's theory that all plays are thrillers seems to be confirmed when the very play that he is in quickly turns into one; it appears to revolve around solving the mystery of Mallot's whereabouts. Yet, rather than solving this riddle, the play only deepens it, thereby offering itself as an example of a new kind of theater.

The answer to Choubert's question about the possibility of a new theater is furnished by Nicolas d'Eu, himself a writer. During his lengthy conversation with the detective, he elaborates a theory of theater that corresponds to Ionesco's. This new theater should be non-Aristotelian and oneiric; it must free itself from outmoded forms and adopt "a different logic and a different psychology." As for action and causality, they should be abandoned, at least in their old-fashioned, obvious form. Finally, the old categories of drama and tragedy must be replaced: "No more drama, no more tragedy: the tragic's turning comic, the comic is tragic, and life's getting more cheerful" (159). Given these theoretical pronouncements within the play, it is obvious that the play offers itself as an example of just the kind of theater Nicolas (speaking for Ionesco) is espousing.

The unfavorable critical reception accorded to Ionesco's new theater is cleverly alluded to directly in the play. In the first scene, for example, Madeleine agrees that Choubert has some original ideas, but she suggests that he should find out what the "experts" think. When Choubert asks who they might be, Madeleine answers (in a humorous jab at Ionesco's critics), "Oh, there's bound to be someone, among the cinema enthusiasts, or the professors at the College de France, the influential members of the Agricultural School, the Norwegians, or some of those veterinary surgeons . . . A vet, now there's someone who should have a lot of ideas" (120). The audience's lack of comprehension and appreciation of this new theater is also portrayed in the scene in which Madeleine and the detective become spectators of Choubert's play-within-a-play. Madeleine's reactions—"A lot of bad parnassian-symbolic-surrealism"; "My dear, we'd far better spend the rest of the evening at a cabaret . . ." (143)—are exactly those of many spectators and critics of Ionesco's earlier plays. Finally, Ionesco includes a reference to himself: Nicolas says that he doesn't need to write because "we've got Ionesco and Ionesco, that's enough!" (162). On one level, this assertion means that Nicolas doesn't have to write because he and the other characters have already been "written" by Ionesco. At the same time, it is a double-edged kind of praise; it can mean either that Ionesco is so good that we don't need any more writers, or that just one writer of this kind of theater is plenty. At any rate, these direct allusions to his own theater indicate that Ionesco had already achieved a measure of success as a playwright.

Ionesco's First Dream Play

One key to understanding the play can be found in the conversation between Nicolas and the detective about contemporary theater. Nicolas tells the detective, "The theatre of my dreams would be irrationalist" (157). Contemporary theater, according to the poet, is still a "prisoner of outmoded forms," trapped in an outmoded psychology. The new theater that Nicolas would create would be surrealistic, but only "in so far as surrealism is oneirical": "Inspiring me with a different logic and a different psychology, I should introduce contradiction where there is no contradiction, and no contradiction where there is what common-sense usually calls contradiction. . . . We'll get rid of the principle of identity and let movement and dynamic psychology take its place" (158). Here Nicolas is describing precisely the play in which he appears; *Victims of Duty* is Choubert's nightmare, the first of Ionesco's autobiographical (or autopsychological) dream plays. It has all the vivid clarity of detail of a nightmare and exhibits that different logic that governs dreams; Ionesco told Claude Bonnefoy that, when he was writing the play, he was "within the extraconscious logic of the dream" (*ENT* 68), "in a nightmare" (69). By turning inward to his own dreams, he will break through the "crust" of conventional realism to find new dramatic forms that would reach the level of archetype and myth: "I hope I have rediscovered in my own mind the permanent basic outlines of drama. . . . The discovery of forgotten archetypes, changeless but expressed in a new way" (*NCN* 131). "I believe that the social crust and discursive thought conceal man from himself and cut him off from his most deeply repressed desires, his most essential needs, his myths, his indisputable anguish, his most secret reality and his dreams" (*NCN* 223–24).

One feature of the play that identifies it as a dream is the instability and fluidity of the characters' identity. The police detective, for example, is an extremely mutable character: he is at once the representative of a repressive totalitarian society, Choubert's father, the son Madeleine and Choubert never had, and a scapegoat who stands in for Choubert as a victim of duty. When he first enters the Chouberts' apartment, he is very deferential and timid. The Chouberts comment on how well he is dressed and how handsome he is:

> Madeleine: Beautiful eyes, such a gentle look. Hasn't he?
> Choubert: A nice man you feel you can trust. With the face of a child. (123)

After he enters the room, however, he becomes increasingly rude and tyrannical; he addresses the couple disrespectfully (using first names and, in the French version, the familiar form of address) and orders them about. Madeleine must bring him coffee, and Choubert must find "Mallot with a 't.'" He will be Choubert's authoritarian guide as the search for Mallot is quickly transformed into a journey through Choubert's own past. The detective then plays the role of Choubert's father in the extended sequence that constitutes the heart of Choubert's psychodrama. First, the detective and Madeleine act out a scene from Choubert's childhood in which his father forces his mother to drink poison. Choubert then pleads with his father for reconciliation and mutual understanding: "She forgave you, but I went on and carried out *her* revenge myself. . . . What's the good of taking vengeance? It's always the avenger who suffers. . . . I was wrong to despise you. I'm no better than you are. . . . Let's make it up! Let's be friends! Give me your hand!" (136). In a long monologue, the detective-father answers, explaining how much he had loved his son: "I had forgiven the world, for love of you. Everything was saved, because now nothing could ever wipe out the fact of your birth into the living universe" (138). He asks for and grants forgiveness, but Choubert is unable to hear him: "Father, why don't you speak, why don't you answer me! . . . How sad to think that never, never again I shall hear your voice. . . . Never, never, never, never. And I shall never know . . ." (139).[12] The detective then shifts roles abruptly, becoming first a spectator of the play in which Choubert continues his descent/search, then a cruel doctor/inquisitor. When Nicolas d'Eu turns on him Choubert becomes a child again as Madeleine tries in vain to defend him, calling him "Poor boy" and "My pet" (164–65), just as though he were her son. She points out that he is only twenty and that Nicolas "could have been his father" (164).

Madeleine is as polymorphous as the detective, evolving in rapid succession from sharp-tongued contemporary to ravishing young seductress to ancient wife. She becomes Choubert's mother, making explicit the Oedipal nature of their relationship, and she repeats the role of mother with the detective. Nicolas d'Eu is a character straight out of a dream. His name is a play on words triggered by the line immediately preceding his entrance. "Deux" (two) is a homonym of "d'Eu"—he is the double for both Choubert and his father. The detective asks whether he is Nicholas II, Czar of Russia, alluding to his status as authority figure. He appears as Choubert's defender precisely when Choubert is the most vulnerable—Madeleine (his mother) has been sent out for coffee and is no longer there to protect him—and he represents a greater authority and power than that exercised by the detective. Furthermore, he is a poet, a writer, a double for Choubert ("Schubert"), also an artist.

Read as Choubert's dream, the play is rich in psychoanalytic material. According to Freud, all dreams represent some degree of wish fulfillment; wishes and desires that have been repressed into the subconscious appear, but in altered, disguised form. Freud theorized that the mechanisms of condensation and displacement operate in dreams both to disguise and to reveal to the explorer (the analyst) the partially repressed dream thoughts that lie beneath the dream content. Condensation means that one object or character in a dream incorporates many different significant traits that have been drawn from a number of sources in the dreamer's psyche and concentrated in this one object. Displacement means that, since the repressed thought or wish cannot be fully and openly expressed even in the dream, elements in the manifest dream content are often displaced (onto another person, for example) or reversed; Freud theorized that the greater the repression, the greater the reversal or displacement in the dream. Applying these principles to Choubert's dream, we would find that Choubert's guilt stems from the childhood trauma of watching his father force his mother to drink (*swallow*) poison. During the course of his descent into his psyche, Choubert regresses completely to the infantile state, where, according to Freud, the source of the most powerful emotions lies. Just as his father forced his mother to swallow the poison, the detective forces him to swallow the bread, recreating the father's cruelty. Even as he fears his father, however, Choubert desires his love and approval, so his hatred and rage are displaced onto the character of Nicolas d'Eu, who performs the ritual murder of the father with a knife. Yet Nicolas is also the feared father who kills (castrates) his son, the detective ("He could have been your son"), and continues to punish Choubert for his forbidden wishes (to kill his father and sleep with his mother). The silent woman is both an example of the inexplicable object that Ionesco deemed necessary for the creation of the atmosphere of a dream and a character who represents Choubert's absent mother, no longer able to speak or intervene because she is dead. Yet she is also young and unmarried, therefore still available as an object of erotic desire to the son she has not yet had.

The dream (the play) seems to end on a negative note—Nicolas's murder of the detective enacts both sides of the Oedipal drama between father and son: the castration feared by the son and the son's ritual murder of the father. Guilt for wishing this murder is reinstalled, reinforced this time even by the silent woman who joins in the chorus of "Chew, swallow." Yet the dream is not entirely negative. In the father's monologue the answer that the son desires to hear is proffered: "You can reject me and blush for me and insult my memory as much as you like. I'll not blame you. I'm no longer capable of hate. I can't help forgiving. I owe you more than you owe me. I wouldn't want you to suffer, I want you to stop feeling guilty. Forget what you consider to be [your] faults" (139). Even though he is unable to hear his father in the dream, it is *he* who has dreamed the father's answer, thereby gaining the forgiveness and love he had sought.

The play is rich in other elements typically found in dreams. For example, proper names have great, if hermetic, significance: Mallot with a "t," the strange "Nicolas d'Eu," the long series of place-names that Choubert recites during his journey (144–45), and the list of Mallot's aliases—Marius, Marin,

70

Lougastec, Perpignan, Machecroche (154). As in dreams (or poetry), these proper names are generated both metaphorically (through association with the sea, for example) and metonymically (through phonetic slippage). This second kind of wordplay was already quite frequent in Ionesco's earlier plays, as we have seen. In *Victims of Duty,* however, the words (in the original French) have a magical power to generate characters and actions that is particularly characteristic of dreams. The detective's line "Now it's between us two!" ("A nous *deux!*") (154; emphasis added) created Nicolas *d'Eu,* the double of both Choubert and the detective. Similarly, the alias Machecroche (in conjunction with the childhood trauma of watching the mother swallow poison) generates the bizarre punishment of chewing and swallowing the hard bread.[13]

Lightness versus Heaviness

Ionesco has spoken and written on several occasions about a fundamental tension that informs his theater; it is the opposition between feelings of lightness, euphoria, transparency, and evanescence on the one hand and heaviness, despair, denseness, and entombment on the other. When Claude Bonnefoy remarked to him that there is a lot of mud, a lot of sinking in his theater, Ionesco answered that he alternates between feeling light and heavy, or too light or too heavy (see note 8). This is precisely how the detective characterizes Choubert toward the end of the play: "He's heavy when he ought to be light, too light when he ought to be heavy, he's unbalanced, he's got no grip on reality!" (154). At one level, the feelings of lightness and evanescence are positive, associated with euphoria and freedom, while heaviness and denseness are negative, associated with claustration and death. Just as chairs choked the stage in *The Chairs,* the stage in *Victims of Duty* is inundated with coffee cups—guilt expressed as proliferation of matter. The mass of bread that Choubert is forced to swallow is another example of a concrete correlative of oppression. Commenting on such proliferation, Ionesco wrote: "What is light grows heavy, the transparent becomes dense, the world oppresses, the universe is crushing me. A curtain, an impassable

wall stands between me and the world, between me and myself; matter fills every corner, takes up all the space and its
weight annihilates all freedom. . . . When words are worn out,
the mind is worn out. The universe, encumbered with matter,
is then empty of presence: 'too much' links up with 'not enough'
and objects are the materialization of solitude, of the victory
of the anti-spiritual forces, of everything we are struggling
against" (*NCN* 163–64).

Choubert's odyssey reflects the contrast between heaviness
(mud) and lightness (flying). The first part of his journey into
his own past is a descent into sticky mud: "I'm walking through
the mud. It's sticking to the soles of my shoes . . . my feet are
so heavy! I'm afraid of slipping" (129). As he moves closer to
the trauma of his childhood, he sinks deeper and deeper until
he is entirely submerged in the mud that represents guilt and
death; Madeleine urges him downward, saying, "Go right under. Stretch out your arms in the mud, move your fingers about,
swim through the deep and find Mallot, whatever you do . . .
Down . . . Down . . ." (132). Sinking into the mud is a motif that
recurs in Ionesco's work (see especially the film *The Mire*, made
for German television), and it symbolizes for him the "difficulty of being" (*ENT* 36). After this descent into the dark un-
derworld, Choubert climbs an invisible mountain (represented
in Mauclair's production by a chair atop a table)[14] until he
reaches the summit and emerges into a dazzling light "mightier
than the sun": no longer afraid of death (149), he is able to fly
(151).[15] With the stage in total darkness (since Choubert has
climbed out of sight), we hear him say, "I'm bathing in the light.
The light is seeping through me. I'm so surprised to be, surprised to be, surprised to be . . ." (151). This euphoric evanescence ("the easiness of being") is the opposite emotional state
of sinking into the mud; it is the first transcription into
Ionesco's theater of a euphoric experience that he has recounted
several times in his journals and interviews:

> I was about 17 or 18. I was in a small provincial town.
> It was June, around noon. Suddenly I got the feeling
> that . . . I was in another world, one that was mine in
> a way the old one wasn't, an infinitely brighter one; . . .

it seemed to me that the sky had become extremely dense, that I could almost feel the light, that the houses had a gleam no one had ever seen before, an unusual sparkle, truly out of the ordinary. . . . I experienced an enormous joy. . . . Then I said to myself, "I'm not afraid to die anymore." I felt an absolute, definitive truth. . . . I felt that gravity no longer existed. I walked along effortlessly, taking long strides, great leaps. (*ENT* 32–33)[16]

Lightness and the dream of flying, on the one hand, and heaviness and the horror of sinking into the mud, on the other, are not mutually exclusive poles, however. Rather, each represents one aspect of Ionesco's "astonishment at being," the existential consciousness of the contingent nature of being.[17] As Ionesco told Bonnefoy, "Lightness is euphoric evanescence that can become tragic or painful when anguish is present" (*ENT* 36). In his most recent memoirs, he elaborates on this ambivalence: "The world free of gravity used to be able to give me a kind of euphoria. Freedom. Internal flight. Now, this spiritual weightlessness reveals to me the inhuman precariousness of everything. Between emptiness and the too-full, it's hard to prefer one, to choose one's anguish, one's fear. Fear of too much, fear of not enough, fear of thick mud or the solid earth, or fear of its holes?" (*Quête* 21–22). Thus Choubert's ascent into the dizzying heights and blinding sunlight of the mountain top is not without its own suffering; when Madeleine and the detective literally drag him back to the earth, they are dragging him back from weightless nonbeing into the reality of being. That the realm of earthly being is not completely negative is indicated by Choubert's description of a marvelous garden that he glimpses when he reaches the very deepest point of his journey into the past: "The wind shakes the forests, lightning rends the thick gloom, and there on the horizon, behind the storm, a gigantic curtain of darkness is heavily lifting. . . . and there, appearing in the distance, gleaming through the shadows, still as a dream in the midst of the storm, a magic city. . . . or a magic garden, a bubbling spring and fountain and flowers of fire in the night . . ." (142–43). This nostalgia for a lost earthly paradise had already appeared in *The Chairs* and recurs in various forms in later plays, including *The Killer, Hunger and Thirst,* and *A Hell of a Mess!.* The ambivalence surrounding the lightness/heaviness dichotomy is also expressed through the oxymorons and contradictions Choubert uses to describe his surroundings and feelings: "the light is dark . . . the stars are dim" (141); "Joy . . . and pain . . . tearing you . . . healing you . . . Fullness . . . And emptiness . . . Hopeless hope. I feel strong, I feel weak, I feel ill, I feel well, but I feel, above all, I feel myself, still, I feel myself . . ." (143).

Critique of Totalitarian Society

The detective, like the Professor in *The Lesson,* is another incarnation of the grotesque authority figure who appears time and again in Ionesco's theater. As he said in one of his journals, "Everything that represented authority seemed to me, and is, unjust" (*PP* 17). Like all father figures in Ionesco's personal archetypal symbolism, the detective is a monster and a tyrant.[18] A member of the secret police in a totalitarian state, he already seems to know everything about the Chouberts (Madeleine's name, for example, and Choubert's political beliefs) before he enters their apartment. He begins his interrogation by having Madeleine remove her husband's necktie, belt, and shoelaces, signifying that Choubert is under arrest, but there is no warrant or any hint that Choubert enjoys any rights at all. The sadistic detective subjects Choubert to psychological and physical torture as he forces him to find the mysterious Mallot: the abuse is both verbal (for example, he calls Choubert "fathead," "poor wretch," and "nonentity" [152–54]) and physical (he pulls Choubert up by the ears and forces him to eat bread crusts that are as hard and rough as the bark of oak trees [156–62]).

Madeleine also represents authority in her primary role as Choubert's wife. At the beginning of the play, for example, Choubert expresses his skepticism regarding the government's latest "friendly recommendation" (that the citizens of big towns "cultivate detachment"): "We know how suggestions suddenly come to look like rules, like strict laws" (118). Madeleine acts as the apologist for authority: "Well, my dear, you know, the law *is* necessary, and what's necessary and indispensable is *good,* and everything's that [*sic*] good is *nice.* And it really is very nice indeed to be a good, law-abiding citizen and do one's duty and have a clear conscience! . . ." (118). She is the detective's accomplice throughout the play as she joins him in urging Choubert to find Mallot. As wife, she is sharp-tongued and highly critical of her husband, using her sexuality only to entice him to obey the detective's orders. During the scene in which Choubert is acting out his descent into the deepest level of his past, it is Madeleine and not the detective who is very critical of Choubert's performance: "He's an old ham! It's ridiculous! Unthinkable! He's a liar!" (143).

Whereas the Old Woman in *The Chairs* was for the most part the good mother, Madeleine represents the wife as bad mother. She speaks with the voice of the superego, scolding her husband as though he were a bad little boy: "You ought to be ashamed of yourself, talking to Monsieur Chief Inspector like that! . . . And now I suppose you're going to have the cheek to tell Monsieur Chief Inspector you're not trying to get your own back" (153–54). When Choubert protests at the end of the play that he doesn't want to continue the search for Mallot under Nicolas's direction, Madeleine browbeats him as she would a child: "I don't like husbands who won't do as they're told! What do you mean by it? You ought to be ashamed!" (166). The tender feelings that Madeleine expresses are directed toward the detective when, at the end of the play, he comes to represent the son that she and Choubert do not have. Thus it is only through displacement (the detective stands in for Choubert and Madeleine for Choubert's mother) that Choubert can receive from his wife the love he wanted from his dead mother.

The third authority figure in the play is Nicolas d'Eu. Although he seems at first to be a champion and avenger as he uses his superior age and strength to rid Choubert of his tormenter, he is immediately taken up in the larger system that demands obedience. The detective dies "a victim of duty," and, as Madeleine says at the end of the play, "We're all victims of duty!" (166). Thus the play's critique of authority is not limited to the psychoanalytic plane. Rather it is society itself that is targeted, for it places the collective good (here the need to find Mallot) above the individual's private needs and aspirations (here Choubert's desire to confront and reintegrate his past). Herein lies the significance of the "politics of detachment" recommended by the government that Choubert discusses with his wife at the beginning of the play. Choubert objects to this politics of renunciation because it requires "the sacrifice of some of our creature comforts," but Madeleine responds, "Sacrifice isn't always so difficult. There's sacrifice *and* sacrifice. Even if it *is* a bit of nuisance right at the start, getting rid of some of our habits, once we're rid of them, we're rid of them, and you never really give them another thought" (119). As the detective brutally tells Choubert when the latter begs to linger awhile in his own past in order perhaps to find out his father's answer, "Moaning won't do any good. What's your personal life to do with us?" (139). This conflict between the demands of a collective society and the individual's personal dreams and desires will remain an important element in the plays that follow, especially in *The Killer* and *Rhinoceros*.

Amédée, or How to Get Rid of it

Ionesco finished writing *Amédée* in August 1953 just after attending and speaking at a colloquium on new theater held at Cerisy-la-Salle. Like *Victims of Duty,* it is adapted from a short story ("Oriflamme") published in *The Colonel's Photograph*. It premiered on 14 April 1954 at the Théâtre de Babylone in a production directed by Jean-Marie Serreau. Although it reworks much of the thematic material from earlier plays, it marks a turning point in several respects. It is Ionesco's first three-act play; it contains far less wordplay than previous works do; and it is fantastic rather than nightmarish, relying on special effects for its optimistic surprise ending. Whereas the giant growing corpse of the first two acts is an effective and powerful device, the problems associated with staging the end of the play weaken its overall impact considerably. As with *Victims of Duty,* the fact that the play was adapted from a story is, no doubt, the source of these technical problems. (Similar problems arise later with *A Stroll in the Air.*)

The curtain rises on a sparely furnished, modest room where Amédée Buccioni and his wife Madeleine live and work; he is a playwright who has managed to write only two lines in fifteen years, and she is a telephone operator working at a switchboard in their living-dining room. The structure of a mystery is established from the beginning with Amédée's discovery that poisonous mushrooms (connected somehow with a mysterious presence in the bedroom offstage left) have begun to grow in the living room. Dialogue between Amédée and Madeleine establishes that the mysterious presence is a corpse that has been there for fifteen years. Only twenty years old when he died, he has been growing older and larger all this time, so that he now has a long white beard and threatens to outgrow the bedroom where he is hidden. Fearful of discovery, the Buccionis have neither received any visitors nor left their apartment in fifteen years; Amédée does the marketing by lowering a basket out the window, and when the postman attempts to deliver a letter, Amédée claims that it must be for another Amédée Buccioni living at another 29, rue des Généraux. The corpse is growing geometrically ("the incurable disease of the dead" [28]), and the first act ends in crisis as the giant feet burst through the bedroom door and begin to invade the living room.

When the second act begins, the right side of the stage is filled with all the furniture pushed out of the bedroom by the growing corpse, and the left side is filled with the huge feet and legs that are advancing in spurts across the stage. Each time they move, Amédée marks the progress with a chalk line on the floor. Everywhere giant mushrooms are also growing, so that there is less and less space left for the middle-aged couple. Faced with an ultimatum (Madeleine will divorce him if he doesn't get rid of the corpse), Amédée finally agrees to dispose of it as soon as night falls. While they wait for darkness, Amédée dozes off, and younger versions of Madeleine and Amédée appear in a dream sequence that explains the radical difference in temperament that has always characterized the couple: the young Amédée is a lyric poet who sees the world as light, freedom, and air, while Madeleine is bogged down in mud, darkness and fear. When it is dark enough, Amédée laboriously drags the corpse feetfirst out the window to the street below; his plan is to throw it into the Seine.

The setting in the third act is the street outside.[19] As Amédée is struggling with the unwieldy corpse, he is befriended by an American soldier and a French woman of ill repute named Mado. He is discovered and then pursued by a crowd of onlookers and two policemen. Suddenly, however, the corpse turns into a huge balloon or banner that carries him away, out of the reach of the crowd below, including Madeleine. The play ends as two onlookers say that it's time to go to bed because the show is over.

The Corpse

According to Ionesco, the origin of *Amédée* was a dream about a cadaver stretched out in a long corridor of a house he was living in at the time. The play grew up around that initial image, which may account for its loose structure: as the playwright remarked, "it's the corpse that gives the play its meaning. Everything else is just a story woven around it, even if the story has some meaning of its own" (*ENT* 83). As in a dream, the explanation for the corpse's presence is shrouded in ambiguity. In Madeleine's version, he was her lover, murdered by Amédée in a moment of jealous rage (36). Amédée is unsure that this was the way it happened: "I get everything so mixed up, dreams and real life, memories and imagination" (38). He offers a series of possible alternative explanations: perhaps he is the baby a neighbor left in their care years ago, killed by accident or negligence; perhaps he is the young lover, dead of a heart attack brought on by sexual excitement; perhaps he is the body of a young woman who drowned when Amédée didn't bother to rescue her (38–40). Whatever the circumstances of how the cadaver came to be there, however, Madeleine points out that they would still be guilty of hiding the body (40). Thus the corpse's significance is not reducible to that which it would have in some murder mystery; it functions rather as a symbol.

The central symbol in the play, the corpse is the objective correlative of guilt and remorse. As was the case in the previous two plays, proliferation of matter (the corpse, the poisonous mushrooms, the mounds of furniture in the second act) leaves no space for human life, joy, or dreams.[20] Here, however, the sin and guilt are much more precise, if no less enigmatic, than in *Victims of Duty*. At one level the cadaver is a metaphor for the death of love between Amédée and Madeleine and for the wasted years of their marriage: "All those wasted years, they're a dead weight" (41). Significantly, the corpse lies in their wedding bed. The corpse is the bitterness and resentment that have grown between them over the years; as Madeleine says, "He still has a grudge against us. The dead are terribly vindictive. . . . A bit more every day, every day a bit more, it all adds up" (19). For Amédée, love is the magical ecstatic state that would release them from this prison: "If we really loved each other, none of this would be important. Why don't we try to love each other, *please,* Madeleine. Love puts everything right, you know, it changes life. . . . I know it does! . . . Love makes up for everything" (52–53).

On a metaphysical level, the corpse symbolizes original sin—the Fall, in a literal sense, from timeless paradise into mortality.[21] As in *Victims of Duty,* the two emotional states underlying Ionesco's work (heaviness and depression versus lightness and euphoria) are of central importance here. Weighted down by the guilt and remorse that the corpse symbolizes, Amédée has become heavy and tired: "I feel so tired, so tired . . . worn out, heavy. I've got indigestion and my tummy's all blown out! I feel sleepy all the time" (7). He has not been able to write since the corpse has been there: "Write in the state I'm in! A man should be in a state of elation to do creative work" (8). The dream sequence illustrates how different Amédée was as a young man. Then, his emotional state was just the opposite of this crushing fatigue: "An insubstantial universe . . . Freedom . . . Ethereal power . . . Balance . . . airy abundance . . . world without weight . . ." (50).

As a symbol of love that might have been, however, the corpse contains within it the possibility of redemption and salvation. Its eyes are beautiful and luminous: "His eyes haven't aged. They're still as beautiful. Great green eyes. Shining like beacons" (15). Because Amédée is unable (or unwilling) to keep the eyelids closed, the eyes give off a pleasant greenish light that grows in intensity as the corpse grows larger. By nightfall the light from his eyes illuminates the stage. The corpse is also the source of a strange music that Amédée identifies as singing. Thus the light and song associated with love are not entirely dead. In the sudden reversal of the play's ending, evanescence is materialized as the corpse becomes a balloon that lifts Amédée into the sky in a gorgeous display of light and fireworks. Just as the Fall (original sin) is literalized through the cadaver, so is salvation, taking the form of ascension and resurrection. In the end, the corpse becomes Amédée's ally rather than his enemy; the real enemy is elsewhere.

The Couple

Amédée is perhaps the most misogynistic of Ionesco's major plays. Here the ambivalent attitude toward women developed in the preceding plays has come full circle since *The Chairs*. (There is, in fact, an intertextual allusion to the earlier play: the two characters in the play Amédée is writing are an old man and an old woman.) In contrast to the self-effacing, nurturing mother figure that was the dominant strain in the Old Woman, Madeleine is a nagging harpy who repeatedly scolds and berates her husband for his failure to write. She complains constantly that he is a worthless good-for-nothing who has brought all this trouble upon them, while she, entirely blameless, must work to earn them a living and keep house. She opposes her "realism" to his "silly 'look on the bright side'" (7). The vestiges of sexual attraction and vulnerability that remained in the character of Madeleine in *Victims of Duty* have disappeared in this second Madeleine. The dream sequence reveals that she repelled Amédée's sexual advances even when they were first married: "Don't come near me. Don't touch me. You sting, sting, sting. You hu-urt me!" (47). She is brutally antiromantic—"Where does love come into it? Lot of nonsense! Love can't help people get rid of their troubles!" (53)—and immediately represses the one tender expression that escapes her mouth:

Madeleine: Please, please darling, do something. . . .
Amédée: What did you say?

80

> Madeleine (annoyed again): I simply said "Do some-
> thing" because something has got to be done, that's
> all. . . . (41)

Even as he is being carried away by the corpse/balloon at
the end of the play, she cannot stop berating him: "You may
have gone up in the world, but you're not going up in my esti-
mation" (77, 89).

Madeleine, more so even than the corpse, is the heavy matter that holds Amédée down. The dream sequence is one of the
most misogynistic passages in all of Ionesco's theater. In it,
the woman is associated with every negative element;
Madeleine's depressive pessimism is an obstacle in stark opposition to Amédée's fundamental optimism and lyricism. As a
young newlywed, Amédée II approaches his bride with a radiant vision of light and joy: "Madeleine, let's wake up, let's pull
the curtains, the spring is dawning . . . Wake up . . . the room
is flooded with sunshine . . . a glorious light . . . a gentle
warmth! . . ." (47). Madeleine II counters with her vision of
reality: ". . . night and rain and mud! . . . oh, the cold! . . . I'm
shivering . . . dark . . . dark . . . dark! . . . you're blind, you're
gilding reality! Don't you see that you're *making* it beautiful?"
(48). Where Amédée sees green valleys full of flowers where
people dance, Madeleine sees dark, damp, swampy valleys full
of mushrooms where people are sinking into the mud and
drowning; where Amédée sees a "house of glass, house of light,"
Madeleine sees a "house of brass, house of night" (51–52). It is
clear that the airy, timeless, radiant sphere of abundance and
joy is the domain solely of the man and that the woman represents the dark, heavy mud of existence leading inevitably to
death. Once Amédée manages to drag the corpse out of the
presence of Madeleine, its value becomes positive instead of
negative, and Amédée can escape from his wife and his marriage.

The other couple set up as a parallel to Amédée and
Madeleine are the American soldier and Mado, the French
woman he picks up in the brothel-like bar of the third act. Once
again it is the man who is portrayed as the poetic soul who
longs only for love, while the woman is venal and earthbound,

interested in her material well-being; Mado uses her sexuality to persuade the soldier to take her to America with him.

Time

More than any previous Ionesco play, *Amédée* foregrounds the passing of time. The play's action respects the classical unity of time, unfolding within the space of twenty-four hours. A large clock face whose turning hands record the passing minutes and hours is a prominent part of the set. The subjective nature of lived time is conveyed through the changing speed of the hands, as they accelerate to indicate the faster pace of life while Amédée and Madeleine are engaged in the morning's work. By contrast, time slows to a standstill while Amédée waits for midnight, when he can begin to dispose of the corpse: "Oh! If only the time would pass more quickly!" (45). The clock face also serves to underscore the relationship between the dramatic (fictional) time of the play and the real-world time of the audience, emphasizing in metatheatrical fashion a dramatic convention that remains masked and implicit in more traditional plays. (This emphasis on the relation between time of the play and time of the performance will become a major feature of *Exit the King*.)

If the cadaver itself represents original sin and the death of love, its uncontrollable growth represents time.[22] Its relentless progression reflects the impossibility of halting or reversing the inevitable decline into old age and death. Indeed, the Fall in Christian mythology is precisely the Fall from timelessness into time, from immortality into mortality.

Space

As in the preceding two plays, spatial structures play a significant role. The interior space is claustrated and airless, particularly for Madeleine, who complains that she is suffocating. More willing to compromise with (or to close his eyes to) the reality of their situation, Amédée maintains that all he needs is a "little space, a tiny little corner to live in" (35), much like a fetus in the womb. Amédée and Madeleine have not left the apartment or received any visitors in fifteen years, as was noted earlier; the shutters of the main window are closed, and the bedroom where the cadaver is kept is "hermetically sealed." The room has become a prison, and they are prisoners of their own guilt.

The exterior space threatens their existence. Offstage left the growing corpse threatens to engulf them, while the world offstage right represents the possibility of discovery and punishment. Again, Amédée (the intellectual) is less concerned about their surroundings or what the neighbors might think than Madeleine, who is so solidly grounded in the material and social world. Maintaining the increasingly untenable status quo requires that the barriers separating the living room from the exterior (the two doors and the main window) remain closed and intact. This tenuous false security is breached at the very beginning of the play with the appearance of the first poisonous mushroom in the living room, a sign that a change in their situation is imminent. Shortly thereafter the barrier of the other door falls with the postman who enters to deliver their first letter in fifteen years, and the corpse breaks out of the bedroom in two directions (its head breaks the bedroom window, and its feet invade the living room).

In the first act, the menace came from the outside, and the problem was keeping the outside out. Once the security of the apartment is violated, the situation is reversed, so that in the second act the threat is inside the apartment and the problem is how to get it out. The exterior space thus acquires a positive value that is affirmed in the last act when the exterior becomes Amédée's pathway to escape.

The interior space in the play is strongly associated with Madeleine. It is clearly her domain; she is able to work there, while Amédée is not, and it is she who does the housekeeping. Even if she feels confined, it is she, not Amédée, who fears the outside. The interior is a woman's space also insofar as it functions as a womb. The long labor of expelling the corpse through the central window has many parallels with childbirth—in this case, a difficult breech birth, since the cadaver is dragged out feetfirst. Once the umbilical cord is severed, Amédée and the corpse become independent of Madeleine and go on to pursue their own adventure in the extrauterine world.

Equally important as tension along the horizontal axis (inside versus outside) is the tension along the vertical axis (down versus up). Gravity and sinking in the mud are linked to the interior space and to Madeleine (as shown in the dream sequence), while weightlessness and flying are concretely linked to Amédée's poetic lyricism (both in the dream sequence and in the final image). Whereas escape from the interior space (the womb) meant falling to his death for the Old Man in *The Chairs*, Amédée's escape is just the opposite—he flies away.

The Role of the Artist

A final parallel among the three major plays of this period is the fact that the three protagonists are all artist figures: the Old Man in *The Chairs* is a storyteller, poet, and writer; Choubert's artistic temperament is inscribed in his name, he is ardently interested in literary questions, and his best friend (and double) is a poet; Amédée is a professional playwright, albeit an astonishingly unproductive one. Like his antecedents, Amédée is a failure and a target for satire; an obvious parody of both Ionesco and Beckett, the play Amédée is writing has, after fifteen years, only two lines: "The old woman says to the old man, 'Do you think it will do?' and the one I managed to write today, the one I've just read you: The old man replies, 'It won't do by itself'" (8). Here as before, the artist is portrayed as ineffectual, lazy, and childlike, dependent on others to tend to the practical matters of existence.

If he is a practical failure, however, Amédée represents the positive value of art and especially poetry. When he tells Madeleine that love can save them and change their lives (52), he is offering her an alternative way of seeing the world, a poetic vision that has the power to transform reality. He is sensitive to the beauty of the night sky that floods the stage when the main window is opened: "Look, Madeleine . . . all the acacia trees are aglow. Their blossoms are bursting open and shooting up to the sky. The full-blown moon is flooding the Heavens with light, a *living* planet. The Milky Way is like creamy fire" (59). Madeleine, on the other hand, is the philistine whose only answer is "Don't waste time. What's the matter with you? The night air's coming in. We shall both catch cold" (60). Finally, he is literally carried away (against his will, he protests) by his poetic inspiration, or alter ego, as the corpse is transformed into a beautiful balloon.

Notes

1. The same extended family reappears in the sequel to this play, *The Future Is in Eggs* (*L'Avenir est dans les oeufs*), first produced in 1957. In the later play, Jack and Roberta II have married and, coerced and exhorted by their parents, are producing massive numbers of eggs (offspring). The eggs proliferate out of control and engulf the stage at the end of the play.

2. See Ruby Cohn, *From* Desire *to* Godot (127–28).

3. This note is absent from the English version. See the French edition (1991), 167.

4. J. S. Doubrovsky, "Ionesco and the Comic of Absurdity," rpt. in Rosette C. Lamont, ed., *Ionesco: A Collection of Critical Essays* 15.

5. In his excellent article "Designation and Gesture in *The Chairs*" (in *The Two Faces of Ionesco,* ed. Rosette C. Lamont and Melvin J. Friedman), Robert Champigny recommends that the role of the Orator be performed by a puppet, "or a human actor made up and acting as a puppet." He observes that "the human appearance of the orator will tend to emphasize, instead of playing down, the difference between full-fledged and blank characters" (164).

6. This womb-like image echoes one of the archetypal dreams recounted in Ionesco's interviews with Bonnefoy. In the dream in question, Ionesco is a sort of astronaut, nude, in a celluloid cabin, seated in a fetal position: "I'm a fetus and an astronaut at the same time. I know I'm going to another planet. Infinite space surrounds the cabin" (*ENT* 34).

7. Confusion between exterior scenic space and exterior dramatic space can lead to an interpretation like that of David Mendelson, for whom the play is science fiction. See "Science and Fiction in Ionesco's 'Experimental' Theatre (An Interpretation of *The Chairs*)" in Rosette C. Lamont's *Ionesco* 64–98.

8. Ionesco has commented repeatedly on the opposition between the two fundamental states of consciousness that dominate his life

and work. In "My Plays and I," he writes, "These basic states of consciousness are an awareness of evanescence and solidity, of emptiness and of too much presence, of the unreal transparency of the world and its opacity, of light and of thick darkness" (*NCN* 162). Speaking with Claude Bonnefoy, he said, "You have said that there is a lot of mud, a lot of sinking in my theater. That corresponds precisely with one of my two states. I feel either very heavy or very light, or else much too heavy or much too light" (*ENT* 36).

9. See Champigny's article, especially p. 158: "In my eyes, the main technical and semantic interest in *The Chairs,* as in some other plays of the fifties, lies in the way designative meaning, while not disappearing, is ruined and gestural meaning correlatively brought into relief."

10. Ingrid H. Coleman, "Memory into 'Message'" 61.

11. As Ionesco said in an interview in 1960, "One must not allow oneself to get bogged down in sentimentality. One needs to be somehow cruel and sardonic with oneself. What is most difficult is not to get too attached to oneself or one's characters—and yet continue to like them. One has to be able to regard them with a lucidity that is not malevolent but ironical" (*NCN* 123).

12. This poignant scene is intensely personal and autobiographical. Ionesco's parents had fought bitterly before his father deserted them; as a small child, he had witnessed a scene like the one in the play, except that Ionesco's father stopped his mother from drinking the poison; Ionesco hated and resented his father in the same way that Choubert did, and his father died not long before Ionesco wrote *Victims of Duty,* foreclosing any possibility of reconciliation.

13. The *mache* in Machecroche comes from the French verb *mâcher,* meaning to chew. *Croche* has several different associations. It contains the word *roche* (rock), evoking the hard crusts; it is also phonetically close to *croquer* (to eat, to swallow) and to *croûte* (crust). Finally, it comes from the verb *crocher* (to bite into, to hold), which evokes the idea of the bread's sticking and scraping on its way down Choubert's throat.

14. Ionesco talks about the origin of this mountain-climbing dream in his interviews with Bonnefoy. His friend Mircea Eliade had told him to dream this archetypal dream in order to relax and go to sleep (*ENT* 34).

15. In the French version, he reaches a mythic ladder connecting the earth to the sky.

16. This same experience is central to *The Killer.* It also figures in *Amédée, A Stroll in the Air, Hunger and Thirst,* and *A Hell of a Mess!.*

17. In his book *The Existential and Its Exits,* L. A. C. Dobrez compares Ionesco's sense of wonder to Heidegerrian angst; the realization of the uncanny confronts us with the *fact* of existence. (See chapter 7, especially 151–53.)

18. "The great, auspicious symbols that arise from the depths of the psyche are in my case reversed; they are sinister and baleful. Is my unconscious a peculiar one?

"Thus, normally, the father-figure is an auspicious, benevolent one, the father is a guide; for me the father is a monster, a tyrant" (FJ 133).

19. The published text offers a choice between two possible endings. The second is essentially the same as the first but easier to stage and shorter; it calls for no intermission between the second and third acts.

20. The other one-act play that relies primarily on proliferation of matter for its effect is *The New Tenant (Le Nouveau locataire)*. Written in 1953, it was not premiered until 1955, in Finland, in a Swedish-language version directed by Viveca Bandler. The English-language version premiered in London in 1956 on a double bill with *The Bald Soprano,* directed by Peter Wood. The French version was not produced until 10 September 1957, at the Théâtre d'aujour d'hui; it was directed by Robert Postec. In this play, a nearly mute, ordinary-looking man is moving into a new apartment overseen by an extremely loquacious concierge whose chatter is filled with clichés, nonsense, and contradictions. Movers begin to bring the man's furniture into the room, slowly at first. The rhythm accelerates rapidly, and by the end of the play, the man is invisible, literally buried under the huge piles of furniture that choke the stage. The furniture, we learn, has even clogged the Seine and all the streets of Paris.

21. "For me, the corpse is transgression, original sin" *(ENT 83)*.

22. "The growing corpse is time" *(ENT 83)*.

CHAPTER FOUR

Ionesco and the Critics:
Improvisation

Throughout his career, Ionesco's attitude toward theater critics, indeed toward critics in general, has ranged from contempt to outright hostility. As a young man he was an active participant in the lively literary scene in Bucharest, where many rival movements and journals competed for backing and for an audience. A critic himself, he created a scandal with the publication of *Nu* (No) in 1934. This series of essays (translated into French only in 1986) staged an ironic attack on three prominent Romanian writers in order to demonstrate that the whole enterprise of literary criticism is arbitrary and unrelated to the literary texts under discussion. "The critic is a stupid animal," he wrote. "There are two ways of being stupid and they are exactly alike. One can either think, say and do things that have absolutely no relationship to reality, or think, say and do what everyone else thinks, does and says and which can be either true or false—in fact, whatever everyone agrees about is always false. The stupid man is one for whom the evidence is opaque. The literary critic has to be stupid" (*Non* 197). Ionesco did not exempt himself from this attack on critics, but he announced that he would continue to write criticism—why not? At about the same time he published the first part of a projected "ironic biography" of Victor Hugo in which his goal was to demystify one of the greatest members of the literary establishment. It was first published in French (*Hugoliade*) in 1982; an English translation (*Hugoliad*) appeared in 1987.

Improvisation

As soon as Ionesco became a playwright, he was embroiled in an ongoing polemic with his critics. His first plays were condemned by the conservative bourgeois press: Robert Kemp and Jean-Jacques Gautier in particular attacked him as a fraud. Writing for *Le Monde* (18 October 1955), Kemp called him "a very minor curiosity of contemporary theater. . . . The butcher would call it second-class." Gautier, in the conservative *Le Figaro* published the same week (16 October 1955), wrote, "I don't believe that M. Ionesco is a genius or a poet; I don't believe that M. Ionesco is an important author; . . . I don't believe that M. Ionesco has anything to say. I believe that M. Ionesco is a practical joker, . . . a charlatan, a fraud." While some critics of the left (Jean Pouillon, for example, writing for the Marxist *Temps moderne*) at first embraced his work and hailed him as a fresh voice in the theater, they soon turned against him. Roland Barthes and Bernard Dort were among those who attacked him. Influenced by Jean-Paul Sartre and Bertholt Brecht (whose plays were first performed in French in the early 1950s to great acclaim), they criticized Ionesco for his aversion to politically engaged "committed" theater and accused him of empty formalism. Ionesco responded in many essays, lectures, and articles, always defending the autonomy of the individual artist and denouncing ideology of any and every kind. He counterattacked in 1955 with the play *L'Impromptu de l'Alma, ou le caméléon du berger* (*Improvisation, or The Shepherd's Chameleon*), in which Gautier, Barthes, and Dort are singled out for parody and the theories of Sartre and Brecht are held up to ridicule. The play premiered on 20 February 1956 at the Studio des Champs-Elysées in a production directed by Maurice Jacquemont, who played the role of the character Ionesco.

The curtain rises to reveal a playwright named Ionesco asleep amid a pile of books and papers. Bartholomeus I, a theater critic who sounds very much like Bernard Dort, enters and asks him about the new play he is writing. After stalling a bit, Ionesco tells him that the play will be a tragic farce called "The Shepherd's Chameleon" and that it will be an improvisation in which he will put himself on stage to explain his own ideas about the theater, drama criticism, and so forth. He then proceeds to read the beginning of his play, which is an exact replica of the beginning of *Improvisation*. He is interrupted by the arrival of Bartholomeus II and III (Roland Barthes and

89

Jean-Jacques Gautier), and the play quickly becomes a biting satire of Marxist and structuralist theories of literary and dramatic criticism. The three Doctors are abysmally stupid and pretentious, and they browbeat Ionesco until the playwright is completely cowed and demoralized, forced to wear a dunce's cap and bray like a donkey. At the same time, the three Doctors are quarreling violently among themselves. Marie, Ionesco's neighbor and cleaning lady, finally forces her way into the room and puts an end to the nonsensical slapstick, pushing the three critics off the stage. Suddenly Ionesco calls a halt to the action, announcing that the play is over and calling the actors back on stage. He explains that he has taken the critics' words straight from their own writings (from *Théâtre populaire* for Bartholomeus I and II—both pedants— and from *Le Figaro* for Bartholomeus III—an idiot without pedantry): "If you have been bored, I can hardly be held responsible; if you have been amused, I can claim no credit" (149). He then begins to read from a prepared text that expounds his own ideas about theater. His text and demeanor soon become pedantic and pompous themselves, however, and Marie and the critics chide him for taking himself seriously and succumbing to the temptation to pontificate. The play ends with his apology and a promise that he will never do it again.

Satire of Critics

The three critics are all buffoons. As a representative of the conservative bourgeois press, Bartholomeus III is dim-witted and unashamed to admit that he understands nothing: he doesn't know who Plato, Aristotle, Shakespeare or Molière were; he is grotesquely xenophobic; and he is as confused by the tirades of the other two critics as is the character Ionesco. While the two others praise Brecht, he extols the virtues of Bernstein, a writer of boulevard plays. While he sympathizes with Ionesco's inability to understand what the other two critics are talking about—"I don't understand: there's an expression I *do* understand . . . or at least, it's one I *use*" (117)—he recognizes the necessity to remain united with his colleagues against "the enemy" (that is, the playwright).

Bartholomeus I and II echo Dort and Barthes as they spout pseudoscientific-sounding jargon. These critics claim scientific status for their theories. As Bartholomeus I tells Ionesco at the beginning of the play, he has been charged with directing the new play "according to the latest dramatic theories. Theories worthy of a people's theatre in this ultrascientific age we live in" (111). Ionesco must be subjected to all the latest theories of "theatrology," "costumology," "decorology" and "spectatopsychology." One target of parody is Sartre's rhetoric that plays upon paradox. Bartholomeus II tells the bewildered Ionesco, for example, that the only way to get out of a vicious circle is to close oneself inside of it; and Bartholomeus I explains, "That is to say, one is inside when one is outside, outside when one is inside, or popularly speaking, I mean. . . . and dialectically speaking, it's called: The Being-In-on-the-Outside-and-Out-on-the-Inside. It's also the Being of not-Being and the Not-Being of Being in the Know . . ." (117–18).

Also held up to ridicule are the dramatic theories of Bertholt Brecht. Brecht's Berliner Ensemble had come to Paris in 1954 and performed *Mother Courage* to great acclaim at the Théâtre des Nations (a previous visit in 1951 had passed almost unnoticed). Dort and Barthes were among the critics who championed Brecht most fervently, and the journal *Théâtre populaire* (to which both frequently contributed) devoted a special issue to Brecht in January-February 1955. In Ionesco's play, the learned Doctors decide to educate the ignorant playwright by consulting the "treatise of the great Dr Bertholus" (136). According to Brecht's theory of epic theater, the audience should always be reminded of the concrete social and historical circumstances in which dramatic action unfolds. Theater should not succumb to mimetic illusion but should always foreground its own artifice; the audience must always be conscious that they are watching a play, not some imitation of everyday reality. Specific techniques used to achieve this result included the use of placards and projections onstage to label places and to summarize the political and social significance (the "Gestus") of the action. Brecht also advocated a certain acting style (variously known as distanciation, alienation, or *Verfremdungseffekt*) that would maintain an ironic distance between the actors (and therefore the audience) and their roles. The two critics' misguided enthusiasm for the "great Dr Bertholus" is one of the sources of the play's hilarious slapstick comedy. Bartholomeus I and II label everything onstage with placards: they first put up signs reading "A Playwright's Education" and "Stylized Realism" to label the action, and then they label everything with signs indicating its facticity—"False Table," "False Place," and so on. They instruct the character Ionesco in a properly alienated acting style: to answer the door, he must take two steps backward for each step forward, until he reaches the side of the room farthest from the door. Furthermore, he must not identify too closely with himself:

> Bartholomeus I: Watch yourself acting . . . Be Ionesco not being Ionesco!
> Bartholomeus II: Look at yourself with one eye, listen to yourself with the other! (143)

When Ionesco complains that he can't do this, they tell him to squint (in the French version, they tell him to cross his eyes), which he does to their great satisfaction.

Another source of humor is the play's parody of Barthes's article "Les Maladies du costume de théâtre" ("The Diseases of the Costume"), published in *Théâtre populaire* in 1955. In the article, Barthes proposed to sketch a "pathology" or an "ethics" of the theatrical costume: "I shall propose a few very simple rules which may permit us to judge whether a costume is good or bad, healthy or sick" (41).[1] He said that a costume must never be an "alibi," and he listed three common illnesses, or alibis, that afflict costumes: hypertrophy of the historical function, hypertrophy of the aesthetic function, and hypertrophy of sumptuosity. The costume must always be an argument; the vestimentary sign may suffer from illnesses of nutrition (it may be poorly fed, overfed, or underfed). He concluded by commending Brecht's theater for its "healthy" costumes. Such jargon almost begs to be parodied, and *Improvisation* uses many words, phrases, and sentences lifted directly from Barthes's essay to comic effect in a burlesque scene. When the pedantic critics decide to educate Ionesco, "costumology" is the field they choose, and they determine immediately that his costume is sick, suffering from hypertrophy of the historical function: "Your costume is just an alibi. It's shirking its responsibility!" (141). When Ionesco protests that he has always dressed this way, they tell him that an author's costume must be a sign (they pin signs on him reading "Poet" and "Scientist"), that his clothes are badly nourished and need careful treatment— whereupon they try to take his pants off. They tell him that his costume must "tear at the heart" (a term lifted from Barthes), and he begs them not to tear his pants any more than they already are torn, since it's the only pair he has (142). In sum, the playwright responds to his critics by making their jargon into slapstick and turning it back upon them.

The play satirizes the critics' bent for stating obvious truths as though they had discovered them, only to distort them in a way that defies common sense. Addressing the audience at the end of the play, the character Ionesco says, "I blame these doctors for discovering elementary truths and dressing them up in exaggerated language so that these elementary truths appear to have gone mad" (149). For example, when Bartholomeus II takes it upon himself to explain what a play is to Ionesco, he says, "My dear chap, plays are written to be performed, to be seen and heard by the public, in a playhouse, like this one for example. . . ." Bartholomeus I congratulates him for the profundity of his insight, and a very confused Ionesco responds, "I don't know whether . . . whether it's profound, but it's certainly correct. Why, even I, in my ignorance, I thought *I* knew that" (135). If theater is destined to be performed in public, however, its goal must be only to instruct the audience, never to entertain them, say the learned Doctors: "The public shouldn't enjoy themselves at the theatre!"; "Those who enjoy themselves will be punished!" (125).

The Impromptu

The impromptu (or improvisation) is a form of French theater that goes back as far as Molière; Ionesco's play is, in certain respects, a tribute to the great seventeenth-century playwright. (There are, in fact, several direct allusions to Molière in Ionesco's play: when Bartholomeus II tells Ionesco that he had been writing prose all along with knowing it, he is quoting a famous line from Molière's *Le Bourgeois Gentilhomme,* and the playwright character pays homage to Molière's comic genius when he says, "As Molière still amuses, I thought him of universal, of eternal interest" [121].) In *L'Impromptu de Versailles* and *La Critique de l'Ecole de Femmes,* Molière put himself and other members of his company onstage in order to respond to the criticisms leveled against his theater. The form was revived by Jacques Copeau in *L'Impromptu du Vieux colombier* (1917) and has been used by several other French playwrights in this century, including Jean Giraudoux (*L'Impromptu de Paris,* 1937) and Jean Cocteau (*L'Impromptu du Palais-Royal,* 1962).

Ionesco's play contains many parallels with and allusions to Molière's plays, particularly *L'Impromptu de Versailles.* As in Molière's play, the underlying pretext for *Improvisation* is that the author is being commissioned to write a play—in Molière, it is the King who has requested a play; in Ionesco, it is a group of theater directors. In both plays, one of the roles is that of the play's author, and in both plays, it is the "impromptu" itself that becomes the play which fulfills the author's commission. Marie, the cleaning lady, is a character found in nearly all of Molière's comedies—the sensible, earthy, outspoken servant who is the voice of common sense and reason. By the time she succeeds in forcing her way into Ionesco's study in the play, all four men are wearing dunce caps, braying like donkeys, and dancing around the stage. She takes one look at the pandemonium and demands that they clean up the mess they made, leave M. Ionesco alone, and get out. She tells him that the three Doctors have only been making fun of him and chases them off the stage with her broom; when Ionesco explains that his costume was sick, she tells him that all he had to do was send it to the cleaners. It is Marie who brings Ionesco back to earth at the end of the play, when he begins to sound pompous himself while expounding his own theory of theater.

There are several notable differences between Ionesco's play and Molière's, however. Ionesco's is a much more physical, broader farce than Molière's, using a burlesque slapstick found in Molière's pure farces. Further differentiating the twentieth-century play from its ancestor is the fact that the character Ionesco steps out of his role before the play is over. He addresses the audience directly, thereby making *The Shepherd's Chameleon* a play-within-a-play inside the larger impromptu. This move undermines the pretense of dramatic illusion even more than was the case in the earlier play, reflecting Ionesco's penchant for mise-en-abyme—self-conscious, reflexive metatheater. Ironically, Ionesco's play is as alienated as the Brechtian theater it holds up to ridicule, albeit in a different style; like Brecht, Ionesco insists on "showing the strings" behind the play and never allows the audience to forget that they are watching theater, not some mimetic copy of their own lives.

Ionesco's Art of Drama

The last part of *Improvisation* contains a straightforward statement of Eugène Ionesco's opinion of the proper role of literary criticism and a succinct defense of his theater. Criticism, he says, must be descriptive, not normative; it is the critic's job to move into the poetic universe of the work of art, not to establish dogmatic criteria by which artistic creation will be directed and judged. His own theater is, he says, "the projection onto the stage of the world within: it is in my dreams, my anguish, my dark desires, my inner contradictions that I reserve the right to find the stuff of my plays" (150). This emphasis on the absolute freedom of the individual artist and this deep hatred of all dogma mark all of Ionesco's writings; he has been engaged in an ongoing public dispute with critics throughout his career. In the French press, it took the form of a debate between Ionesco and critics of the left (Barthes, Dort, Renée Saurel, Jean Vannier) about avant-garde theater. As Ionesco's plays began to be performed outside of France, it led to the famous exchange of articles that became known as the London Controversy.

The London Controversy

Kenneth Tynan, the prominent British drama and film critic, was an early champion of Ionesco in England. In a 1956 review, he called *The Bald Soprano* "explosively, liberatingly funny," "a little masterpiece"; and about *The New Tenant* he said, "Nowhere is there a fuller and funnier portrait of introversion" (*Curtains* 149–50). His review of a 1957 production of *The Chairs* was also favorable; in it he called Ionesco a "superb and classical" comic inventor (*Curtains* 178). By June 1958 Tynan had changed his mind and was warning his readers about the dangers of an Ionesco cult. Reviewing a double bill of *The Chairs* and *The Lesson,* he called Ionesco the "founder and headmaster of l'école du strip-tease intellectuel, moral, et social" (*Curtains* 407). He condemned Ionesco for preaching that communication is impossible and for leading theater into a blind alley, "a bleak new world from which the humanist heresies of faith in logic and belief in man will for ever be banished" (*Curtains* 408). Tynan now preferred the realism of Arthur Miller, Brecht, or John Osborne to the anti-theater of Ionesco and Beckett.

In Ionesco's response ("The Playwright's Role," published in July 1958 in *L'Express*), he attacked Miller, Brecht, and Osborne for being "representatives of a left-wing conformism as lamentable as the right-wing sort." He condemned all ideology, saying that society itself ("le social"), or politics, is what raises barriers between people. Ideology must be absent from works of art: "Every work of art (unless it is a pseudointellectualist work, a work already comprised in some ideology that it merely illustrates, as with Brecht) is outside ideology, is not reducible to ideology" (*NCN* 92). The critic's proper role is to allow the work "to speak, uncolored by preconception or prejudice" (*NCN* 91–93). The controversy continued when *The Observer* published a number of reactions to Ionesco's reply on 6 July. In "Ionesco and the Phantom" Tynan expressed his regret that Ionesco denied the connection between art and life. Ionesco, he feared, "is on the brink of believing that his distortions are more valid and important than the external world it is their proper function to interpret." He is in danger of "locking himself up in that hall of mirrors . . . known as solipsism" (*Curtains* 409). In the same issue, Philip Toynbee took Ionesco to task for saying that society is a barrier between human beings; he called Arthur Miller "an important playwright" and Eugène Ionesco "a lesser one" (*NCN* 97). One week later Orson Welles jumped into the fray, refuting Ionesco's claim that the artist must evade politics. "An artist," wrote Welles, "must confirm the values of his society; or he must challenge them" (*NCN* 99).

The London Controversy ended with Ionesco's second reply, prepared for *The Observer* but not published there. (It was published in French the following winter and reproduced in *Notes and Counter Notes.*) In "Hearts Are Not Worn on the Sleeve," he reiterates his objections to "realist" art, saying that that kind of realism "no longer captures reality and must therefore be exploded" (*NCN* 104). He condemns social realism as just another form of bourgeois art and defends what he calls the avant-garde (nonmimetic, nonrepresentational art) as being the only truly revolutionary form of art.

The Debate Continues

Ionesco's debates with his critics did not end with the London Controversy. Rather, they entered a new phase as Ionesco's theater evolved. With *Tueur sans gages* (*The Killer*, written in 1957, premiered in 1959) and *Le Rhinocéros* (1960), Ionesco's theater became more and more humanized, even classical. Some critics (Guy Leclerc and Gilles Sandier, for example) regretted the loss of the earlier style. Even Robert Kemp, who had never approved of the earlier plays, wrote in a review of *The Killer*, "Symbolism, look what you've done! You have robbed an original and petulant playwright of much of his energy and appeal" (*Le Monde,* March 1959). Other critics of the bourgeois press who had attacked the early plays were converted and became supporters. In a 1966 review of *Le Roi se meurt* (*Exit the King,* 1962), Jean-Jacques Gautier, one of the targets of *Improvisation,* called the play a "Shakespearian tragi-comedy," full of "great poetry," and urged the bourgeois readers of *Le Figaro* (7 December 1966) to see it. Critics of the left remained hostile, even when Ionesco's most political play (*Rhinoceros*) came out. Tynan called it "a bad social play" (*Tynan Right and Left* 34), and Hans Mayer, writing in *Théâtre Populaire* (no. 50, 1963), called Ionesco "an ideologue nursing the illusion that he is fighting all ideology."

As Ionesco's fame and stature grew (he was elected to the Académie française in 1970), he continued to publish numerous articles and essays in which he explained the importance of his personal metaphysical anguish for his theater and defended the autonomy of the individual against mass movements of any kind. Beginning with *Notes and Counter Notes* (first published in 1962), many volumes of his collected writings both polemical and personal have appeared: *Journal en miettes (Fragments of a Journal)*, 1967, *Présent passé. Passé présent (Present Past Past Present)*, 1968, *Découvertes* (Discoveries), 1969, and *La Quête intermittente* (The Intermittent Quest), 1987, consist largely of excerpts from his journals and personal musings. *Antidotes* (1977) and *Un Homme en question* (A Man in Question), 1979, are collections of articles, essays and speeches with a highly polemic tone. *Le Noir et le blanc* (Black and White), 1981 (reissued in 1985 as *Le Blanc et le Noir*), is a collection of Ionesco's drawings accompanied by personal, journal-like entries in which he meditates on the failure of language to express the inexpressible. (*Découvertes* also contains several of Ionesco's drawings.) Finally, Ionesco has granted many interviews, the most penetrating and illuminating of which were conducted by Claude Bonnefoy. First published in 1966 under the title *Entretiens (Conversations with Eugène Ionesco)*, they were updated, expanded, and reissued under the title *Entre la Vie et le rêve* (Between Life and Dreams) in 1977. There is perhaps no contemporary European author who has spoken so publicly and so often about his work and beliefs. Even when he voices reservations about certain of his own earlier plays, he continues to defend the autonomy of the individual artist against critics who would label or evaluate works of art according to political, extraaesthetic criteria.

Note

1. "The Diseases of Costume," in Roland Barthes, *Critical Essays*, trans. Richard Howard (Evanston: Northwestern University Press, 1972) 41–50.

CHAPTER FIVE

Humanized Theater: The Bérenger Cycle

Between 1957 and 1962 Ionesco wrote four major plays whose main character is named Bérenger: *Tueur sans gages* (*The Killer*), *Le Rhinocéros* (*Rhinoceros*), *Le Roi se meurt* (*Exit the King*), and *Le Piéton de l'air* (*A Stroll in the Air*). While they exhibit a certain continuity with the earlier plays (fear and hatred of authority, for example, and noticeable—if subdued—use of physical humor), these plays mark a shift in Ionesco's theater. The extravagant word play and outrageous nonsense of the early plays are nearly gone, replaced by a language that is coherent, "literary," and often lyrical. All but *Exit the King* were adapted from short stories, and the action and structure of those three plays are therefore more complex than in previous works. The protagonist is in each case a fully humanized character, and metaphysical anguish in the face of death becomes the central focus. These plays—especially *Rhinoceros* and *Exit the King*—brought Ionesco widespread public acceptance and recognition as a major playwright; by 1962 he was no longer an outsider or iconoclast but was well on his way to becoming a contemporary classic.

The Killer

Written in London in 1957, *The Killer* premiered in February 1959 at the Théâtre Récamier in a production directed by Jose Quaglio. Adapted from the short story "The Colonel's Photograph," it is Ionesco's second three-act play; like *Amédée* (his first three-act play), it suffers from a certain lack of focus and dramatic cohesion, particularly in the second act and the beginning of the third. (Ionesco's dramatic gifts seem to be best suited to the one-act form; with the exception of *Rhinoceros,* the longer works tend to lose tautness and intensity.) Like *Victims of Duty, The Killer* has a nightmarish quality; its greatest strength as theater lies in the skillful use of lighting, first as the sole element of decor for representation of the Radiant City and, at the end of the play, in the confrontation between Bérenger and the Killer. Of dramatic interest are the parody of the thriller genre in the second act (Does Edouard have in his briefcase the clues needed to capture the Killer?) and the darkly comic satire of fascist crowd hysteria in the third act.

In the first act, Bérenger, an ordinary, rather naive Everyman, has stumbled upon a gloriously beautiful neighborhood by accident. The Architect (who is also the chief of police, a physician, and a sociologist) is showing him around the Radiant City, where the weather is always beautiful, in marked contrast to the rest of the city, which is always damp, dark, and cold. Bérenger is overwhelmed with a joy that culminates in his impetuous declaration of love and proposal of marriage to the Architect's secretary Dany. (He proposes before she even appears on stage.) There is a worm in this earthly paradise, however; a mysterious killer is stalking the population, drowning several victims a day in a pool that appears only after the Architect draws Bérenger's attention to it. The Killer lures his victims to the pool by promising to show them photographs of the Colonel and offering them assorted cheap trinkets. Bérenger's horror and distress at this discovery are compounded when Dany becomes the Killer's next victim—despite the Architect's warnings, she had quit her job and thereby forfeited the protection enjoyed by everyone who works for the government. Bérenger vows to track down the Killer in order to avenge the death of the girl he imagines to be his fiancée and to eradicate the evil that has made the Radiant City uninhabitable.

The second act is set in the dark and gloomy confines of Bérenger's apartment. After an extended opening sequence involving exchanges between the Concierge and several offstage passersby, Bérenger returns home and is surprised to find his friend Edouard waiting for him. When Bérenger tells his friend about his remarkable discovery, Edouard says that everyone already knows about the Radiant City and the Killer and that he had never told Bérenger about it because he assumed that it wasn't worth mentioning. Edouard, a funereal figure who is suffering from tuberculosis, has with him a large black briefcase. When the briefcase flies open as the two men are leaving to go out for a walk, they discover that it is filled with photographs of the Colonel, cheap trinkets, the Killer's photo, his identification and business cards, and a list of all the victims' names and addresses. At first professing total ignorance about how the Killer's belongings came to be in his possession, Edouard goes on to pull out of his clothing ("like a magician") the Killer's personal journal detailing each crime and a map indicating the spot of each killing. Pressed for an explanation, Edouard suddenly remembers that the Killer had sent him all this material long before the crimes began, asking him to publish it in a literary journal, but that he had forgotten all about it. Bérenger is determined to go to the police station with this evidence and put an end to the Killer's reign of terror. They leave the apartment, but Edouard leaves the briefcase behind.

In the third act, Bérenger encounters a series of obstacles on his route to the police station. A large political rally is going on, several passersby have black briefcases, and two gigantic policemen stand in Bérenger's way. Finally Bérenger sends Edouard back for the forgotten briefcase and persuades the policemen to let him pass. Alone on the deserted street with night falling, Bérenger has just decided to turn back when the Killer suddenly appears. All of Bérenger's efforts to confront him and establish some sort of dialogue are met with glacial silence. When the Killer draws his knife, Bérenger takes out two pistols but is unable to use them. Powerless, he falls to his knees and submits to the silent Killer as the curtain falls.

An Unpaid Killer

The French title of the play (*Tueur sans gages*) contains a play on words that is not conveyed in the usual English translation.

Tueur à gages is the French term for hired killer; the change from *à* to *sans* (without) creates a phrase that emphasizes the gratuitous nature of the murders committed by this killer, who kills not for money but solely for pleasure.

Allegorically, this unpaid killer is death itself. Like death, he is inhuman, merciless, immune to pleading or reason, arbitrary in his choice of victims, invincible. Metaphysical anguish in the face of the inevitability of death is a theme that recurs constantly in Ionesco's journals; it dominates many of his plays as well (*Exit the King* and *The Killing Game,* for example).

Bérenger is the only person in the dream-like world of the play sensitive enough to be horrified and indignant about death. For him, as for Ionesco, mortality (the lurking Killer) is what poisons the joy of human existence (symbolized by the Radiant City). When the Architect tells him to calm down, get a grip on himself, and face up to reality, he explains, "I can't remain indifferent. . . . What I'm suffering from doesn't show, it's theoretical, spiritual" (36–37). The Architect is the methodical bureaucrat who reasons that we cannot allow ourselves to dwell on all the evil and unhappiness in the world, that we should look on the bright side of things and get on with the business of living. Likewise, Edouard reacts with indifference when Bérenger tells him the horrible news about the Killer. He, like everyone else, has known about it all along: "The whole town knows the story. I'm surprised even, you didn't know about it before, it's old news. Who doesn't know? . . . There didn't seem any need to tell you" (63). Certainly Edouard is sorry, but it's not worth getting upset, he says, since there's nothing anyone can do about it. Bérenger is horrified by Edouard's resignation and tells him several times how disgusted he is by his friend's indifference.

Bérenger, on the other hand, is the sensitive poet; as he tells the Architect, he is not like other people, "unconsciously suffering from being alive. But *I* was aware of the sickness of life" (20). He is the sole idealist in the play, the only one indignant enough to try to track down and vanquish the Killer. In his long closing speech (more monologue than dialogue), Bérenger tries every possible stratagem to convince the Killer to stop the murders—appeals to reason, pleas for mercy, promises of sympathy and help, and finally threats. All is futile, of course, and Bérenger pays with his own life for his idealism.

Light and Darkness

In his interviews with Claude Bonnefoy, Ionesco explains that the Radiant City is "light, the city of light. Light is the world transfigured" (*ENT* 30). From the moment the curtain rises on a nearly empty stage, it is evident that light is to play a major role in *The Killer*. As Ionesco's lengthy stage directions indicate, lighting will constitute the sole element of decor in the first act. Before any actor enters, the lighting changes from dull gray to a strong white light illuminating a brilliant blue sky. Bérenger perceives and describes the city primarily in terms of light: "light and beautiful, this neighborhood beyond compare, with its sunny streets and avenues bathed in light . . . this radiant city within the city . . ." (11). In a very concrete sense, light equals energy and life; it is associated with joy, warmth, and dryness. It is the objective exteriorization of the energy and life force that Bérenger once felt but had long ago lost: "Well, you see: once upon a time there was a blazing fire inside me. The cold could do nothing against it, a youthfulness, a spring no autumn could touch; a source of light, glowing wells of joy that seemed inexhaustible" (20). He goes on to describe to the Architect the intense joy he had experienced on a number of occasions, always associated with a certain quality of light: "And then, oh what indescribable bliss took hold of me! The light grew more and more brilliant, and still lost none of its softness, it was so dense you could almost breathe it, it had become the air itself, you could drink it like clear water . . ." (22). When he was young, the memory of these epiphanous moments was enough to keep him going when he was feeling depressed: "When I was in a gloomy mood, the memory of that dazzling radiance, that glowing feeling, gave fresh life to the force within me, to those reasonless reasons for living and loving . . . loving what? . . . Loving everything wholeheartedly . . ." (21). He had experienced the last of these moments of intense joy at the age of seventeen or eighteen, when "everything was a mingling of airiness and plenitude, perfectly balanced. . . . I walked and ran and cried: I *am,* I *am, everything* is, everything *is!* . . . Oh, I'm sure I could have flown away, I'd lost so much weight, I was lighter than the blue sky I was breathing" (23–24). Bérenger's description echoes not only the euphoric weightlessness experienced by Choubert in *Victims of Duty* during his dream of climbing the mountain but also a personal experience—a feeling of sheer astonishment at the "miracle of being" that Ionesco has described on several occasions in his journals and in interviews.[1] The effect of light on Ionesco was as vivid as for Bérenger; he describes it in his journal as "the intensity of a burning, pervasive total light that was trying to escape from the forms that contained it. . . . Suddenly I felt as if I had received a blow right in the heart, in the center of my being. A stupefaction surged into being, exploded . . ." (*PP* 154).

This light contrasts strongly with Bérenger's everyday life in another part of the city. The bleak, grayish light of the very beginning of the play (before the appearance of the Radiant City) had reflected the atmosphere that reigned in the rest of the city, where "the sky's as grey as the hair on an old woman's head" and dirty snow lines the sidewalks (13). The decor of the second act is gloomy, "heavy, realistic, ugly; it contrasts strongly with the lack of decor and the simple lighting effects of Act I" (43). As is the case throughout Ionesco's work, the positive pole (the miracle of being) can be experienced only rarely in privileged moments of joy, serenity, and plenitude. This emotional state is always ephemeral, inevitably giving way to its opposite—the dull heaviness of mortal existence, symbolized in the play by Bérenger's dark, humid apartment and the gray monotony of the city. Darkness represents fatigue and death; it is associated with despair, cold, and humidity. In his neighborhood and, more specifically, in his apartment, "everything is damp: the coal, the bread, the wind, the wine, the walls, the air, and even the fire" (13). As the Architect rightly points out, this state of affairs is not coincidental but is the concrete manifestation of depression and despair.

The dichotomy between light and darkness is a concrete extension of the conflict between the two poles or emotional states within Bérenger himself. In his lengthy explanation of his newfound joy, Bérenger establishes an identity between interior world and exterior world:

> A setting, *that's* just superficial, an artistic consideration, unless it's, . . . a background that would answer some profound need inside, which would be somehow. . . . the projection, the continuation of the universe inside you. Only, to project this universe within, some outside help is needed: some kind of material, physical light, a world that is objectively new. Gardens, blue sky, or the spring, which corresponds to the universe inside and offers a chance of recognition, which is like a translation or an anticipation of that universe, or a mirror in which its own smile could be reflected . . . in which it can find itself again and say: that's what I am in reality and I'd forgotten, a smiling being in a smiling world . . . Come to think of it, it's quite wrong to talk of a world within and a world without, separate worlds; there's an initial impulse, of course, which starts from us, and when it can't project itself, when it can't fulfil itself objectively, when there's not total agreement between myself inside and myself outside, then it's a catastrophe, a universal contradiction, a schism. (18–19)

This identity between interior and exterior serves as the basis for the dramatic tension in the play. In the internal and external radiance that he discovers in the Radiant City, Bérenger believes he has finally found "total agreement between myself inside and myself outside." This total agreement is shattered by Bérenger's discovery of the Killer's crimes; as he had said, without agreement, there is "catastrophe, universal contradiction, a schism." The environment that Bérenger had thought was his accomplice has become his enemy, and he is plunged again into darkness, now all the more intolerable because he has just experienced radiance.

Contrast between light and dark extends even to two secondary characters, Dany and Edouard. Each functions as a complement to one of Bérenger's emotional states. Dany's blond hair, "luminous face," and physical presence in the Radiant City link her with the positive pole of his existence (light, warmth, love, hope, joy). She appears as if by magic precisely at the moment when Bérenger desires to fall in love—he proposes to her before they even meet. Her death at the Killer's hand plunges Bérenger into despair, but her memory inspires him to seek revenge and to restore the earthly paradise symbolized by the Radiant City. Edouard, on the other hand, is dressed in black and clings to the large black briefcase containing the Killer's belongings; he is hidden at first by the darkness in Bérenger's apartment. Close to death himself because of his tuberculosis, he is resigned to and matter-of-fact about the Killer's presence in the Radiant City. Although he is ostensibly Bérenger's friend, it is he who seals Bérenger's fate, first by precipitating the futile trip to the police station and then by leaving the briefcase behind, so that Bérenger will be left to face the Killer alone.

The Killer is a creature of darkness, and the final confrontation scene stands in symmetric contrast to the beginning of the play. As in the beginning, light is almost the only element of decor, the rest of the set having faded into obscurity to leave Bérenger alone in the dim twilight. Just as the brilliant light of the Radiant City was the exteriorization of confident energy and hope, this gloomy darkness is the exteriorization of Bérenger's vulnerability and fatigue. The gloom of the play's ending balances the radiance of the beginning; the radiance, Bérenger's accomplice in his quest for life, is finally vanquished by darkness. Bérenger finds an enemy rather than a benevolent collaborator in his environment, and the triumph of darkness over light is the triumph of death over life—the catastrophe that Bérenger had earlier feared. Such is the power of darkness that it is possible, as Ionesco suggests, to stage the final scene without using a human actor to portray the Killer: "Or possibly there is *no Killer at all*. Bérenger could be talking to himself, alone in the half-light" (98).

Paradise Lost

The Radiant City is another version of the lost earthly paradise that appears so often in Ionesco's work. Bérenger's joy

106

there echoes the joy Ionesco knew as a child in La Chapelle-Anthenaise, an idyllic experience that he has described quite often in his journals. The pastoral qualities of the Radiant City—clear blue sky, lush greenery (blue and green are "the colors of joy" for Bérenger [12]), beautiful flowers, silence, warmth—suggest the Garden of Eden. For Ionesco, however, paradise always contains original sin, leading inevitably to the Fall from grace into the quotidian.[2] For Adam and Eve, expulsion from the garden signified mortality; Bérenger and ultimately all the residents of the Radiant City are expelled from this earthly paradise by lurking death. Nostalgia for a prelapsarian state of grace is what drives Bérenger; as he tells Edouard, "I thought I'd found everything again, got it all back. . . . All I'd lost and all I hadn't lost. . . . I thought the spring had returned for ever . . . that I'd found the unfindable again, the dream, the key, life . . . all that we've lost while we've gone on living" (61). Furthermore, he experiences the loss of his dream of "another universe" specifically as a fall: "Once again everything fell into chaos . . . in a flash, in a flash! The same collapse, again and again . . ." (62).

Paradoxically, it is precisely this longing for joy and immortality that causes Bérenger such suffering. Unlike the pragmatists around him (Edouard and the Architect), Bérenger is unable and unwilling to accept life as it is. As Edouard observes, "You've always been dissatisfied, always refused to resign yourself" (61). His exalted nature makes him incapable of settling for anything less than the intense joy in being alive that he (like Ionesco) felt during rare privileged moments of his youth. When he finally does stumble upon the fabled Radiant City, only to lose it, his pain is too great for him to bear: "My life is over. It's a wound that will never heal" (60). For Bérenger, living without hope is worse than dying. Thus his quest to retrieve paradise by eliminating the Killer is doomed before it begins; it can end only in his own death.

The Individual versus the Collective

Juxtaposed somewhat awkwardly with the central theme (metaphysical and emotional anguish in the face of death) is a satiric denunciation of bureaucracy and demagoguery. Although this play is not totally successful in integrating these two currents, they are not unrelated. For Ionesco, politics—more precisely, an excess of politics—is what has led to a society of individuals who are "spiritually and metaphysically handicapped": "Perhaps politics is the devil. It is evil. It contributes powerfully to supporting evil" (*Homme* 49). Whereas the earlier plays had as their focus the microcosm of the couple, *The Killer* broadens the horizon to include the widest perspective on society at this point in Ionesco's career. Bérenger is a loner in a way that the Old Man, Choubert, and Amédée were not, and he is at odds with an unresponsive, unsympathetic, impersonal society.

In "Culture and Politics," Ionesco called upon society to refocus its attention on metaphysical and spiritual matters, saying that the proper role of politics is limited to administration—the ideal administrator would be a computer (*Homme* 49). The Architect seems at first glance to fulfill this role admirably well. It was he whose beneficence and creative intelligence devised the Radiant City, for which Bérenger is exceedingly grateful and admiring. He is chief of police, physician, psychiatrist, and sociologist as well, yet he is as unfeeling and impersonal as a computer. He views the inevitable death of the city's residents as an unfortunate glitch in the system. A pragmatist and a consummate bureaucrat, he says that the only thing to do is accept reality and move on to the next project. Furthermore, he (and everyone who works for the Administration) is immune to the Killer's threat, symbolizing the detachment and isolation from humanity that characterize all bureaucracies. It is precisely this detachment that Dany finds so intolerable: "Surely you can understand that I can't go on sharing the responsibility. It's too much for me" (29).

The lengthy dialogue among offstage voices that opens the second act portrays a society composed of disheartened, "spiritually handicapped and amputated" individuals who have nothing better to do than pass the time by exchanging empty talk. The Concierge is a prying, hypocritical gossip who beats her dog. Above all, she says to one of her tenants, "Do without feelings too, how are we meant to find room for them? They don't enter into our account of things. How would feelings help *me* sweep my staircase?" (46). Other voices are heard arguing, insulting each other, spouting platitudes, singing silly songs, or telling the kind of nonsensical anecdotes found in *The Bald Soprano* and *The Lesson.*

In the first half of the third act, as in the beginning of the second act, social and political satire displace Bérenger and his quest as the center of attention. Authority appears in the form of two gigantic policemen and their huge paddy wagon that block Bérenger's route. These agents of society hinder rather than help Bérenger in his quest to bring the Killer to justice. Their sole function is to preserve order.

Even more menacing is the guignolesque Mother Peep, the leader of a political rally that dominates the beginning of the third act. Peep is exhorting a cheering crowd to hand power over to her and her geese. She is a vicious demagogue who speaks in Orwellian double-talk: "We won't exploit men, we'll make them productive. We'll call compulsory work voluntary. War shall change its name to peace and everything will be altered, thanks to me and my geese. . . . When tyranny is restored we'll call it discipline and liberty. The misfortune of one is the happiness of all!" (77). Another of the grotesque, monstrous authority figures that appear so often in Ionesco's theater, Mother Peep spouts a rhetoric that satirizes political propaganda of both the right and the left: "We'll replace the myths . . . by slogans . . . and the latest platitudes!" (80). Her name echoes not just Mother Goose but also Brecht's Mother Courage, and much of her speech parodies the Marxist rhetoric of Sartre, Brecht, and other of Ionesco's bêtes noires. She will demystify the people by offering a new mystification that will be invulnerable: "The new one will be fool proof and cause nothing but misunderstanding. We'll bring the lie to perfection" (76); "To disalienate mankind, we must alienate each individual man . . . and there'll be soup kitchens for all" (77). Nazism is also evoked in the goose-stepping and the antiintellectual slogans: "As for the intellectuals, . . . we will make them do the goose-step" (78). The one person courageous (or stupid) enough to denounce Mother Peep is a drunkard who is torn to pieces by the angry geese when he dares to say that he does not think like everyone else. Here Ionesco is attacking all forms of political demagoguery and tyranny. Mass movements are dangerous because they distract attention from the spiritual and the metaphysical and because they subordinate individual freedom of thought and action to an abstract collective good. This theme—the fate of the individual caught in the midst of mob hysteria—has its roots in Ionesco's own experience of the rise of fascism in Romania; it becomes the central focus of his next major play.

Rhinoceros

Rhinoceros was adapted from a short story of the same name first published in *Lettres nouvelles* in 1957 (later to be included in the volume entitled *The Colonel's Photograph*). Its world premiere (in German) took place in Dusseldorf on 6 November 1959; it opened in France at the Odéon-Théâtre de France (a theater subsidized by the French government) on 22 January 1960 in a production directed by Jean-Louis Barrault. The play was a great international success; the London production was directed by Orson Welles and starred Sir Laurence Olivier and Joan Plowright, while the New York production, starring Zero Mostel and Eli Wallach as Jean and Bérenger, was filmed and released as part of the American Theater Festival series. The most intelligible and accessible of Ionesco's plays to date, *Rhinoceros* marked a decisive turning point in his career, situated as it was exactly at the midpoint between the scandal of *The Bald Soprano*'s premiere and the official canonization of Ionesco's election to the Académie française. It won him the respectability of having his plays produced on the stage of a national theater as well as his first large popular audiences. While it may be considered Ionesco's most political play in some respects, it is, in fact, an elaboration of the aversion to politics that he expressed in the London Controversy.

Act 1 is set in the square of a small provincial town around noon on a Sunday. The brilliant white light and blue sky create a peaceful atmosphere reminiscent of the Radiant City in *The Killer*. In contrast to the openings of Ionesco's previous plays, at the beginning of *Rhinoceros* a large number of actors and a detailed outdoor set (a small grocery and a sidewalk café, with a church steeple visible in the distance) occupy the stage. Bérenger, disheveled and hung over, arrives at the café (late, as usual) to meet his friend Jean, a fastidious, overbearing pedant who berates Bérenger for his lack of self-discipline, willpower, and ambition. The calm of this peaceful Sunday afternoon is soon shattered, however, by the sudden appearance of a rhinoceros running at top speed down the opposite sidewalk. Everyone is shocked except Bérenger, who pays little attention to this surprising occurrence. When a second rhinoceros rushes by and tramples one woman's pet cat, shock becomes outrage, and Jean in particular demands that the authorities do something about the rhinoceros problem. Jean and Bérenger quarrel about which kind of rhinoceros (African or Asian) has one horn or two, and Jean leaves in a huff as Bérenger orders another cognac.

Scene 1 of act 2 takes place the next morning in the office where Bérenger is employed, a firm that publishes legal texts. The employees include Botard, a retired teacher and outspoken critic of the management; Daisy, the beautiful secretary with whom Bérenger is in love; and Dudard, an ambitious, well-educated and self-possessed young man who is Bérenger's rival for Daisy's affections. Bérenger arrives late and just manages to escape the attention of M. Papillon, the office manager, who is involved in a discussion about whether or not a rhinoceros in fact appeared in the town the previous day. Mme Boeuf arrives to announce that her husband will be absent from work; she is out of breath because a rhinoceros has chased her. When the animal demolishes the staircase, she recognizes it to be her husband and jumps down to ride away on his back. Stranded upstairs, the remaining employees phone the firemen to come to their rescue and discover that rhinoceroses have caused similar predicaments throughout the city. Bérenger announces his intention to visit Jean and mend their friendship. The following scene takes place in Jean's apartment, where a horrified Bérenger watches as Jean is transformed into a rhinoceros before his eyes.

The last act finds Bérenger barricaded in his apartment as more and more of his fellow citizens and coworkers succumb to rhinoceritis. First Dudard comes to visit, then Daisy, to discuss the growing epidemic of rhinoceritis. When Dudard rushes out to join the rhinoceroses, Daisy and Bérenger discover their mutual love and, like a new Adam and Eve vow to fight rhinoceritis. Daisy lacks the strength to resist, however, and she leaves Bérenger alone on stage, surrounded by the stylized silhouettes and almost musical roaring of the horde of beasts outside. Even though he is tempted at the last minute to join them, he is finally defiant, swearing as the curtain falls that he will never give up.

An Allegory of Nazism?

It is well known and widely noted that *Rhinoceros* was inspired by Ionesco's own bewilderment and horror at seeing nearly all his colleagues and compatriots in Bucharest succumb to fascism between 1934 and 1938. "Imagine that one fine morning you discover that rhinoceroses have taken power," he wrote in his private journal around 1940 (*PP* 67). In the play, the rhinoceros is a symbol for the fascist Iron Guards whose rise to power in Romania paralleled the rise of Nazism in Germany. Jean's transformation into a rhinoceros dramatizes Ionesco's own experience of seeing a colleague turn into a fascist: "I spoke to him. He was still a man. Suddenly, beneath my very eyes, I saw his skin get hard and thicken in a terrifying way. His gloves, his shoes, became hoofs; his hands became paws, a horn began to grow out of his forehead, he became ferocious, he attacked furiously. He was no longer intelligent, he could no longer talk. He had become a rhinoceros" (*PP* 80).

Certainly the analogies between the Nazis and the rhinoceroses of the play are obvious. As Jean makes clear in justifying his decision to join the rhinoceroses, the rhinoceros mentality glorifies nature and dismisses outdated moral standards: "Nature has its own laws. Morality's against Nature." When Bérenger asks him if he is suggesting that we replace our moral laws by the law of the jungle, Jean answers, "It would suit me, suit me fine. . . . We've got to build our life on new foundations. We must get back to primeval integrity" (67). Like the Nazis, these are brutal beasts who glory in their strength and trample the weak—the cat, for instance—under foot. They are bullies who rampage through the streets and destroy civilization.

Each of the characters who contracts rhinoceritis has a reason that echoes the rationales or excuses of various groups who became fascists. Jean is a zealous conformist who speaks and thinks only in platitudes. He is an overbearing bully, and therefore it is not surprising that he is among the first to convert. He is, moreover, a racist; when Bérenger maintains during their argument in the first act that "Asiatics are people the same as everyone else," Jean becomes livid and screams, "They're yellow!" (31). Botard is also an ideologue, a left-wing activist who sees conspiracies everywhere and claims to know the secret behind the sudden appearance of the rhinoceroses. As Dudard points out, Botard's passionate and overly simplified attitudes are "entirely dictated by hatred of his superiors" (83). Despite his early opposition to the rhinoceroses, he converts in order to "move with the times" (89). Dudard, on the other hand, represents the type of intellectual for whom "to understand is to justify": "My dear Bérenger, one must always make an effort to understand. And in order to understand a phenomenon and its effects you need to work back to the initial causes, by honest intellectual effort" (83). Dudard's transformation parallels the conversion of Ionesco's antifascist friends to fascism "because in the beginning they gave in on one little detail." "This is the way they all begin. They admit certain things, with complete objectivity. You must discuss things with them reasonably and objectively. In reality they give in a little, to the right, to the left, without realizing it" (*PP* 79–80). Dudard is a tolerant relativist who maintains in his discussion with Bérenger that as mere humans we are not competent to judge what is normal or abnormal: "Who can say where the normal stops and the abnormal begins? Can you personally define these conceptions of normality and abnormality? Nobody has solved this problem yet, either medically or philosophically" (84). Other characters (Daisy and M. Papillon, for example) are ordinary, otherwise decent citizens who go along with the rhinoceroses because everyone else is doing it or because they are afraid.

The Individual Versus the Collective: Politics and
Metaphysics

Read as an allegory, the play may appear to be a politically engaged work denouncing fascism—Ionesco's response to the demands of Tynan and others that he write socially relevant plays. Yet, as Ionesco has repeatedly averred, the target of his critique is not just fascism but all mass movements that subordinate the individual to the collective: "*Rhinoceros* is certainly an anti-Nazi play, yet it is also and mainly an attack on collective hysteria and the epidemics that lurk beneath the surface of reason and ideas but are none the less serious collective diseases passed off as ideologies" (*NCN* 199). Like Mother Peep's geese in *The Killer,* the rhinoceroses are a faceless mob (with the lone exception of the Logician, distinguishable from the others by his straw hat).

Rather than offering counterarguments or a political alternative to rhinoceritis, Ionesco is attacking ideology, or politics, itself. Responding to the critics who reproached him for failing to provide Bérenger with an ideology to justify his resistance, Ionesco wrote, "If I set up a ready-made ideology in opposition to other ready-made ideologies, which clutter up the brain, I should only be opposing one system of rhinoceric slogans to another" (*NCN* 210).[3] The reason that Bérenger resists the rhinoceroses is precisely because he has no arguments (that is, no dogma) of his own to oppose to the arguments of Jean or Dudard. He is in every sense an ordinary man—"I'm content to be what I am," he tells Jean (75). Like Ionesco, Bérenger is an essentialist who knows intuitively that "the human individual" (68), whatever time and society he may live in, is always "identical in his essence" (*NCN* 78) His aversion to the rhinoceroses is visceral—"Just the sight of them upsets me" (78). Inarticulate, he counters Jean's defense of rhinoceroses not with argument but with feeling: "It's hard to say why; it's just something you feel" (66). In other words, what sets Bérenger apart is quite simply his humanity.

Alone among the characters, Bérenger suffers from the metaphysical anguish that, for Ionesco, defines the human condition. "I can't get used to it," he tells Jean. "I just can't get used to life" (7). While Jean is concerned solely with the veneer of social function (he is meticulous about his appearance and dedicated to projecting a virtuous image), Bérenger is grappling with the fundamental problem of existence—the fact that each human being is a solitary individual facing mortality. Like Ionesco, Bérenger feels heavy, mired in despair that can be relieved only by drinking: "I don't like the taste of alcohol much. And yet if I don't drink, I'm done for; it's as if I'm frightened, and so I drink not to be frightened any longer. . . . It's a sort of anguish difficult to describe. . . . I'm conscious of my body all the time, as if it were made of lead, or as if I were carrying another man around on my back. I can't seem to get used to myself" (17–18).[4] Jean, on the other hand, feels "as light as a feather," even though he weighs considerably more than Bérenger. Bérenger is the only one with a conscience, the only one who experiences guilt.

Rather than criticizing any *particular* ideology or system, *Rhinoceros* attacks all systems or ideologies because they obscure what is truly important (the human condition, metaphysical anguish) and reduce individuals to functions or ciphers. Politics serves to divide individuals over squabbles about problems that are solvable rather than allowing them to contemplate together what really unites them—the problem of existence. Again and again in his writing and interviews, Ionesco emphasizes the primacy of the individual over the collective: "I believe that the reason why people throughout the world have loved this play is that all countries—in the West as well as in the East—are more or less collectivized now. Somewhat unconsciously, I've put my finger on a terrible problem: depersonalization. So, in all modern societies, collectivized people long for solitude, for a personal life" (*ENT* 128). Like Ionesco himself and nearly all of his protagonists, Bérenger is uncomfortable at best living in society; he is a loner. As Ionesco wrote in *Notes and Counter Notes,* "Several times I have said that it is in our fundamental solitude that we rediscover ourselves and that the more I am alone, the more I am in communion with others; whereas in organized society, which is an organization of functions, man is merely reduced to his function, which alienates him from the rest" (78). If Bérenger remains alone at the end of the play, despite his last-minute wish to join the others, it is because the rest of the world around him has become impersonal and dehumanized: "Bérenger finds himself alone in a dehumanized world where each person tried to be just like all the others. It's just because they all tried to be like each other that they became dehumanized, or rather depersonalized, which is after all the same thing" (*ENT* 128).

Reason versus "Logic"

When the play premiered, critics attacked Ionesco for failing to provide a rational defense against rhinoceritis, for mocking the human capacity to reason. Yet the true object of the play's satire is not reason so much as the perversion of reason wherein a system (logic) supplants reality. Bérenger is like the *raisonneur* in Molière's comedies—the one character who speaks with the voice of common sense; he is the only one to point out the basic truth that it is normal to be human and absolutely abnormal to become a rhinoceros. His aversion to the rhinoceroses is founded in his essential humanity and not in some dogma. The dogmatists—Jean, Botard, the Logician—succumb to a system because they cannot exist outside a system. It is dogma that reverses the terms, making the irrational "logical" and perverting reason into irrational rationalizing.

The character of the Logician is the prime example of this kind of antilogic. During the first act, he gives the Old Gentleman a lesson in logic, warning ironically that logic is a very beautiful thing "as long as it's not abused" (19). He then undertakes to teach the old man what a syllogism is, but he makes an elementary error, reversing the last two terms: "The cat has four paws. Isidore and Fricot both have four paws. Therefore Isidore and Fricot are cats" (18); "All cats die. Socrates is dead. Therefore Socrates is a cat" (19). The Logician's antilogic, founded on a rigid system of false syllogisms, leads him to deny the obvious and lose contact with reality:

> Old Gentleman: So then logically speaking, my dog
> must be a cat?
> Logician: Logically, yes. . . .

Old Gentleman: So Socrates was a cat, was he?
Logician: Logic has just revealed the fact to us. (18–19)

Certainly the Logician is an object of satire, like the learned Doctors in *Improvisation;* like them, he is a fool and a pseudointellectual. The fact that he is honored as an intellectual authority satirizes a society so easily duped; this does not mean, however, that the play condemns the human intellect and its capacity to reason. On the contrary, it is the perversion of human reasoning that leads to disaster. When the Logician says that "there are no limits to logic" (21), he is issuing an implicit warning about the danger of allowing any mechanical system to take precedence over obvious truths. As Ionesco told Claude Bonnefoy, "Obviously, logic is external to life. Logic, dialectics, systematologies contain all possible mechanisms, all possible forms of madness. Everyone knows that systematologies lose touch with reality" (*ENT* 121).

Dreams and Nightmares

In the same interview cited above, Ionesco opposes the natural logic of dreams to the madness of so-called logical systems: "Dreams are natural, they're not mad" (121). Like so many of Ionesco's protagonists, Bérenger is a dreamer; as he tells Jean, "I do dream. Life is a dream" (14). At the beginning of the play he is nearly somnolent, hung over, apathetic. His contact with waking life is tenuous and painful at best—"Solitude seems to oppress me. And so does the company of other people"; "I sometimes wonder if I exist myself" (19). He feels "out of place in life, among people" and uses alcohol to "forget" (17). So wrapped up is he in his own anxieties and musings that he hardly notices the first passage of the rhinoceros. While all the other characters exclaim and react with surprise and indignation, he merely yawns. As the play becomes more and more like a bad dream, however, Bérenger "wakes up," so that the initial situation is reversed by the end of the play. Asleep in a "normal" world, Bérenger wakes up as the world becomes a nightmare.[5] By the end he is as much out of place as he was in the

117

beginning, but the normal-abnormal polarity has been reversed.

The nightmarish proliferation of rhinoceroses, progressing geometrically at an increasingly frenzied pace, echoes the proliferation of matter (chairs, eggs, furniture, mushrooms, coffee cups, the growing corpse) in other Ionesco plays that have the quality of a bad dream. Metamorphosis of a human being into an animal is reminiscent of Kafka, an even more disturbing invasion of the human domain than the proliferation of objects because animals are living beings, like humans. As the animal becomes the norm and the human the aberration, the scale of values is reversed. The rhinoceros norm becomes attractive, even to Bérenger, who in a penultimate reversal of attitude tries but fails to become a rhinoceros himself.

Space and Decor

Like *The Killer, Rhinoceros* opens in a brightly lit exterior setting. Whereas the bright light in the earlier play was the objective correlative of the protagonist's euphoric emotional state, however, the light in the later play has no effect on Bérenger's psyche, mired as he is in his own darkness. Moreover, the sets of the first two scenes in *Rhinoceros* are realistic, crowded with scenery, characters and props—quite a departure from what audiences might have expected from Ionesco. For the first time in Ionesco's theater, the main character is shown working in a public office with others, solidly placed within the larger context of society; both the light and the decor of the first two scenes reflect human activity and the normal bustle of daily life. As rhinoceritis spreads in the last two scenes, however, the lighting becomes gloomier, reflecting Bérenger's increasing distress and isolation, and the set returns to the claustrated interior room found in so many earlier plays.

The set also becomes progressively more stylized and less realistic as the human domain (the "normal") is displaced by rhinoceroses (the "abnormal"). Beginning with Jean's physical transformation near the end of act 2, rhinoceros horns and then rhinoceros heads appear on stage. By the end of the last act,

rhinoceros silhouettes surround the stage, and the entire upstage wall is covered with stylized rhinoceros heads that, "in
spite of their monstrous appearance, seem to become more and
more beautiful" (94). After Daisy leaves, Bérenger takes some
pictures of human beings out of a cupboard and hangs them on
a wall in an effort to find a reflection of his own human image,
but "the ugliness of these pictures is in contrast to the rhinoceros heads which have become very beautiful" (106).

Sound effects also have a major role in representing the displacement of the human realm by the rhinoceroses. In the first
two scenes, the rhinoceroses are represented primarily by the
deafening roar of their hooves as they run by, the sound of
which momentarily drowns out human conversation. The roaring and trumpeting of the beasts punctuate the third act, signifying the rapid spread of the epidemic. Only annoying and
intermittent in the beginning, they become increasingly intru-
sive; toward the end, their sounds invade the room through
both the telephone and the radio. As the stylized heads became more beautiful, so the noises become more musical and
melodious as the rhinoceroses become the norm: "Powerful
noises of moving rhinoceroses are heard, but somehow it is a
musical sound" (94); "all these disquieting sounds are nevertheless somehow rhythmical, making a kind of music" (101). It
is this music, in fact, that finally seduces Daisy to join the
rhinoceroses:

> Daisy: Listen, they're singing!
> Bérenger: They're not singing, they're roaring.
> Daisy: They're singing. . . .
> Bérenger: You can't have a very musical ear, then.
> Daisy: You don't know the first thing about music,
>   poor dear—and look, they're playing as well, and
>   dancing. . . . They're beautiful. . . . They're like
>   gods. (104)

The organization of space, both onstage and offstage, reflects the tension and conflict between human and animal
realms. The appearance of the rhinoceroses divides space verti-
cally, with the rhinoceroses occupying the lower level (the street)
and the humans occupying second-story rooms. It is only in the

first act that human beings appear at street level. The death of the housewife's pet cat is a signal that the street belongs to the rhinoceroses. Staircases—the link between upper and lower levels—figure prominently in the last three scenes. In the second scene, M. Boeuf destroys the stairs leading up to the office, trapping Bérenger and his colleagues. In the last two scenes, the staircases outside Jean's and Bérenger's apartments are visible to the audience. When a character (Bérenger, Dudard, Daisy) mounts them, it symbolizes that character's humanity. Inversely, descending the staircase signifies becoming a rhinoceros; all the characters who become rhinoceroses run down the stairs to join the others on the ground. While the location of the human domain on the upper level signifies human superiority, it also leads to isolation as the rhinoceroses take over the entire ground level and cut off all avenues of escape.

A similar tension between interior and exterior space underlies the play. As the rhinoceroses take over the exterior space, the humans are driven inside by the dust they raise, the noise they make, and the danger of being trampled. While the rhinoceroses are confined to the offstage exterior space in the first two scenes, they invade the onstage space in the last two. Interiors function as both prison and shelter. The humans are trapped in the office in the second act, and Bérenger feels trapped inside Jean's room when Jean becomes a rhinoceros and rhinoceroses block the exits. At the end of act 2 Bérenger is desperate to escape from Jean's room, while in act 3 he is barricaded inside his room, trying to keep the rhinoceroses outside. The barriers that separate inside from outside are easily penetrated, however; the rhinoceroses call Bérenger on the phone, their sounds enter the room over the radio as well as through the walls and windows, the dust they raise fills the room, and their stylized heads eventually cover the entire back wall. The shelter afforded by Bérenger's room is precarious at best, for the rhinoceroses are quite capable of knocking down any wall—Bérenger, Dudard, and Daisy report seeing them demolish the walls of the fire station (92).

An innovation in organization of space is the extension of the offstage space into the auditorium. In both Jean's and

120

Bérenger's rooms an empty window frame faces the audience in the foreground. Part of the invisible wall that separates the stage from the auditorium, the frame serves both to emphasize Bérenger's isolation from the human world and to involve the audience implicitly in the growing mass hysteria. Jean tries at one point to escape through this window in the second act, but his way is blocked by "a large number of rhinoceros heads" "crossing the orchestra pit at great speed" (70). On several occasions in the third act, Bérenger, Dudard, and Daisy look out through the empty frame into the auditorium, gesturing toward the audience as they describe the rhinoceroses whose heads can be seen passing underneath the window; Bérenger exclaims, for example that, "a lot of them started like that!" while pointing to the audience (98).

A Tragic Farce

Although *Rhinoceros* has no subtitle, the term tragic farce would be equally appropriate for this play as for *The Chairs*. Ionesco disliked the American production because it turned the play into a silly comedy. "I have read the American critics on the play and noticed that everyone agreed the play was funny. Well, it isn't. Although it is a farce, it is above all a tragedy" (*NCN* 208).

The grimness of the play's basic theme is thrown into relief by use of farcical elements, in keeping with Ionesco's conviction that the comic should be submerged in the tragic and vice versa. The first act in particular is broadly farcical. The contrast between the physical appearance of the two principal characters (Jean is large, pompous, and immaculately groomed, and he is wearing yellow shoes; Bérenger is slim, groggy, disheveled, and rumpled) is an immediate source of humor; they are in this regard reminiscent of Laurel and Hardy. Slapstick and physical humor are prominent: Bérenger spills his drink on Jean, Jean knocks the Old Gentleman into the Logician's arms while flapping his arms like a bird, and the waitress drops a full tray of glasses when she is startled by the passage of the second rhinoceros. While the succeeding scenes become somewhat less farcical as the rhinoceroses become more threatening, physical humor persists throughout the play, from the large Mme Boeuf's leap onto the back of her rhinoceros husband to Jean's transformation into a rhinoceros, as comic as it is terrifying, to Bérenger's constant checking under a bandage he wears on his forehead for any trace of a horn. This broad slapstick humor is probably the primary explanation for the widespread appeal and popularity of the play among mass audiences throughout the world.

Although the outrageous nonsense of the earlier plays is absent, verbal humor is another important source of comedy in *Rhinoceros*. The Logician's idiotic false syllogisms and his lengthy explanation to the Old Gentleman about what happens when you take legs away from cats are very funny, as is the silly argument about which variety of rhinoceros has one horn and which has two. Equally amusing is the contrapuntal dialogue of the first act, in which two simultaneous conversations—one between Jean and Bérenger and the other between the Logician and the Old Gentleman—overlap so that each pair occasionally repeats the words of the other. The rapid-fire repetition of certain exclamations and the accelerated pace of the dialogue add considerably to the comic effect. The twisted logic of Jean's and Dudard's rationalizing explanations of the rhinoceroses is as funny as it is distressing. Even in the last act, comic touches remain. Daisy and Bérenger fall in love, quarrel, and part in a very short space of time; as Bérenger says, "Oh dear! In the space of a few minutes we've gone through twenty-five years of married life" (104).

Other touches of Ionesco's wit appear as well. When Dudard looks in the paper to find out what really happened the day before, for example, he consults the "dead cats column" (39). As is so often the case, Ionesco does not resist a small reference to himself.[6] When Jean urges Bérenger to improve his mind, he recommends seeing an interesting play—one by Ionesco: "There's one playing now. Take advantage of it" (23).

It is the play's humor that saves it from pathos and sentimentality. Bérenger is a derisory antihero; a well-meaning but inept weakling with a drinking problem, he cannot explain his own resistance to the rhinoceroses. He even tries at the last minute to join them, unsuccessfully. As Ionesco said about the type of character he prefers, "He must be as comic as he is moving, as distressing as he is ridiculous. . . . One has to be able to regard [him] with a lucidity that is not malevolent but ironical" (*NCN* 123). The one unbreakable rule for writing comedy, he said, was that "one must not allow oneself to get bogged down in sentimentality. One needs to be somehow cruel and sardonic with oneself" (*NCN* 123). It is exactly this irony, this sardonic twist, that makes the play a tragedy of derision rather than of grandeur. Read in this light, Bérenger's final words— "I'm the last man left, and I'm staying that way until the end. I'm not capitulating!" (107)—are not heroic so much as they are desperate.

Exit the King

Ionesco dictated *Exit the King* during two ten-day periods between 15 October and 15 November 1962. It premiered only one month later (on 15 December 1962) at the Théâtre de l'Alliance française in a production directed by Jacques Mauclair. Reviews were glowing for the most part, full of comparisons with Shakespeare's *King Lear* and of praise for what can be called the most classical of Ionesco's plays. Consisting of an intense, tightly structured single act, it portrays the last two hours in the long life of King Bérenger I.

Despite its being a one-act play, *Exit the King* has the structure and characters of a classical tragedy. In a very brief prologue, the Guard (who acts as the chorus throughout the play) introduces the characters: King Bérenger I; his two wives, Marguerite (an older, severe authority figure) and Marie (young and beautiful); Juliette (the Nurse and confidante); and the Doctor (surgeon, bacteriologist, executioner, and astrologer), representative of fate or destiny. As befits tragedy, this play has as its protagonist a king whose fate should inspire terror and pity. It observes strictly the classical unities of action, time, and place: it is set in the King's throne room, the sole action is King Bérenger's passage from denial to acceptance of his own death, and the time of the action corresponds exactly to the time of the performance (approximately two hours in most productions). The action, although linear and without breaks, can be divided into five movements that correspond roughly to the five acts of classical tragedy.

The beginning of the play (7–18) is an exposition of the situation. Without ever mentioning death directly, the Guard, Juliette, Marguerite, Marie, and the Doctor make it clear that the King's death is imminent. His power has waned so much that the sun no longer obeys him, the castle and his entire kingdom are falling to pieces, and even the cosmos is in a state of total chaos. Marguerite reproaches Marie for failing to prepare the King for his inevitable fate and says that she will guide him through his final moments.

The equivalent of a second act (18–35) begins with the King's entrance. Marguerite and the Doctor inform him that he is going to die, not at some time in the distant future but in ninety minutes—at the end of the show. Bérenger refuses to believe them at first, abetted in his denial by Marie. The evidence laid before him finally convinces him that they are telling the truth, and he begins to plead for his life. The Guard's proclamation that the "ceremony" is beginning marks the next stage in the action (35–54). Bérenger experiences anger, abject fear, and despair; he regresses to childhood. Finally, he asks to learn resignation, and the fourth "act" (54–77) begins. This part of the play is a ritual of resignation and renunciation in which Bérenger gradually gives up his attachments to life and begins to overcome his fear. At the beginning of the final movement (77–95), the King has fallen silent and the other characters speak of him in the past tense. First Marie, then the Guard, Juliette, and the Doctor vanish as Bérenger's senses cease to function. In a kind of reverse childbirth, Marguerite cuts the cords that still bind him to life and guides him through the last steps of his journey to death before disappearing herself. The play ends as Bérenger and the entire set vanish into a mist of grayish half-light.

An Apprenticeship in Dying

Both a meditation on and a clinical description of the process of dying (the literal translation of the French title is "The King is Dying"), *Exit the King* has its origins in Ionesco's lifelong obsession with death as well as in the specific circumstances of its composition. Ionesco wrote the first part of it after having been confronted with his own mortality as the result of an illness; he then suffered a two-week relapse before finishing the play. As he told Claude Bonnefoy, personal anguish was the point of departure for this "trial apprenticeship in dying": "I told myself that one could learn how to die, that I could learn how to die. . . . It seemed to me the most essential thing that we can do since we're all dying people who can't accept that we're going to die" (*ENT* 77–78).

The conflict between Marguerite and Marie is a conflict between two possible attitudes toward death. Marie wishes to live eternally in the present; for her, there is no point in interrupting the pleasures of life to contemplate the horror of death. She urges the King to cling to the present moment, since "until Death comes, you are still *here*. When Death is here, *you* will have gone. You won't meet her or see her" (66). For Marguerite, however, "death has always been here, present in the seed since the very first day" (66). She advocates a stoic apprenticeship in dying: "[It's your fault if you've been taken unawares, you ought to have been prepared. . . .] You'd been condemned, and you should have thought about that the very first day, and then day after day, five minutes every day. It wasn't much to give up. Five minutes every day. Then ten minutes, a quarter, half an hour. That's the way to train yourself" (37). For Marie, the dominant metaphor for life is a party, a celebration, while for Marguerite, it is a journey with death as its goal. If the King is not prepared to die, she says, Marie is partly to blame. According to her, the King should never have been permitted to "lose sight of his destination" (11). "He's been like one of those travelers who linger at every inn, forgetting each time that the inn is not the end of the journey" (13). Asked to adjudicate between the two, the Doctor says, "What you both say is true. It depends on the point of view" (67). In the context of the play, however, it is Marguerite who prevails. She is the last character remaining with Bérenger, and she guides him through the last steps of his journey, up a slope and over a footbridge into death (92–94).

Bérenger's initiation into death takes the form of a ritualized ceremony, orchestrated by Marguerite and punctuated by the Guard's proclamations and announcements.[7] Like the classical chorus, the Guard addresses the audience directly. He introduces the other characters; announces the stages in the action (for example, "The ceremony is about to commence" [35], "The Queen and the Doctor no longer owe the King obedience" [72], "His Majesty is officially blind" [85]); and delivers a long speech in which he lists the King's prodigious accomplishments, which include inventing gunpowder, extinguishing volcanoes, founding the world's major cities, and splitting the atom (73–74). He serves to make of the King's death a public, ceremonial event, thus by implication universal rather than particular or private. The outward symbols of power (crown, scepter, cloak, and throne) also play an important role in this reverse coronation—divestiture instead of investiture. As the ceremony progresses, the King's scepter becomes a cane, his crown is replaced by a sleeping cap, a wheelchair takes the place of his throne, and blankets and hot water bottles surround him instead of his cloak. Liturgical language and forms also serve to underscore the ceremonial nature of the play, as when all the characters invoke the help of those who have died in teaching the King resignation (54–57). Indeed, the stage directions accompanying this passage are explicit in this regard: "The following dialogue should be spoken and acted as though it were ritual, with solemnity, almost chanted, accompanied by various movements, with the actors kneeling, holding out their arms, etc." (54).

The goal of the ceremony is to teach the King serenity and acceptance of death, reflecting Ionesco's own interest in non-Western mysticism.[8] Marguerite, the Doctor, and even Marie reassure the King that "life is exile" and death is only a return to "his own country": "You'll go back where you came from when you were born. Don't be so frightened, you're sure to find something familiar there" (56). Marguerite is like a Zen master who teaches that life is a burden or an entangling web; her job is to help the King free himself from its confines: "I'll cut him loose. I'll untie every knot and ravel out the tangled skein. I'll separate the wheat from the tenacious tares that cling to him and bind him" (66). The final journey described by Marguerite is indeed a painless, even euphoric, return to the womb. First she cuts the cords that still bind the King with a pair of invisible scissors, as though severing an umbilical cord that attaches him to life. She then removes a whole series of invisible symbols of the King's earthly existence, "all those messy little things that worried you" (91): a ball and chain from his leg, a heavy sack from his shoulders, a pack from his back, his boots, his tools, and his weapons. She tells him to stand up straight and climb higher and higher as he mounts the steps to his throne, reversing the descent down the birth canal. When he has nearly reached the throne, she commands him to give her his body: first his legs, then his fingers, then his arms, his chest, his shoulders, and his abdomen. Her final instruction to him before disappearing is to "take his place" on his throne, which becomes symbolically the womb, the land that preceded his birth.

Although the goal of the ceremony is clear, the play offers no answers about whether the ceremony is successful from the King's point of view. By Ionesco's own testimony, writing the play did not help him at all to relieve his anguish (*ENT* 78). Despite all the help he receives, the King continues to resist stubbornly and cling tenaciously to life until the very end. His last words are "Blue, blue" (93)—that intense color associated throughout Ionesco's work with the pure joy and astonishment of existence, indicating that he has not yet given up his life (abdicated) willingly.[9] The gray mist into which the King and set vanish also contributes to the ambiguity of the ending. Ionesco had at one point considered bright light for the end— in his own vocabulary, that would have symbolized euphoria, serenity, plenitude, and redemption. But the King, the throne, and the entire set disappear in darkness at the end of the play. We have no way of knowing what Bérenger feels or experiences at the moment of death; the play represents the process of dying and can tell us nothing about death itself other than its unknowability. The impenetrable veil of darkness means that death must still remain forever unknowable to the living.

Acting in tandem with Marguerite, the Doctor offers a clinical perspective on death that balances and lightens its metaphysical aspect. It is he who delivers the diagnosis and prognosis: "He's in a typically critical condition that admits no change" (16); "Sire, you are now incurable" (24). He knows "every phase of the disease" (81) and charts the stages of the King's illness from crisis to crisis (36, 46, 57–58, 59, 66, 70, 72, 76, 80–81, 85). As astrologer and meteorologist, the Doctor is also the voice of destiny and is therefore concerned with keeping track of Bérenger's relationship with time and the cosmos. Twice he becomes concerned that Bérenger is running late—"If this was a good old heart attack, we wouldn't have had so much trouble" (72)—but Marguerite reassures him that "it was all to be expected, all part of the program" (72) and that "the timetable allows for holdups. Some delays were expected, you know" (76). Along with Marguerite, he is concerned that the King's death be dignified and edifying for the sake of posterity: "We'll credit him with some edifying maxims. We'll watch over his legend" (41).

The stages Bérenger passes through in dying parallel in many respects the experience of terminally ill patients as it is described by Dr. Elisabeth Kubler-Ross in her 1969 study *On Death and Dying*. His first reaction to the announcement of his death is denial: "It's because I never used my will power that everything went to pieces. Sheer neglect. It can all be put right" (31). Confronted with the undeniable evidence, he then reacts with a mixture of abject terror and anger. He screams out the window for help from his people, provoking Marguerite to remark that "what was once a king is now a pig that's being slaughtered" (40), and he angrily blames a vague "they" for tricking him: "They promised me *I* could choose the time when I would die" (36); "I've been trapped. I should have been warned, I've been trapped" (37). He then begins to bargain, first begging for someone to come forward to "give up his life for the poor old King's" (41) and then hoping for "a ten to one chance, one chance in a thousand," reminding the others that he "often used to win the sweepstakes" (44). Bérenger's plea for help from those who have already died signals the passage from disbelief to belief in the inevitability of his death: "Help me, you countless thousands who died before me! Tell me how you managed to accept death and die. . . . teach me your indifference and serenity, teach me resignation" (54). As long as the King continues to talk, however, he gives no evidence of

128

having received an affirmative answer to his plea. For Bérenger, "it's not natural to die, because no one ever wants to. I want to exist" (57). He then interrogates Juliette about her life of privation and hard work, rapturously noting every detail in support of his contention that "life can never be bad. It's a contradiction in terms" (61). He finally does renounce one small earthly pleasure—stew—and fear gives way to despair. As the Doctor puts it, "His *death* will kill him now, and not his fear" (66). At this point the only response the King can offer to the other characters' entreaties is, "I'm dying" (67–70). A final pang of nostalgia culminates in a sorrowful farewell to a little ginger cat, "My poor little cat, my one and only cat" (76). Whether the King ever reaches the final stage of serene acceptance is an open question; certainly the text is ambiguous enough to accommodate diverse readings by individual directors.

A Solipsistic Universe

One of the accusations leveled against Ionesco by Kenneth Tynan during the London Controversy was that he was guilty of solipsism: "M. Ionesco is in danger of . . . locking himself up in that hall of mirrors which in philosophy is known as solipsism."[10] While Ionesco himself is not guilty as Tynan charges, the word *solipsism* is particularly appropriate in the case of *Exit the King,* for the identification between the main character and the external world is so close as to be solipsistic. In King Bérenger's world, the boundaries separating internal from external worlds have disappeared, carrying to an extreme the identification evoked by the earlier Bérenger of *The Killer.* As the Doctor points out, Bérenger suffers from "a well-known disease of the psyche: narcissism" (86). "He imagines that no one's ever died before," comments Marguerite scornfully, but Marie defends him with the observation that "no one *has* died before" (41), alluding to the unknowable, unique experience of each individual who must face death and the disappearance of the universe alone. The play thus presents a powerful vision of the process of dying from the perspective of a character whose whole world vanishes along with him.

The entire world of the play exists solely as a function of Bérenger's will, an exteriorization of the character himself. All the other characters repeatedly emphasize that Bérenger and his kingdom grew up together, and they are vanishing together. His kingdom was "boundless in space," reflecting the limitless scope of his aspirations, but "bounded in time": "at once infinite and ephemeral" (78), says Marguerite, like human life. Bérenger in the play is literally every man—the founder of every important city, creator of every important invention, the force behind every significant event of human history (73–74). Furthermore, he played the role of God in this world, having created the seasons, trees, flowers, colors, oceans, mountains, the sun, fire, stars, the sky, people, faces, buildings, rooms, beds, light and dark, war and peace (79–80).

As the King's health has worsened, his kingdom has fallen into ruin and chaos: the cows in the stable can no longer give milk, the only children left are severely handicapped, the country's borders and mountains are shrinking, and the whole kingdom is dying. Ruin extends even beyond the kingdom into the cosmos itself. Mars and Saturn have collided; snow is falling on the sun's north pole; the Milky Way is congealing; and the comet, exhausted and moribund, has curled up with its tail around it, like a dog dying (17). As Juliette puts it, "The earth collapses with him. The suns are growing dim. Water, fire, ours and every universe, the whole lot disappears. . . . He drags it all with him into the abyss" (79).

The identification between the character and his environment is represented not only by the spoken text but through the use of decor—sets, sound effects, and lighting. Before Bérenger even appears, his imminent death is reflected in the state of disrepair into which the palace has fallen. The floor is covered with dust and cigarette butts; during the night, a crack has appeared in the wall, and all efforts to repair it have proved futile. Toward the end of the play, it is the widening of this fissure that signals the last stage in Bérenger's decline. After his kidneys stop functioning, the loud beating of his heart literally shakes the palace, causing the walls to tremble and fall (81). As the King loses memory and consciousness, the other characters and most of the set disappear; finally, the King and his throne vanish, leaving nothing on stage except a dull grayish light.

Mirror imagery (recalling Tynan's remark about the hall of mirrors) further reinforces King Bérenger's solipsism. After he has become blind, Marguerite urges him to look beyond the surface of things; what he sees is a mirror within himself in which everything else is reflected. When she orders him to look beyond the reflection, all he can see is himself: "Behind everything, I exist. Nothing but me everywhere. . . . am I in every mirror or am I the mirror of everything?" (85–86). Just as he is about to die, Marguerite orders him to look at her: "Look right through me! Gaze into my unreflecting mirror" (94). The mirror that sends back no image is the universe that has disappeared, the void that returns nothing.

Time

Mortality is indistinguishable from time; the play is a meditation on the relative and elusive nature of time. Many passages from Ionesco's journals testify to his obsession with the subject; typical are the following excerpts from *Fragments of a Journal:*

> When did I first notice that time "passed"? The sense of time was not at first associated with the idea of death. . . . A day, an hour, seemed to me long, limitless; I could see no end to it. When they talked to me about next year I had the feeling that next year would never come. When I was at La Chapelle-Anthenaise I felt outside of time, in a sort of Paradise. (10)

> At fifteen or sixteen it was all over, I was in time, in flight, in finiteness. The present had disappeared, there was nothing left for me but a past and a tomorrow, a tomorrow which I was already conscious of as past. . . . Familiarity smooths down time, so that you slip on it as on an over-polished floor. A world that is new, a world that is for ever new, a world that is for ever, young for ever, that is Paradise. Speed is not only infernal, it is hell itself, it is the Fall, accelerated.

The present has been, Time has been, neither present
nor Time exist any longer, the geometrical progression of our fall has flung us into nothingness. (11–12)

Here as elsewhere in Ionesco's work, time is a cancer and
mortality is the price of original sin, described in Biblical terms.
Throughout the play, subjective lived time is contrasted with
concrete chronological time. Bérenger never had the time, he
protests, to think about death; his life has passed much too
quickly (although he is over 400 years old): "I came into the
world five minutes ago. I got married three minutes ago. . . . I
came to the throne two and a half minutes ago" (45). Marguerite counters with the calendar time elapsed: 283 years since
his marriage, 277 years since his coronation. Pressed to begin
preparing to die, he says that it might be possible if he still
had a whole century to do it, but the doctor points out that
since lived time is subjective, a brief moment can be as infinite as a century can be fleeting: "A well spent hour's better
than whole centuries of neglect and failure. Five minutes are
enough, ten fully conscious seconds" (38).
    The contradiction between subjective and chronological time
is underscored by the opposing views of Marie on the one hand
and Marguerite and the Doctor on the other. Marie urges upon
the King a Camusian commitment to the present moment: "Remember, there's only a present that goes right on to the end,
everything is present. . . . *Now* you exist, you *are*" (50–51). She
attempts to give him a Proustian sense of time recaptured by
evoking a privileged moment they had spent together: "I im-
plore you to remember that morning in June we spent together
by the sea, when happiness raced through you and inflamed
you. You knew then what joy meant: rich, changeless and undying. If you knew it once, you can know it now. You found
that fiery radiance within you. If it *was* there *once,* it is *still*
there *now*" (51–52). Marguerite and the Doctor, on the other
hand, are meticulous timekeepers, constantly attentive to the
calendar and the clock. They refer constantly to the exact
amount of time remaining in the play (and therefore in
Bérenger's life): "You're going to die in an hour and a half,

you're going to die at the end of the show" (24); "In one hour
and twenty-five minutes, you're going to die. . . . In one hour,
twenty-four minutes and forty-one seconds" (34). (See also 38
and 59.) This metatheatrical twist adds considerable intensity
and urgency to the King's dilemma, putting him in the position of a condemned man waiting for his execution and adding
to the play's dramatic impact.

Bérenger receives no consolation from either side, being
equally unable to forget as to conceive of and prepare for his
death. For Bérenger, as for Ionesco, the thought of death is
literally intolerable because it poisons every moment, past and
future: "Why was I born if it wasn't forever? Damn my parents!" (45). If he must die, he wails, let him be remembered
forever. Yet time itself will also come to an end one day, eras-
ing even the possibility of posterity: "It's all the same whether
it's tomorrow or in countless centuries to come. What's got to
finish one day is finished now" (50).

The Role of Dreams

Ionesco told Bonnefoy that *Exit the King* did not originate
with a dream (as did several of his other plays, including *The
Chairs, Victims of Duty,* and *Amédée*); rather, it was the most
"wide awake" of his plays (*ENT* 77). What was at work in the
play, he said, was a very conscious fear of death. Nevertheless,
dream material plays a definite role.

One of Marguerite's tactics for easing the King's exit from
life is the suggestion that life is a dream: "Sometimes you have
a dream. And you get involved, you believe in it, you love it"
(89). Upon awakening, she says, "You no longer know what it
was that was there all around you." The King responds, completing the analogy between waking from a dream and dying:
"I no longer know what was there all around me. I know I was
part of a world, and this world was all about me. I know it was
me and what else was there, what else?" (89). Marguerite will
then proceed to sever the King's last ties to life, announcing
shortly thereafter that "the dreamer comes out of his dream"
(91): the passage from life to death is like awakening from a
dream.

Indeed the King adopts the demeanor and discourse of a half-wakened dreamer—a sleepwalker—in the last section of the play. In his last extended speech, Bérenger recalls a dream he used to have, and the stage directions specify that he should "give an impression of being dazed, in a kind of dreamy stupor" (76). When he then rises from his wheelchair to begin the final journey, "he already begins to look rather like a sleepwalker. The movements of a sleepwalker will become more and more pronounced" (84).

The dream that Bérenger recounts is in fact a very abridged version of one of Ionesco's own dreams from 1959 (*PP* 102–3). In both dreams, the dreamer remembers a small cat sleeping on the burning coals of a fireplace without catching fire; in both versions, the beloved cat later dies, causing great grief.[11] For Bérenger, as for Ionesco, the small cat symbolizes both unqualified love and the King's life itself, the loss of which is so painful: "How I missed him! He was good and beautiful and wise, all the virtues. He loved me, he loved me. My poor little cat, my one and only cat" (76). Bérenger's dream differs strikingly from Ionesco's, however, in that the fireproof cat in the King's dream emerges from the fireplace transformed into a frightening creature: "It was a different cat, fat and ugly. An enormous she-cat. Like his mother, the wildcat. A bit like Marguerite" (77). Bérenger's dream is not only a melancholy farewell to life that adds a touch of pathos; it also neatly incorporates into the primary theme of the play the deeply ambivalent attitude toward women that subtends it.

Death: The Good versus the Bad Mother

Perhaps nowhere in Ionesco's theater is the complex relationship between the male protagonist and women so clearly mapped as in *Exit the King*. Marie and Marguerite embody, respectively, the pleasure principle versus the reality principle, life versus death, the good mother versus the bad mother in the economy of the King's infantile projections.

By the time the play begins, the King has lost all power and virility; all references to his power are negative ones (9, 14, 19, 26–29, 31–34). He has regressed to childhood: he's like a "schoolboy who hasn't done his homework" (39), "a small child, a little boy again" (44), a "poor little chap, poor child!" (47). He exhibits all the rage of infantile narcissism when he vacillates between demanding that everything die so that nothing will survive him and demanding that everything endure forever to perpetuate his memory (48–49, 65, 69–70). He is "cold, frightened, crying" (42) and wants to feel arms around him (49–50) holding him as though he were a baby. He even tells Marie that he wants to "make a fresh start": "I want to be a baby and you can be my mother" (47).

Marie is a phantasmic ideal mother figure totally acquiescent to the infantile wishes of the King. She refers to him repeatedly as if he were her child—"my dear little King" (34), "poor little King" (40), "my little King" (70), and so on. As he describes their relationship, she was the good mother who comforted him when he had nightmares, put him back to bed when he would wander out of his room on sleepless nights, share his colds and illnesses with him, finish his sentences, rub his back, comb his hair, shine his crown, and choose his ties for him (70–71). She is herself a child, as he longs to be, concerned solely with pleasure—dancing, parties, charity balls—and the present moment. She is also young, fertile, and sexually desirable.[12] She invokes irrational love as the inebriating antidote to death: "Love *is* mad. And if you're mad with love, if you love blindly, completely, death will steal away" (68).

Yet Marie is ultimately no help to the King. She has no power or agency of her own; she exists solely as a projection of his desire, and then only because Marguerite authorizes her presence. She is as narcissistic as the King in her determination to keep him alive: "I'm nothing if he forgets me. I can't go on living if I don't exist in his distracted heart" (81). This is why she is so obstinate in opposing Marguerite and urging the King to cling to life with a strength he no longer has. As Marguerite puts it, "She thinks of no one but herself" (67). From Marguerite's point of view, Marie is one of "those messy little things that worried" Bérenger (91), an encumbrance preventing him from completing his journey. The image of woman as a sticky mud that prevents a man from rising into the air that appeared earlier in *Victims of Duty* and *Amédée* reappears here, but this time it is a woman who gives voice to the image. Early on, she tells the King, "You got stuck in the mud of life. You felt warm and cozy" (36). Referring to Marie and Juliette as "these two weeping women," she says that "they only push him deeper in the mire, trap him, bind him, hold him up" (53). Later she pulls the King away from Marie, telling him "You're stuck in the mud, caught in the brambles" (82).

If Marie is the phantasmic good mother, Marguerite is a phantasmic evil mother who incorporates many attributes of the feared and dreaded father. Older and more severe than Marie, Marguerite is the first of the King's wives and the one agent in the play to exercise power. She is the forbidding authority figure, the voice of reason, the embodiment of the reality principle. (Her repeated gesture of cutting the ties that bind the King to life make her a castrating figure as well as a midwife/mother in the reverse birth process.) Where Marie is soft, she is hard; where Marie has clearly feminine sexual attributes, she is asexual or even vaguely masculine. Marie is the champion of irrational love, while for Marguerite love is "sentimental superstition" (32); it was she who allowed the King's beloved little cat to be killed by the neighbor's dog: "I hated that sentimental, timorous beast" (76). The King fears and hates her and associates her (rightly) with death. "You've always wanted me dead," he tells her (25), and in his dream, Marguerite is a fat, ugly wildcat (77).

In the end, however, it is Marguerite's image that endures and Marie's that fades. Confronted with both wives near the end of his life, Bérenger is unable to identify Marie—"Who are you? Are you my mother? My sister? My wife? My daughter? My niece? My cousin?"—but he recognizes Marguerite immediately: "You hateful, hideous woman! Why are you still with me? Go away, go away!" (83). Marguerite has claimed all along, though, that she is the only one who can help the King. Closely associated with death, she assumes the role of nurturing mother who firmly but gently guides the King into death as she did into life. According to Marguerite, Marie was a distraction for the King; it is she who has been concerned with his welfare, dignity, and comfort. Like the stern authoritarian parent, she claims to know what is best for him, even if he refuses to accept it, whereas Marie thinks only of herself.

Still, the ambiguity surrounding both women characters remains, just as the ending of the play is ambiguous. If the play's ending is an affirmation of serenity and acceptance in the face of death, then Marguerite has indeed fulfilled her self-described role as supportive good mother, despite all of her negative features. If death is the unspeakable, inconceivable horror that Bérenger fears, then Marguerite becomes an Angel of Death who drags Bérenger out of life against his will. As elsewhere in Ionesco's work, this ambivalence regarding women and particularly mother figures is fundamentally unresolvable; it is one of the basic tensions that underlie most of Ionesco's work.

Language and Humor

Exit the King is the most "classically literary" of Ionesco's plays (*ENT* 187). The language (whether lyrical or comic) is always articulate, with no trace of incoherence or disintegration. While this clarity has made the play one of Ionesco's most accessible and popular, it caused Ionesco himself to wonder later whether he had not perhaps been "too discursive and too clear": "I've often wondered in recent years . . . if I wasn't wrong to use so much rhetoric, such literary language in certain plays, like *Exit the King*. . . . Those plays were understood too soon, too quickly, and they no longer hold any mysteries" (*ENT* 171).

As might be expected in a play whose theme is death and dying, some of the language is lyrical and poetic. Marie refers to life, for example, as "a brisk walk through a flowery lane, a promise that's broken, a smile that fades" (45); full of appreciation for the simple pleasures of life, the King is moved to say, "The market's a medley of green lettuce, red cherries, golden grapes and purple eggplants . . . all the colors of the rainbow! . . . It's extraordinary! Incredible! Like a fairy tale!" (63). Other lyrical passages go beyond imagery and use internal rhyme, which is not easily translatable. Speaking of death, Marguerite says, "She is the shoot that grows, the flower that blows, the only fruit we know" (66–67); later, she tells the Doctor not to worry that the King is falling behind schedule: "His little tricks, these kicks against the pricks . . ." (72).[13]

Invocations, repetitions and refrains serve both to add a lyric quality to the language and to underscore the ceremonial character of the King's death, as does frequent use of stichomythia:

> King: Let time turn back in its tracks.
> Marie: Let us be as we were twenty years ago.
> King: Let it be last week.
> Marie: Let it be yesterday evening. Turn back, time! Turn back! Time, stop!
> Marguerite: There is no more time. Time has melted in his hands. (35)

> Juliette: You statues, you dark or shining phantoms, ancients and shades. . .
> Marie: Teach him serenity.
> Guard: Teach him indifference.
> Doctor: Teach him resignation.
> Marguerite: Make him see reason and set his mind at rest. (54; this passage continues through 57)[14]

At the same time, however, verbal wit and wordplay prevent the play from lapsing into solemnity or pathos. As Ionesco has said, "In my plays, you must never let go of what is strange in favor of pathos. You must avoid pathos; mockery and irony should predominate" (*ENT* 162). The constant use of anachronisms is one device that undercuts any sense of tragic grandeur from the beginning: Juliette insists on calling the throne room the "living-room," much to Marguerite's annoyance, and its floor is covered with cigarette butts (8); the kingdom is dotted with "burnt-out swimming pools" (15); the King calls Marguerite and the Doctor Bolsheviks (28); when the King complains that the palace has no washing machine, Marguerite explains that they had to pawn it (61); and Marguerite, dismayed that Marie and the King would fight over his choice of neckties, exclaims, "How suburban!" (73). Slang and vulgar expressions that clash with the context in which they appear also add to the play's humor. Lamenting the loss of his power to regulate the weather, for example, the King says, "There's an idiotic cloud that can't restrain itself. Like an old man, weak in the bladder" (19). Marguerite in particular has a very sharp tongue in reproaching Marie for her immaturity. She criticizes her in several speeches that contain the kind of lists found in earlier plays: "This is the end of your happy days, your high jinks, your beanfeasts and your strip tease" (13); "With your fun and games, your dances, your processions, your official dinners, your winning ways and your fireworks displays, your silver spoons and your honeymoons!" (11).[15]

Another comic device is the use of puns, some of which lose much of their humor or even disappear in translation. The former category includes puns such as "Many people have delusions of grandeur, but you're deluded by triviality" (16) or (Marie) "You count. And you will be counted," to which the King responds, "I'll never be the accountant" (69). An untranslatable pun accounts for Juliette's somewhat cryptic remark about her broom: "I need a new one. I could really do with twelve brooms" (20).[16]

In addition to the verbal humor, slapstick and physical humor turn parts of the play into pure farce. Both Marguerite (28) and the King (45) remark at different moments, "What a farce!," meaning that life is essentially nothing more than a bad joke. The King's weakness makes him the butt of humor in several scenes, as for example when he orders various characters' heads to fall off to no effect, only to lose his own crown when he orders Marguerite's to fall off (31). In two scenes (28–29 and 58–59) Bérenger repeatedly struggles to stand up only to fall down, accompanied by the alternating announcements "The King is dead!"/"Long live the King!" or "The King is down!"/"He's up again!" As the stage directions to the first of these scenes indicate, "This scene should be played like a tragic Punch and Judy show" (29), recalling the guignolesque quality of other tragic farces such as *The Chairs*. Unlike the heroes of classical tragedy, King Bérenger is completely human—contemptible, childish, egotistical, craven. Far from being exceptional, he is, like the Bérengers who preceded him, an Everyman whose dilemma will be all the more moving because he is so ordinary.

A Stroll in the Air

Ionesco wrote *A Stroll in the Air* in the summer of 1962, before he wrote *Exit the King*. It did not have its French premiere, however, until 8 February 1963, in a production directed by Jean-Louis Barrault at the Odéon-Théâtre de France. (A German version opened in Dusseldorf in December 1962.) Like the first two plays in the Bérenger cycle, it was adapted from a short story. It is a baroque assemblage of elements taken from the circus, operetta, puppet shows, and vaudeville; and its staging requires elaborate sets, masks, costumes, sound, lighting, and many special effects. It is written in one act, with abrupt scene changes achieved through lighting and moving set components. Even more cumbersome to produce than *Amédée,* this play suffers from a certain failure to present effective theatrical correlatives for the fantastic events recounted in the short story.

The curtain rises on a beautiful English countryside illuminated by bright sunlight under a brilliant blue sky, a setting that recalls the opening scenes of *The Killer* and *Rhinoceros*. On a fresh green grassy down overlooking a valley there is a small house described as having a naive dreamlike quality; indeed, the entire play is like a dream that turns into a nightmare. In a humorously self-conscious exposition, an assortment of English people out for a stroll inform each other that they are in Gloucestershire, England, that it's a beautiful Sunday morning, and so on. A Journalist comes to interview Bérenger, the famous French playwright who is vacationing in the cottage. Pressed by the Journalist, Bérenger explains that he is suffering from writer's block caused by his doubts about the value of literature and his fear of death.[17]

The next scene is a dream of Bérenger's wife Josephine who comes on stage wearing a dressing gown, accompanied by her "Doctor-Uncle" and a funeral home employee. The Doctor-Uncle tells her that her father, who had been killed in the war, has risen from the dead (much to the chagrin of the funeral home employee, who threatens a lawsuit). When the Doctor-Uncle points out Josephine's father, however, she cannot see him. The last words of these characters are drowned by the deafening roar of an airplane as the stage becomes dark. The airplane drops a bomb on Bérenger's cottage, and when the lights come up he is seen standing in its smoking ruins. Josephine and Marthe, the Bérengers' daughter, are on the right, wearing their Sunday best, and all the English characters (two old ladies, two sets of parents, a little boy and a little girl, and John Bull, who looks like an enormous puppet) are lined up along the back of the stage.

The central section of the play is a dizzying three-ring circus juxtaposing and intertwining the Bérengers' stroll in the country with the comings and goings of the English characters. Alternating comedy and pathos, familiar themes (guilt and innocence, euphoria and despair, freedom and imprisonment, fear of death, and so on) are elaborated in a complex structure of contrapuntal dialogue and action that is strewn with metatheatrical jokes and special effects. The two groups of characters come together when Bérenger, literally carried away by joy and beauty, rediscovers how to fly and offers to teach the others. He eventually flies out of sight for a "stroll in the air."

As Bérenger is returning to earth, the stage darkens, the lighting turns bloodred, and the sounds of bombs mark the beginning of the next scene. It is a series of six nightmares being dreamt by Josephine despite Marthe's efforts to convince her that these visions are not real. They all focus on death, guilt, and hatred. The dreams end as they began, and the lighting that accompanies Bérenger's return to earth is dim and melancholy, reflecting his despair at what he has seen on his journey. It was an apocalyptic vision of hell, beyond which is nothing but the void. The only glimmer of light left at the end of the play is Marthe's tentative expression of hope that perhaps this fate is not inevitable: "Perhaps it will all come right in the end. . . . Perhaps the . . . the gardens . . . the gardens . . ." (117).

Dreams and the Imagination

Ionesco has said that one of the principal sources for *A Stroll in the Air* was a recurring dream of flying (*ENT* 63, 73), and it is the most thoroughly oneiric of his plays since *Victims of*

Duty. (In this respect, it resembles Ionesco's later dream plays.) The entire play has all the precision and clarity characteristic of dreams. For Ionesco, dreams are "imaged thought" (*ENT* 12), and the stage directions are clear about the sort of painterly quality the set should have: "The dreamlike effect should be achieved . . . by the methods used by a Primitive artist, consciously naive. . . . Everything is fully lit, and so there should be nothing dim and no gauze, etc. . . ." (12). This clarity corresponds to the penetrating insight dreams afford the dreamer, the very quality Bérenger alludes to when he says, "If we were as sharply conscious of things all the time as we are in our dreams, we couldn't go on living" (35).[18] As in dreams, the colors are bright and props are deliberately artificial-looking and fantastic; laws of physics are suspended; objects and characters (the Visitor from the Anti-World, the Silver Bridge, the bicycles, and so forth) appear and disappear magically; and an internal logic reigns—as when Bérenger knows what Josephine dreamt without her telling him (30, 35). As in dreams, the characters are fluid and unstable; disguised by grotesque masks and costumes or slightly distorted by lighting, the English characters play multiple roles. John Bull in particular is a polymorphous, menacing authority figure, a caricature who looks like an "enormous puppet."

In addition to the overall dreamlike quality, the play contains two staged dream sequences—Josephine's nightmares. These nightmares all concern abandonment (by her father [25–27] and by the English people who mock and deride her [95–96]), guilt (she is judged and condemned by two Kafkaesque tribunals without knowing what her offense has been [97–100, 103–105]), and death (telling them they might as well get it over with sooner than later, John Bull murders the English characters with a machine gun [100–103] and the Executioner and Man in White invite Josephine to mount the scaffold [103–105]). When Bérenger returns from his stroll in the air, the two levels of dreaming converge as his euphoric dream of flying has turned into the same kind of nightmare of death that Josephine has dreamed.

One key to understanding the significance of dreaming in the play is the link between dreams and the imagination. On the positive side, Bérenger's euphoric experience of flying symbolizes the free flight of the creative imagination and the resurgence of belief in the value of art. On the negative side, Josephine's nightmares are also products of the imagination: as Marthe reminds Josephine while she is dreaming, "It's only real if you believe in it. It's real if you think it is. It's real if you want it to be" (98).

Bérenger, like Amédée before him, is a professional writer, an artist for whom dreaming is equivalent to the positive power of the imagination. When the play begins he is suffering from writer's block and laments the loss of an energy he used to have: "Once upon a time, though I'm really a nihilist, there was some strange force inside me that made me do things and made me write" (20). He asks the Journalist, "What must we do to make literature an exciting voyage of discovery?" (22), indicating that literary inspiration, like dreaming, must be able to escape the confines of consciousness. The Anti-World is a metaphor for the parallel universes that the creative imagination can discover, and Bérenger's explanations of the Anti-World apply equally to the creative power of the imagination: "There are several universes, and they're all interlocking. . . . These worlds interlink and interlock, without touching one another, for they can all coexist in the same space." When Josephine requires more proof, Bérenger and Marthe both insist that "the proof lies in our own minds, in what we discover when we think" (47). Inspired by the appearance of the Silver Bridge ("That's the reason for it, it's all because of that" [62]), Bérenger recovers his creative power. He becomes an "artiste" (a circus performer doing his flying and bicycle tricks) and truly does embark on "an exciting voyage of discovery" when he takes his stroll in the air.

Bérenger's dream of flying turns into a nightmare, however; his return to earth symbolizes the inadequacy of literature (art) to give anything more than "a very dim and feeble picture of how cruel life is in reality" (22). The free flight of the imagination is unable to survive the continuous assault of evil in the world. Bérenger has lost the ability to see beyond hell—"After that, there's nothing" (116). He has returned to the disillusionment of the beginning, when he explained that he had given up writing because "it ought to lead to something else, but it doesn't"

143

(20). The end of the play tends to affirm the Journalist's earlier judgment about the value of art: "Art has lost its power; if it ever had any" (41).

The Lost Paradise of Childhood

At the end of the play, only Marthe retains some belief in the possibility of "the garden," indicating the special status of children. Significantly, this is the first play in which the protagonist has a child; the children in the play are associated with freedom and creativity. Marthe, unlike Josephine, sees the Visitor from the Anti-World right away, and she believes in the power of love to overcome evil: "You must love people," she tells Josephine. "If you stop being afraid of them, they won't be monsters any more. . . . Love them. Then hell will exist no more" (94). The hopeful, creative side of Bérenger is, in fact, the child in him. He delights in toy trains, balloons, and the circus; his interview with the Journalist is staged just like a Punch and Judy show; and the lovely sights (castles, the Silver Bridge) that the Bérengers see on their walk come straight from fairy tales. Here as elsewhere in Ionesco's work, childhood is a lost paradise; the play's pastoral setting and brilliant colors echo the idyllic atmosphere of La Chapelle-Anthenaise.

Arrayed against the children and the artist are the adults. The English adults represent oppressive society. "Well behaved" ("bien élevé," a source for some punning in the French version) is what these adults wish their children to be—not free or happy. John Bull in particular is a grotesque symbol of repression. When the little English girl is reluctant to sing, her mother threatens that John Bull will eat her up if she doesn't (30); in one of Josephine's dreams, the same character captures the little boy and throws him back into a prison cell; in another, he murders both children. He also lacks any imagination or playfulness. A philistine who prefers sausages and his dog to poets (40), he is too clumsy to play, jump, or ride a bicycle, and he is unimpressed by Bérenger's ability to fly. As in *The Bald Soprano,* the stereotyped English characters satirize repressed, authoritarian, middle-class society in general and not just the English in particular (although part of the play's humor comes from jokes that contrast the stuffy British to the "Mediterranean" temperament of the French). This kind of adult society considers art unimportant because it is only child's play: "After all, up to what age can you go on being interested in art? Art and literature, that's kid's stuff" (40–41).

This play introduces a new dimension to the couple, added perhaps by the presence for the first time of a child in the family; the family replaces the couple as the unit that mediates between the solitary individual and the surrounding society. In most of Ionesco's plays the woman represents some aspect of motherhood for the protagonist; here, Josephine is a highly ambivalent character, both parent and child to Bérenger. She is sometimes allied with the adults against the child in her husband: she is unsympathetic when his house is bombed, scolding him for having bought such a flimsy place; she cannot see the Visitor from the Anti-World when he first appears; she disapproves of Bérenger's flying, scolding him as she would a child—"You look so badly brought up" (71). Yet she is herself an orphaned child, constantly in search of the father who abandoned her by dying. Even as a child, she says, she dreaded the future loss of her parents (93). Bérenger can never take her father's place, she says (29), and yet she interprets his flight as a repetition of her father's abandonment of her (91). It is just this desertion that leads to her nightmares in which all the father figures are hideous, murderous authority figures (John Bull, the Judge, the Executioner, and the Doctor-Uncle). Bérenger and Marthe together become child-parents to Josephine, urging her to forget her adult duties for a moment, to enjoy the beauty around her, and to allow the child in herself to be free. Marthe is explicit about this role reversal: "I'm growing up. I'll soon be as strong as your mother was. I'll protect you" (94).

Travel: Claustration and Escape

Metaphors of travel dominate the play. Even before the play begins, Bérenger has come to England to try to escape from writer's block, and his stroll in the air is central to the play. The prelude to Bérenger's flight is the scene in which the Bérengers stroll in the countryside as various pairings of the English characters carry on their own conversations in counterpoint (this is the same technique used in act 1 of *Rhinoceros*);

on both sides, the central theme is claustration and routine versus escape and travel. The Bérengers see and discuss toy trains, the river, sailors and ships' sirens, a red balloon, and so on, while five of the eight conversations among the English treat travel and escape from daily routine explicitly (37–42). The appearances of the Visitor from the Anti-World and the marvelous Silver Bridge further emphasize the importance of travel as an "exciting voyage of discovery."

Yet travel is double-edged, for every trip is also a trip toward death (as Marguerite insisted in *Exit the King*). One of the explanations of the Anti-World is that it is where people go when they die, and the Silver Bridge is a symbol of passage into another world—death (see also *Victims of Duty, Exit the King,* and *Hunger and Thirst* for other instances of this symbolism). In contrast to the brightly-colored toy trains that appear in the background, the real airplane rains destruction down on the cottage, and the sounds of bombs exploding punctuate Josephine's nightmares and Bérenger's return from his walk in the air; Bérenger regrets that today's children prefer rockets to toy trains (38). Death permeates Josephine's dreams and appears in a conversation between the two Old Ladies (42–43). What Bérenger discovers when he finally does take his trip is a lurid and horrifying vision of death and destruction. (Both Bérenger and the First Old Lady use the image of men with the heads of geese to describe their vision of death, recalling Mother Peep's geese in *The Killer.*)

Comedy and Humor

The tone and vision of the play are extremely dark, close to despair, yet it is the most circus-like of Ionesco's plays to that time. Physical humor and slapstick are abundant, often approximating the effect of guignol. Bérenger pops in and out of the window of his house during the interview with the Journalist, just like a puppet; the little English boy pulls off the little girl's hair (she becomes a "bald soprano"); and everyone (including the lumbering John Bull) is hopping about the stage at one point as Bérenger tries to teach them to fly. Masks and costumes make certain characters appear to be life-sized puppets, producing an effect as shocking and frightening as it is amusing. The fanciful set is deliberately artificial-looking, with

146

toy trains and cable cars, a tiny Eiffel tower, turreted castles, and balloons reinforcing the puppet-show atmosphere.

The circus and the music hall are two other sources of entertainment in the play. Bérenger performs bicycle tricks on props that appear magically from the wings while the other characters sit in bleacher seats. When the little girl sings (the sound is the trilling of a mechanical nightingale), all the other English characters join in; later another short passage of dialogue is sung (71). The little girl sends Bérenger off on his voyage with "a kind of English hymn" (87), his return is accompanied by "derisively triumphant" French dance music (107), and the little boy greets him by trying to play a victory march on "a kind of trombone" (108).

Verbal humor is abundant, including puns (some hard to translate), repetition, clichés, and silly non sequiturs. Differences in nationality are satirized, and Ionesco indulges in more metatheatrical joking here (much of it at his own expense) than ever before. The interview with the Journalist is an occasion for Bérenger to expound views already well-known to be those of Ionesco. For example, Bérenger continues the assault on leftist conformism that Ionesco began in *Improvisation:* "All writers, or almost all, and almost all playwrights are denouncing yesterday's evils, injustices, alienations, yesterday's diseases. They close their eyes to the evil of today. But it's no use denouncing an old evil. It's pointless to demystify what has been demystified already. That's just being conformist" (21). The seriousness of this speech is undercut, however, when Bérenger reveals that the real reason he granted the interview was in order to be paid and to get his picture on the front page of the paper. More metatheatrical are numerous implicit and explicit allusions to *The Bald Soprano.* Finally, Bérenger's self-conscious asides and remarks addressed to the audience break the frame and reach beyond the stage into the audience.

A Stroll in the Air is the least successful and probably the weakest of the Bérenger cycle. As one critic has put it, "the play lacks structure and unity. Whatever internal coherence there is is hard for spectators to follow, and the whole thing leaves one with the memory of a brilliant, but facile and often shallow spectacle."[19] Whereas the comic elements in tragic farces like *The Chairs* and *Exit the King* throw the tragic elements into relief, they risk obscuring them here, so numerous and diverting are they.

Taken together, the four Bérenger plays represent a substantial, coherent achievement. Ionesco found a mature literary voice in these plays, by far the most accessible and successful of his entire corpus. Bérenger is recognizably human and appealing despite his weaknesses (an excessive fondness for alcohol, an inclination toward laziness, a lack of courage and energy). The Bérenger of each play carries some of the same psychological (and in *The Killer,* real) baggage as Ionesco himself (for example, guilt and ambivalence toward women, hatred of authority, paralyzing fear of death), but the protagonists have not yet become so thoroughly autobiographical as to become tedious. These plays have nearly universal appeal; it was their success that made Ionesco a contemporary master and led to his induction into the Académie française.

Notes

1. See chapter 3, pp. 72–74.
2. "It's the fall, original sin . . . the loss of the ability to be amazed . . . forgetfulness . . . the hardening of habit: daily life is a gray blanket that hides the world's virginity; it's truly original sin; you can know, but you can't recognize anything or even yourself anymore" (*ENT* 10).
3. It would be, of course, disingenuous to believe that all ideology is absent from Bérenger's resistance. The ideology that informs this play—indeed, all of Ionesco's work—is a libertarian humanism.
4. Bérenger resembles Ionesco in this regard. Writing in his journal, Ionesco said, "I have always felt ill at ease in my own body; hence my need for drink, for euphoric stimulants" (*FJ* 35); "I have never been really happy except when drunk" (*FJ* 19).
5. In *Notes and Counter Notes* Ionesco wrote, "I really do feel that life is nightmarish, painful and unbearable, like a bad dream" (110).
6. In much the same way, Alfred Hitchcock always included a brief shot of himself in his films.
7. An early title for the play was "The Ceremony."
8. In "The Double Apprenticeship: Life and the Process of Dying," Rosette Lamont sees the king's death as metamorphosis into

Bodhisattva. M. S. Barranger follows in the same direction, using Tibetan Yoga as the basis for seeing the end of the play as a triumph rather than a tragedy ("Death as Initiation in *Exit the King*"). Warren Tucker, in *"Le Roi se meurt* et *Les Upanishads,"* uses Hindu mythology as the basis for his equally positive interpretation of the end of the play.

9. The English translation omits the following parts of Marguerite's response to the King's evocation of color: "Colored memories. He's not an auditory person; his imagination is purely visual. He's a painter . . . too partial to monochromy."

10. *The Observer,* 6 July 58, 15.

11. In Ionesco's personal dream vocabulary, fire is a symbol of death (*FJ* 133).

12. See the pictures of the Association of Producing Artists Repertory production in the Grove Press edition, especially those following p. 28, for how the contrast between the two women is emphasized by costume and makeup. Marie's hair is long, uncovered, and her breasts and hips are set off by the low-cut, clinging gown. Marguerite's hair and body are encased in a severe black hooded gown that hides her sexual attributes.

13. In French these passages are, respectively, "Elle est la pousse qui grandit, la fleur qui s'épanouit, le seul fruit" and "Ces retours, ces tours et ces détours."

14. See also 67–70 for repetition of the phrase "I'm dying", 77 and following for use of stichomythia to inventory the king's past accomplishments, 60–65 for the use of repetition and rhythm in the extended conversation between Juliette and the King about her life.

15. In French, "Fini de folâtrer, finis les loisirs, finis les beaux jours, finis les gueuletons, fini votre strip-tease"; "Vos bals, vos amusettes, vos cortèges, vos dîners d'honneur, vos artifices et vos feux d'artifice, les noces et vos voyages de noces."

16. In French, "Beaucoup de gens ont la folie des grandeurs. Vous avez une folie de la petitesse"; "Tu comptes. Tu seras compté" . . . . "Je ne serai pas le comptable"; "Il m'en faudrait un neuf; il m'en faudrait même douze."

17. Ionesco told Bonnefoy that he encountered writer's block with this play: "With *A Stroll in the Air,* I had trouble getting into it because I was trying to make a play out of something non-dramatic" (*ENT* 85).

18. Ionesco wrote, "Dreams are very important to me because they give me a sharper more penetrating vision of myself" (*ENT* 12).

19. Robert Frickx, *Ionesco* 124.

CHAPTER SIX

A Theater in Search of Itself: *Hunger and Thirst, The Killing Game,* and *Macbett*

The note of grim despair sounded at the end of *A Stroll in the Air* dominates the next phase of Ionesco's career. After the prolific output of the 1950s, Ionesco, suffering from depression and writer's block, found it was no longer so easy to write new works for the stage. More and more pessimistic about world affairs and increasingly in the grip of metaphysical despair as he grew older, he could no longer write the comedies that were his early trademark. Along with his growing fame and public acceptance (culminating in his election to the Académie française in 1970) came a much more literary and personal style. With *Hunger and Thirst* his theater reached an impasse of sorts. *Hunger and Thirst* is somewhat disjointed and rambling in structure, reflecting the difficulties Ionesco had in trying to find a theatrical form that would contain the play's epic quest and its personalized obsessions. Having pursued familiar obsessions to their conclusion, Ionesco then turned for the first time to others' works for inspiration (Defoe and Artaud for *Jeux de massacre,* Shakespeare and Jarry for *Macbett*). These adaptations can be seen in retrospect as part of the search for a new tone and form that was to lead to the late dream plays and even later to the abandonment of theater in favor of drawing. *The Killing Game,* with its manic puppet-show-like pacing and episodic structure, is more entertaining, coherent, and effective as theater than *Hunger and Thirst,* while *Macbett* is a grim clown show that lacks most of the spontaneity and verve of Jarry's Macbeth parody, *Ubu Roi.*

Hunger and Thirst

La Soif et la faim (*Hunger and Thirst*) was commissioned by the prestigious Comédie française; with its premiere there on 28 February 1966 Ionesco joined a French tradition that goes back to Molière.[1] The play is complex, very literary, and therefore sometimes difficult to follow. Heavy with symbolism and almost epic in scope, it contains some striking and moving scenes whose effect is diluted at times by long passages of dialogue (as in the show trial of Tripp and Brechtoll). Each of the play's three episodes is self-contained; together, they encompass the protagonist's mythic quest for fulfillment that spans fifteen years and covers enormous distance.[2] With three very different sets and a large number of actors, its production (like that of *Rhinoceros* and *A Stroll in the Air*) requires the resources of a large theater like the national theaters that had come to welcome the work of a former iconoclast.

In episode 1 ("The Flight"), a gloomy, damp, dilapidated interior is the setting for the typical Ionesco couple, named this time Jean and Marie-Madeleine; in a cradle is their baby daughter. They quarrel about why they had to move back to this apartment after having lived for a while in a light and airy one. It is in their old familiar neighborhood, but it is sinking into the ground: for Jean it is a tomb, while Marie-Madeleine considers it a womb or a refuge. She seeks security; he, adventure and passion. They are visited by Aunt Adelaide, who died in a fire but refuses to recognize the fact that she is dead. Her visit arouses in Jean the guilt that is the last straw in making him decide to leave. After a game of hide and seek with his wife, he rips from his heart the branch of roses symbolizing his love for his wife and daughter and disappears. As soon as he leaves, the back wall of the stage parts to reveal a splendid garden with a silver ladder hanging in the air. According to Marie-Madeleine, the paradise he has left to find was right in his own home all along.

The second episode is entitled "The Rendezvous"; in contrast to the dark interior of the first act, its setting is an arid mountain plain inundated with brilliant light. Jean has come,

151

he tells the two museum guards who work there, to meet a woman of indescribable beauty and to visit the splendid (but unseen) museum with her. This mysterious woman is at once an anima figure, a princess, Eve, Jean's Muse, his Neoplatonic missing half—an idealized phantasm of desire. When the museum guards question him, he is unable to provide any specific information about the day or time they were supposed to meet. Pressed for details about her physical appearance, he says that her face is unforgettable but can give only the vaguest metaphoric descriptions—she is like a chapel, a temple, a hill, a swan, and so forth. As it becomes obvious that the woman is not coming, Jean's initial euphoria at having found this beautiful, brilliant, dry setting changes to the pain of unsatisfied desire. Consumed by ravenous hunger and burning thirst, he leaves in search of the magical woman (a quest for the absolute) as the two guards prepare to eat their soup and drink their wine.

Episode 3 ("The Black Masses of the Good Inn") is set in the refectory of an establishment that is both an inn and a sort of monastery-barracks-prison. A "dismal landscape" is visible in the background behind a large gate of iron bars. Fifteen years have elapsed since the end of episode 2. When Jean arrives, exhausted and disheveled, he is greeted and welcomed by Brother Tarabas, "who looks like a monk without looking quite like a monk" (52). Tarabas will be the voice of authority, speaking for the silent Brother Superior, a gigantic, mute, puppet-like figure dressed in white who remains onstage throughout the act. At first Tarabas is humble and solicitous; he begins by washing Jean's feet while the other brothers bring him huge quantities of food and drink. Jean is insatiable, however; the more he eats and drinks, the hungrier and thirstier he becomes. Although Tarabas assures him repeatedly that he owes them nothing, it gradually becomes apparent that they expect him to pay for his meal by telling stories of his adventures. All he can do is utter disconnected words and phrases, but Tarabas tells him that his story was very well told and invites him to enjoy himself by watching a play they will perform for him.

Two old brothers play the roles of Tripp (a devout Christian) and Brechtoll (an atheistic socialist), who are confined in small cages on the stage. Tarabas, wearing a hood and sumptuous cloak of red and black, plays the role of Grand Inquisitor, while Jean and the other brothers become the onstage audience. Tripp's partisans are dressed in black, while Brechtoll's are in red. Aided by two helpers, Tarabas tortures the two prisoners with starvation until they are brainwashed into abandoning their beliefs—Tripp renounces belief in God and Brechtoll embraces it. The lesson conveyed by this didactic play-within-a-play (only the first of thirty, according to Tarabas) is that the price of receiving sustenance in a totalitarian state is the sacrifice of individual freedom and the annihilation of all moral convictions. Once the play is over, Jean tries to leave but finds that he now must discharge his debt by performing some small service for the brothers. At the very moment when Jean is about to learn how much he owes, a rejuvenated Marie-Madeleine and their now fifteen-year-old daughter suddenly appear outside the bars in the same luminous garden that marked the end of the first episode. As they call to Jean to come join them, he learns that he owes the brothers an infinite number of hours serving their meals. The Brother Accountant recites an endless string of numbers that appear on lighted panels covering the set, and all the other characters join in chanting these numbers faster and faster. Marie promises that she will wait for him forever while Jean, dressed now in a monk's habit, serves and clears the table at a frenzied pace.

Desire and Quest

The hunger and thirst of the play's title symbolize the burning desire that drives Jean on his quest for the absolute: "My stomach's a bottomless pit, my mouth a funnel of fire. Hunger and thirst, hunger and thirst . . ." (49). Like Choubert in *Victims of Duty,* Jean consumes massive amounts of food, but no matter how much he eats and drinks, his hunger and thirst continue to grow: "The more I eat, the hungrier I get. The more I drink, the thirstier I get" (62). The very nature of Jean's desire requires that it can never be satisfied, for its continued existence depends on a fundamental absence, a lack of the desired object; what he wants is, by definition, what he cannot have. When he lived in a large and spacious apartment, he complained that the neighborhood was bad and that there was too much space, yet he is even more unhappy when he and Marie-Madeleine return to their former, now shabby, apartment; as Marie-Madeleine remarks, "If it's not agoraphobia, it's claustrophobia" (9). Disappointed by his missed rendezvous at the end of the second episode, however, Jean yearns once more for the confines of the old apartment: "If only I could find that hide-out again where I dragged out my life, so cosy and snug, walled in by my fear of death" (49). The "Good Inn" that had been such a welcome refuge at the beginning of the third episode has become a prison by the end of the play, leaving Jean forever banished from his home that has been transformed into a heavenly garden beckoning to him from behind the bars.

Jean has, in fact, spent his entire life yearning for what is missing: "I only live in the hope that something fantastic will turn up" (13); or, as Marie-Madeleine puts it, "You never could live like everyone else. For you there's always something missing" (13). What he seeks is "boundless joy and ecstasy" (14) (the same ephemeral sensation of euphoric plenitude sought by earlier Ionesco protagonists), so that the mere peace and contentment that Marie-Madeleine offers him cannot possibly satisfy him. From Marie-Madeleine's point of view, Jean already has "what he wants" (that is, her unconditional love and the comforting bonds of home and family), but he is unwilling or unable to see it. This is why the garden will appear only after he leaves. Jean views the entire social component of existence (his home, family, and obligations) as a trap, however, and believes that the only way he can remain true to himself is to escape the routine that others accept: "I don't want to be like them, I won't get stuck in a rut or just drift along like the rest. Their destiny's not mine, my life is somewhere else" (28). In fact, Jean's destiny is to remain unfulfilled. What he says about having a telephone could apply equally to everything in his life: "It's when I've got it, I've got to get rid of it. When I haven't got it, I've got to have it" (13). Because his hunger and thirst are absolute, moreover, everything that he desires is immediately diminished by his proximity: "Everything I wished for would vanish at my approach, everything I tried to touch would wither" (97). As one of the brothers points out, this insatiability leaves Jean both thirsty for everything and disgusted by everything at the same time (97).

Jean believes that his search is a quest for authenticity, for his true self. In the beginning he claims that he must leave in order to remain true to himself: "I am nothing but myself and must myself remain" (30). It soon becomes clear, however, that it is precisely his lost self that he is seeking in his desperate search for the mysterious woman who has spurred him on his quest. She alone can allow him finally to find himself and become a whole person: "She awoke me to myself, she is absolute necessity" (50). As he tells the guards, he is waiting for the woman whose presence will fill the void in his soul: "The absence that I feel in this presence, the emptiness I feel in this plenitude can be nothing other than her absence."[3] This indescribable but unforgettable woman is Jean's anima image, his lost other half.[4] When he mistakes another woman for her he says, "I knew you'd come, after all the time I've been waiting! Since the beginning of time! Since the first time I was born" (48). Her absence is central to his insatiable hunger. That it will never be satisfied is underlined by Jean's insistence in the very final scene that "she" ("the third one") come to join his wife and daughter in waiting for him. Even the vision of paradise that Marie offers him lacks the presence of the mysterious woman, symbol of a phantasmic desire that must always be unfulfilled.

The Prison and the Garden

Spatial configurations merge with metaphors of confinement and escape throughout the play. As is common in Ionesco's work, interior space is either tomb or womb—claustrated prison or secure, cosy refuge, depending on whether Jean feels locked in (as in the first episode) or locked out (as at the end of the second episode). The exterior space of the second episode initially represents the euphoric freedom of flight, but when Jean's soul mate fails to appear, it becomes a threatening and desolate desert—an "empty brilliance," as one of the museum guards puts it. The garden that appears at the end of the first and third episodes, with its silver ladder hanging in the air, holds out to Jean the possibility of escape from the time-bound prisons of his daily life. It can appear, however, only beyond or outside of the space Jean occupies. This paradise is the Garden of Eden, a mythic space defined for Jean by the impossibility of his ever entering it. It has only the positive qualities of both interiors (it is a refuge) and exteriors (the silver ladder is a link with another world, like the shining footbridge in *Exit the King* and *Victims of Duty* or the silver bridge in *A Stroll in the Air*). The "somewhere else" that Jean seeks is that lost Garden of Eden from which man was banished after the Fall, whereas Marie's garden is the love that lies in her heart and in his, if he will only recognize it.

One of the forms Jean's desire takes is the search for a particular kind of dwelling and a particular landscape that would provide a concrete correlative for the inner fulfillment that he (like Bérenger in *The Killer*) desires. The apartment in the first episode is a tomb, sinking into the mud, creating claustration and choking. Jean's fantasy house, by contrast, would float in the air above a river; it would be weightless, giving the euphoric sensation of flying associated with joy throughout Ionesco's work. Only the blooms—not the stems or roots—of flowers would be visible through the windows. Jean's last words before leaving are a vision of the dwelling and landscape of his dreams: "Way above the wintry valleys . . . On the highest spur . . . *there* stands the princess's palace in the middle of a sunlit park" (35). Not only are the dwelling and the landscape elevated and brilliantly lit, but the palace is the home of the princess—the anima figure, Jean's missing half.

When he arrives at the brilliantly lit mountain plain of the second episode, he initially believes he has found just that perfect landscape that his soul has been seeking. In absolute contrast to the dark, damp apartment sinking into the mud, this place is brilliantly lit, dry, open to the sky: "I'm amazed there can be such mountains, and the space, and this sky all round, resting on the peaks, then stretching out over the world" (38). Even here, however, Jean cannot be happy but can only anticipate happiness: "Actually, I'm happy thinking how happy

I'll be in a minute. . . . I'll have all I want in a minute" (39). The external landscape alone is incapable of giving him the *boundless* (in time as well as space) joy he demands.

After the disappointment of missing his rendezvous with his soul mate, Jean is driven by desire to continue his search for her (really for himself). Carrying on the architectural imagery, the setting of the last act is a prison. An armed monk blocks the exit, and prison bars stretch across the back of the stage. In the play-within-a-play, the two clowns are locked inside small cages, making the onstage space outside the cages seem like the exterior. When the play ends, however, that illusion is shattered definitively, and the monastery-prison-hospital is revealed to be a prison with no exit. (This is why the "monks" are so anxious to hear stories of others' travels.) By seeking absolute joy, Jean has condemned himself to a prison that is a grim counterpart of the secure home that he fled.

Both his former home and his present prison are "safe" places, where meals and shelter will never be a problem and Jean will be protected from the vicissitudes associated with adventure. In episode 1, Marie-Madeleine describes their home as a refuge: "We'll bar the door and put a new lock on, with a nice big key, to keep us safe from burglars and disaster. . . . We've reached our destination. Outside this house, outside us two, outside us three, anywhere else is nowhere. . . . I've brought you some pretty pictures, chocolate and cigarettes. Every day I bring you a heart new-born" (28). In episode 3, when Jean says that the brothers look as though they were dragging chains, Brother Tarabas answers, "We don't ill-treat them. They're sheltered from the sunshine and the rain. Protected from war and poverty. Our surgeons eradicated those germs of conflict in them which were ruining their health" (101). Jean fled one prison only to find another much more confining and much worse, for it lacks love.

The prison and the garden are temporally as well as spatially distinct in the play. Jean, like all Ionesco protagonists, feels burdened and imprisoned by the passage of time, while paradise is associated with youth and timelessness. Thus Jean must flee the apartment in the first episode because it is cursed by the rapid disintegration of mortality: "The plaster's crumbling.

I can feel the weight on my shoulders already. . . . Is all this an image of time? Everything disintegrates before our eyes" (14). Acceleration of the passage of time occurs in each episode to signal the fall into mortality associated with prison and hell. In their apartment in the first episode, Jean despairs because time passes so quickly there, excluding the possibility of ecstasy: "And in these surroundings ecstasy is out. We've hardly been here more than twenty minutes. And now I look at you, you've aged already. Your first wrinkles. White hairs you didn't have before. Time goes faster than you think" (14). Jean's disappointment in his soul mate's failure to come to the rendezvous in the second episode is likewise marked by acceleration of time, as hours, days, weeks and seasons pass in seconds (45–49), and the pace of speech and action at the end of the play is absolutely dizzying, recalling the nightmarish proliferation of sounds or objects found in earlier plays.

The past is another temporal prison for Jean. He feels the weight of memory as a chain that he must cast off in order to be free. Speaking of his memories, he says, "My own are a deadweight already: like these walls, or this ceiling weighing us down" (25). Shortly afterwards, he vows, "I'll loosen the knots and slip my bonds. I'll bury my past, lest it buries [sic] me" (30).

Paradise, on the other hand, is timeless. When Jean emerges on the sunlit plain in the second episode, his joy comes from the freshness of experiencing sensations as if for the first time, "As if the waters of oblivion had washed them clean" (38). His pleasure is the pleasure of making "a fresh start," of being "born again" into an eternal present: "I've woken to the wonder of the morning, of *this* morning at least" (39). Finally, the garden in which Marie appears at the end of the play has rejuvenated her, while Jean has visibly aged over the course of the elapsed years.

The Individual and the Community

Jean believes that he must be free from social constraints and obligations in order to find his true self. Faced with the metaphysical anguish of mortality, he feels that his only chance of finding fulfillment is to escape from the demands of society (including duties, deep-rooted affections, and reason). Society for him is what "they" want: "They bore me stiff with their 'experience.' Because *they* never dared, they want *me* to stick in the mud. I'm meant for something better" (29).

Brother Tarabas and the Brother Superior are two monstrous authority figures at the Good Inn who incarnate the worst kind of repressive, totalitarian society. Brother Superior—towering, inhuman, and silent—dominates the stage throughout this episode, recalling an absent but powerful father. (Both Ionesco's absent father and the presence of a vengeful and judgmental God-the-father are implicit in this figure.) His spokesperson is Brother Tarabas, a Grand Inquisitor who uses torture and brainwashing in insidious fashion to crush the individual will and to establish the dominion of the community. The fact that these figures are "brothers" reflects both Ionesco's anticlericalism and his horror of communal societies.

The brainwashing of Tripp and Brechtoll and Jean's enslavement by the community that had at first been benevolent seem to confirm the existence of an irreconcilable dichotomy between individual freedom and the demands of mass society (as in *Rhinoceros,* for example). Jean is no Bérenger, however. Unlike the compassionate protagonists of *The Killer, Rhinoceros,* or *A Stroll in the Air,* he has deliberately severed his ties with his fellow human beings. "I've done away with pity and regret. I've killed all feeling for the sufferings of mankind. I've shared the torments of my fellows far too long: I've cast that millstone off. I'll be light as air and celebrate my new-found liberty in song" (27). Just before leaving he rips from his heart a branch of roses, casting away his love for his wife and baby along with his compassion for all other human beings. (How to stage this action is not the least of the problems confronted by any director of this play.) His narcissism, more than the confining community around him, is at the root of his suffering. It is no wonder that he feels incomplete, unable to be a whole person again until he finds the anima figure who would return to him the loving half of himself that he murdered.

In this play, as in *A Stroll in the Air,* the family unit is a kind of refuge that mediates between the individual and the larger unit of society. (That it is also a sort of prison is true as well. In order to receive the pure, unquestioning love of his wife, Jean must sacrifice his aspirations for the ideal, his thirst for the absolute.) By abandoning his wife and child, Jean lost any protection that this family might give him. Worse, he missed the opportunity to practice and nurture with them the concern for and interest in others that might have saved him from being condemned by the brothers at the Good Inn.

Twice he is judged lacking in this regard by authority figures. In the second episode, the two museum guards reproach him for seeking from the mysterious woman just that compassion that he had vowed to eliminate from his own heart: "Wasn't he the one who said it's silly to suffer? —Who advised indifference to others, or at the most a sneaking regard? —Who said that you should idolise no-one? That not a living soul was deserving of veneration? —Who claimed we should be free from the ties that bind us?" (47). In the third episode, his account of his travels is found wanting precisely because he took no notice of others, helped no one. His infantile narcissism caused him to miss all the wonders and beauty as well as all the suffering around him. The brothers remark that the talents he did have turned to poison because he kept them to himself: "They've stagnated inside him, they've corroded. —They became ulcerated, gangrenous. —It would have been so easy for him to find relief. —They become a disease" (99). Thus the reason why Jean can never be free is, finally, that he carries his prison with him. By trying to cast off his obligations to others, he has enclosed himself in what Brother Tarabas calls the cage of solitude: "We're human beings. We have obligations towards one another, unless we prefer the cage of solitude. But that's not a comfortable place. You can't quite stand up or sit down properly there" (96).

Women and Guilt

Jean, perhaps more than any previous Ionesco protagonist, is weighed down by guilt. His guilt is associated particularly with women and is linked to his deeply-felt need for them, coupled with his fear and resentment of their power over him.

Aunt Adelaide is a startling character straight out of Jean's nightmares, a catalyst for his guilty conscience. She died in a fire in the very room where Jean sometimes slept as a child, and the vision of her engulfed in flames haunts him because he could do nothing to save her: "That's how I always see her, desperate, holding out her arms, in agony. Then she vanishes in smoke and leaves a heap of ashes at my feet. But the next time the fire is lit, there she is again, rising like a phoenix, an eternal reproach" (25). Even his protestation of innocence—"I didn't kill Aunt Adelaide" (24)—indicates the extent to which he feels responsible and guilty, since no one has ever accused him of killing her. When she visits, she does not hesitate to remind Jean of how much she had helped him and his deserted mother when he was small; this adds to his burden of guilt. Rather than being grateful for his aunt's past kindness, he is hostile, refusing to humor her and coldly pressing her to confront the fact of her death. The more compassionate Marie-Madeleine, on the other hand, indulges the dead woman's fictitious accounts of her daily life, her suitors, her fame, and so forth.

One reason why Aunt Adelaide triggers such horror in Jean is that she shares some of his own qualities (a vivid imagination and desire for a better life, fear and refusal of death, irrationality); in reproaching her for these things, he puts himself in the role of the responsible voice of reason—exactly the position he wants to flee. It is her visit that finally pushes Jean to leave: "It's only *here* she's able to find us. . . . I really can't stay in this house any more. I can't stand it . . ." (24).

Death and sexuality are linked in terrifying fashion in Aunt Adelaide. In the course of denying that she is dead, she first exposes her breasts to prove that her flesh is still beautiful and then forces Jean to touch the bloody wound she creates by slitting open her own skull (23). Carnal contact thus becomes a grotesque and repulsive experience, reflecting a fear of sexuality that subtends Jean's ambivalent feelings toward Marie-Madeleine—indeed toward all women.

Marie-Madeleine is an archetypal maternal figure, at once nurturing and smothering, associated both with comfort and with death. In the game of hide and seek, Jean regresses openly to childhood in playing a child's game with his mother. She cajoles and chides him, telling him to take a warm coat and to be sure not to catch cold if he is set on leaving (29), and she addresses him as if he were a child during their game of hide-and-seek: "Jean, my little dear, my darling, my Jeannot!" (33). She is content with an encapsulated and shabby existence in an apartment that is sinking into the mud, as long as she is with Jean. Like the mud (as in *Victims of Duty*), she is that earthy force that drags Jean down into death, the downward pull that resists weightless euphoric flight. She is incapable of understanding, much less sympathizing with, Jean's need for flight and freedom: "Why doesn't he want to be like an old wall, or an oak, covered in moss or ivy? An oak with its roots deep in the earth" (30). Since death is inevitable, she says, it doesn't matter how soon it comes: "What's the difference, whether it takes ten minutes or an hour, a fortnight or a year? We all get there in the end" (14).

When he leaves his home, Jean is fleeing the claustration, guilt, and fear associated with the maternal figure: "I was safe enough in my hide-out, firmly locked in gloom and nostalgia, remorse and anguish, fears and responsibilities, like so many walls all around me" (46). The figure of an old woman reappears during Jean's travels, again as harbinger of aging and death: "a ghastly figure would appear, a ragged old woman leaning on a stick. . . . an old face such as I've never seen before, old age itself" (66). By contrast, the young girl is neither demanding nor sexually threatening. Jean seeks ecstasy and passion, to be sure: "I had to choose between peace and passion. I chose passion, fool that I was!" (46). The passion he seeks is, however, spiritual and largely asexual. Thus the object of Jean's quest is a "princess" who lives "way above the wintry valleys" (35), far removed from the rot and disintegration associated with sexuality and flesh. Even at the end, when his wife and daughter call on him to join them in paradise, he longs for "that other one, she for whom I was neither father, nor son, nor husband" (100). This feminine figure has no physical, carnal relationship with Jean; her innocence removes the guilt and fear he feels around grown women.

Metatheater: "A Sinister Farce"

"What a sinister farce!" says Brechtoll (87), commenting on the play-within-a-play in which he is acting; his remark could apply equally to *Hunger and Thirst* itself. The gloomiest and most somber of Ionesco's plays at that point in his career, *Hunger and Thirst* seems too often to take itself seriously, lapsing at times into pathos or sentimentality. The language is quite literary—often lyrical and poetic, with none of the nonsensical wordplay that leavened earlier works. Mitigating banality and pathos, however, is the distancing provided by surreal dreamlike sequences, episodes of violent slapstick and farce, and the frequent use of metatheatrical, self-conscious form.

Early in episode 1, Aunt Adelaide's scandalous visit undermines any tendency on the part of the audience to identify too closely with the protagonist or to interpret the play too emotionally. Aunt Adelaide is clearly a visitor from the common nightmare in which a dead loved one appears among the living, unaware that she has died. The incongruous disjunction between her outlandish claims (she has many suitors, she is a brilliant and respected author and scholar, she has received many decorations) and her ancient, decrepit appearance is as comic as it is frightening. Her shocking behavior (lascivious posturing, slitting her skull and forcing Jean to feel the wound) combines farce and surreal imagery; she casts a metatheatrical light on the whole episode when she says, "I am an artist, but this is not a performance" (24). Farce and metatheater in episode 2 offset Jean's lyrical transports and self-pitying melancholy. The two museum guards provide comic relief with their down-to-earth reactions to Jean's poetic language (much like the fools and clowns in Shakespeare), and they perform the roles of the various women whom Jean approaches in hopes of finding his "princess."

Episode 3 is the most brutal and grim of the three and therefore the one most dependent on farce and metatheater to lighten the effect. When the play-within-a-play begins, the onstage audience is divided into two camps (those dressed in red are partisans of Brechtoll and those in black, of Tripp). Each side reacts loudly with applause, cheers, or jeers when one or the other of the prisoners makes a point, creating the atmosphere of a prizefight. The play-within-a-play is itself a thinly-disguised, sinister parody of the kind of pedagogical theater so despised by the author of *Improvisation:* Tarabas describes the play to be performed as "a didactic entertainment," produced by "our Pedagogical Brother, who's in charge of our various education and re-education courses" (68). The very name Brechtoll is a clear allusion to Brechtian theater practice, condemned by Ionesco as slavishly ideological. Finally, the ending of the play is stylized slapstick, with the carnivalesque proliferation of lighted numbers on the walls and the rapidly accelerating pace with which bowls of food appear. Much like Charlie Chaplin in *Modern Times* (or even Lucy in a famous episode of *I Love Lucy*), Jean is forced to rush faster and faster to serve the bowls to the other brothers. Despite the seriousness of its subject, its lyrical language, and its tone of gloomy despair, *Hunger and Thirst* remains an example of tragic farce.

The Killing Game

Jeux de massacre (The Killing Game) had its world premiere (in German) at the Schauspielhaus Dusseldorf on 22 January 1970; it opened at the Théâtre de Montparnasse on 11 September of the same year in a dazzling production directed by Jorge Lavelli, the noted Argentine director whose reprise of *Exit the King* in 1976 won the prize for best Paris production of the year. Its title is a play on words that is difficult to render in English; a "jeu de massacre" is the carnival game in which players try to knock over weighted dolls by throwing balls at them. Adapted from Daniel Defoe's *Journal of the Plague Years,* the play is a series of eighteen (seventeen in the standard English edition) blackout sketches that portray the relentless progress of death during a plague epidemic. "Killing Game" translates the gratuitous cruelty of the disease, but it does not convey the sideshow quality of this grotesque and horrific puppet show.

Like *Rhinoceros* and *A Stroll in the Air,* the play begins with a crowd scene. (In Lavelli's original cast, eight women and nine men performed all the roles.) The setting, a town square neither ancient nor modern, indicates the universality of the theme—the horror and inevitability of death. The characters are nonrealistic and puppet-like; Ionesco suggests that "huge dummies, either real puppets or painted papier-mache figures" (3) be used to perform the roles of many of the townspeople. A tall, silent, black-robed monk (Death) crosses the stage to set the action in motion. The other characters do not see him at first. As they bustle about on their daily business, the audience hears snippets of conversation that contain allusions to "that disease," a mysterious ailment that only monkeys can catch. As in a musical overture, various themes (food-associated disease, space travel, spiritual and physical malaise, despair, and claustration) are introduced; elaborations and variations on these themes will supply the bulk of the play's material. Still unseen by the other characters, Death enters and takes center stage, triggering the death of twin babies. Following Ionesco's principles of proliferation and acceleration, the remaining characters fall down and die, one after the other, just like the figures in the game of the play's title. Scene 2 completes the exposition; a public official announces that the disease is an unknown evil, an incomprehensible plague without visible cause. With deaths increasing in geometric progression, the official proclaims draconian measures meant to stem the tide and issues a futile plea for divine mercy.

The fifteen scenes that follow portray the progress of the plague. Long sketches alternate with short ones, poignant with grotesque, humanized with guignolesque, as in a puppet show, culminating in a final scene in which the town is delivered from the plague only to be destroyed in a conflagration.

Structure

Though the sketches that make up the play seem to be randomly ordered and loosely connected, they are in fact highly structured. The action is linear, and the scenes can be grouped into four or five miniacts reflecting the linear progression of rising and falling action. Scenes one and two constitute the exposition (serving as act 1); there follow two consecutive sets of six scenes each (which could be considered acts 2 and 3)

that depict, respectively, the universality and the growing fe-
rocity of the plague. The crisis (structurally, act 4) occurs in
scenes 15 through 17 (the last of which is missing from the
English translation), followed by the denouement (scene 18)
and a brief epilogue.

While the action does progress in linear fashion, the development is based neither in plot nor in character: plot as such
is absent, and the characters (many of whom are one-dimen-
sional and puppet-like) change with each scene. Continuity and
cohesion derive rather from a principle of theme and variation
more characteristic of a musical composition than of a traditional tragedy. The thematic material (claustration and guilt
versus freedom, travel and escape; friendship and love versus
greed and violence; social and political conflict; metaphysical
anguish in the face of death; and so on) is laid out in the first
part of the play (scenes 1 through 7). The extremely brief eighth
scene (in which a passerby tells his friend that two corpses
somehow became eleven in the space of five minutes, reflecting the obsession with acceleration and proliferation found
throughout Ionesco's work) brings this phase of the action to a
close. The next group of six scenes elaborates the thematic
material of the earlier scenes through experimentation with
technique. Doubling and juxtaposition (achieved by using a
split stage), repetition, and direct imitation of the carnival
game that gives the play its name in French are among the
experimental techniques used.

All of the thematic material comes together in scene 16, the
central scene of the play. In this scene, an old couple (the old
couple of *The Chairs* resurrected or ancient incarnations of
Jean and Marie-Madeleine from *Hunger and Thirst*) recapitu-
late all the familiar themes of this play and of all of Ionesco's
theater: the fleeting character of life and joy, love as a means
of vanquishing fear, the conflict between desire for security
and desire for freedom, mystical faith (in the woman) versus
intellectual despair (in the man). With the Old Woman's death
imminent, they say their farewells in a poignant moment that
ends with the old man's affirmation of their love. These two
figures are the most fully developed (therefore the least puppet-like) characters in the play, and their farewell scene comes
dangerously close to pathos.

The near-pathos of this scene is immediately balanced by the appearance of a group of greedy women who, while looting the store of some deceased merchants, begin fighting over the spoils of death in a "colorful, animated tableau" (102). Missing from the English translation is a scene that was added during the play's first production in which extreme famine has pushed the population to resort to cannibalism. The addition of this horrifying, grotesque scene further counterbalances the tenderness of the old couple's farewell; it leads directly to the ironic denouement of the final scene. With the whole cast once again assembled onstage, an official announces that the plague is over. Amid joyous shouts of "We're saved," a huge fire breaks out and traps everyone onstage. The Black Monk (harbinger of death throughout the play) enters and stands stage center as the curtain falls. In the epilogue a man appears in front of the curtain and addresses the audience. He too dies immediately, however, and is unceremoniously thrown into a coffin by two Tough Men who carry the coffin offstage as the audience starts applauding.

In addition to the linear progression underlying the action outlined above, the play is elaborated according to principles of contrast and alternation. Thus poignant scenes are immediately juxtaposed with cynical, grotesque, or violent ones (see, for example, scenes 9 and 10 compared to scene 11; scenes 16 and 17); long scenes alternate with short ones; interior scenes (for example, 3, 4, and 6) alternate with exterior ones (5 and 7). Some characters (for example, the old couple, Alexander and his friends, Jeanne and Jean, Lucienne and Pierre, the mother and her young daughter) are fully humanized and touching, while others are clownlike caricatures, and still others are to be portrayed by life-sized puppets.

One final element that provides continuity and structure in the play is the Black Monk. This silent figure, unseen by the other characters in the play, sets the motion in action and appears periodically (a total of eight times) to signal a shift of scenes or another death. He is onstage both at the beginning and at the end of the play, suggesting the inevitability and omnipotence of death, and he is doubled throughout by other black-robed characters—undertakers, priests, gravediggers, and the like.

Self-Conscious Theater

The Killing Game is more metatheatrical—more self-conscious and specular—than any of Ionesco's preceding plays.
Completely episodic and fragmented, it constantly exposes and
violates traditional theatrical and scenic conventions in order
to transgress the barrier separating the audience from the
stage in conventional theater. The very title of the play establishes an expectation of a Punch and Judy show, in which the
strings behind the performance are clearly visible to the audience. Huge puppets or puppet-like characters (most noticeably,
the Black Monk) frequently replace human or humanized actors and characters, and one entire scene (scene 11) takes precisely the form of a puppet show. In this scene, five windows
light up, one after the other; in each of them a different
minidrama is acted out, just as in guignol. The characters bob
about like puppets and "appear and disappear as in a Punch
and Judy show" (67).[5]

The split stage used in scenes 9 and 10 also serves to break
the theatrical frame. In scene 9 the stage is divided in half,
with the set on each side the mirror image of the other. Two
couples, one on the right-hand stage and one on the left, speak
almost simultaneously the same lines of dialogue: in each case,
the husband (Jean and Pierre) has risked arrest to return to
his wife (Jeanne and Lucienne). When one member of each
couple (Jeanne and Pierre) suddenly falls ill, however, there is
a slight shift of gears. Jeanne's lines are repeated by Pierre
rather than Lucienne, and Lucienne's lines diverge in increasingly ironic counterpoint from Jean's—he is devoted and loyal,
while she abandons her spouse in a panic. The irony of the
ending of the scene is a brutal commentary on the lack of communication between the spouses. The last words of Jeanne,
whose husband stays with her loyally to the end, are "I'm all
alone," while Pierre, whose panic-stricken wife has already
left him, dies saying, "I know I'm not alone" (59).

The next scene also uses a split stage, but in somewhat different fashion. Again two scenes unfold simultaneously: stage
left, a mother encourages her daughter to make herself pretty
for the "secret ball," while stage right represents a room at an

168

inn where a weary traveler has arrived to stay the night. Linking the two scenes is the presence in each of a maid who points out to the other characters that a man in black is passing back and forth outside. Having sent the chambermaid for some beer, the traveler on the right agonizes and dies alone, while the young girl on the left soon succumbs as well. The two deaths cause the two maids to scream, rush in panic through the door of the dividing wall, and bump into each other, thus breaking the frame and exposing the artificiality of the theatrical set.

Other techniques that serve to denaturalize the performance are the use of song to deliver some of the lines, as in *A Stroll in the Air* (see scenes 15 and 18); intricately choreographed crowd scenes that resemble dance; and the deliberate repetition of some lines of dialogue.

Social and Political Satire

As social and political satire, *The Killing Game* is unrelenting in its virulence. As the plague mounts in intensity, the veneer of civilized behavior disappears rapidly, revealing the craven cowardice, avarice, and brutality lurking under the surface. Generosity, charity, and compassion are totally absent from human nature in the play.

Even before the plague claims its first onstage victims, the solid bourgeois citizens reveal how complacent and xenophobic they are: the disease can become comprehensible only if it can be blamed on the moral shortcomings of its victims. Thus, a woman in the first scene assures her friends that "those people" who get the disease "live in total confusion, no morals, no traditions" (4). Likewise, characters in later scenes smugly claim that the epidemic is confined to the slums: "The slums is where it's staying, dear boy. Here we're safe. The slums are, well you know, ignorant . . ." (47). The "unhygienic" slums are teeming with vice, squalor, and poverty, and the citizens in the "safer" neighborhoods have established boundaries "to keep people from highly contaminated areas from coming in to take refuge" (35).

Powerless in the face of the metaphysical anguish of death, the political authorities nevertheless pretend to be in control in scenes 2 and 18 (in which the outbreak and the abatement of epidemic are proclaimed). Policemen—the public representatives of authority—are omnipresent, bludgeoning or shooting anyone who tries to leave a contaminated house. The ultimate authority figure is the Black Monk, however, and his recurring presence silently mocks the ineffectual and pointless brutality of the municipal authorities. Political satire dominates scenes 13 and 14, in which two political orators harangue the crowd. Once again, Ionesco attacks ideology and demagoguery. The first orator is a leftist revolutionary who believes that the plague is an evil plot hatched by the oppressors; his solution is to call for "Revolt! Terrorism! Violence!" (76). The second orator advocates "social justice through peaceful means" (79) and promises everything to everyone without explaining how such a "Kingdom of Heaven on earth" might be achieved.

Even the obvious truth that all living things must die is disputed by the ideologues on the Council of Doctors: "The surging masses do not fear death; it does not exist for those who are strongminded, with strong ideologies to back them, and who look forward, always forward. Death is the temptation of the reactionary" (87). According to this line of thinking, belief in the inevitability of death is only "counterpropaganda": "The victims are the ones responsible in fact; they should have believed us" (88). As is the case throughout Ionesco's theater, however, all political systems and solutions are equally futile in the face of death.

Claustration and Escape

One of the structural and thematic polarities elaborated in the play is the opposition between claustration and escape. Even before the outbreak of the epidemic, one of the characters expresses physical and spiritual malaise as a feeling of being "stuck in a thick fog. . . . I could neither sit, nor stand, nor lie down" (7); the Old Man repeats the same idea much later in similar terms: "Being in the house is unbearable. I can't stand remaining seated or standing or lying" (96). Like many earlier protagonists in Ionesco's theater, he feels imprisoned: "I can't go on living in this city. I'm locked in. . . . I hate homes, all homes. You get locked into them" (95).

Indeed, all the houses in the city are turned into prisons, for the reaction of the municipal authorities in the face of the disaster had been to make all of the citizens prisoners in their homes. Scenes 3 and 6 mirror each other in this regard. In scene 3 a very wealthy man seeks to seal his home hermetically against the plague, making his luxurious home into a prison. When he suddenly drops dead and the servants try to flee, however, they run right into policemen who keep them from leaving the house. Balancing this scene is scene 6, set in a prison. Here the terms are reversed: the real prison is outside, where the plague reigns. When the jailer comes to release the prisoners, one is reluctant to leave because his chance of contracting the disease is less inside than out. Moreover, the entire city has become a prison surrounded by armed guards.

The proliferation of corpses and accelerated pacing add to the sense of claustration. In a brief scene in the middle of the play, a passerby describes the fantastic way the corpses multiply: "When I left my friend's house to go out and buy a newspaper, there were just two of them. When I returned, I opened the door and saw eleven corpses stretched out." "Maybe it was done by computer," suggests his friend (51). Several scenes (1, 11, 15) end with a rapid-fire succession of falling bodies. Associated with claustration in the play are alienation, heaviness, coldness: "The whole world had become like a distant planet, unreal, ice cold, shut tight" (7); "Everything seems black and dirty. Even the stones, heavy with the weight of silence, are caught in their prison" (92); "The world is a great ball of steel, impenetrable" (96).

The only avenue of escape from the claustrated world of the play is death, either from the plague or from the fire that blocks the surviving characters from fleeing the stage at the end. Allusions to travel are numerous, from snatches of dialogue about space travel in the first scene to the three returning travelers in scenes 9 and 10 to the Old Man's recollections of the many times he left home, only to return. Each evocation of travel is negative, however, underscoring the impossibility of escape: "People like us don't fly to the moon. —No, people like us are committed to doom" (8).

171

Knowledge, Power, and Love

One character in the first scene expresses the belief that "knowledge and power are the two great faculties of the human spirit" (6). Reason and logic demand that there be some remedy for the situation. Near the end of the play, however, the First Doctor opens scene 15 by declaring, "Our knowledge is powerless." His colleague immediately protests: "To say that scientific knowledge is powerless will lead to mysticism, which is outlawed" (85). This conflict between knowledge and mysticism subtends the key relationship between the Old Man and Old Woman, a late incarnation of the couple found in so many of Ionesco's earlier plays.

The character of the Old Woman represents the quintessential refinement of woman as nonintellectual being, a creature of pure love, intuition, feeling, and the heart. For her, "every moment of life is enchanting" (91); she is open to that weightless "astonishment at being" alluded to in previous plays. Like the Old Woman in *The Chairs* or Marie-Madeleine in *Hunger and Thirst,* she retains an innocence that keeps the world eternally fresh: "With each sunrise, the world is reborn, clean and pure" (93). A mystic, she is exempt from the anguish associated with intellect: "I feel myself fulfilled by the mysterious presence of the world that surrounds me and by the knowledge that I exist. I never felt the need to know more than that" (93).

Like Jean and Bérenger, the Old Man is nostalgic for a time when he felt this wonder: "In the beginning the world filled me with astonishment" (91); "A long time ago, . . . I seemed to have inexhaustible sources of happiness and I would use these to combat my doubts" (94). For him, however, life has become heavy and dark; like Jean, he has spent his life on a quest without knowing what he was looking for. It is, in fact, the quest for knowledge and power itself that leads the Old Man to despair. For his wife, on the other hand, pure love lights up the world.

This figure of the loving woman provides the only possible shred of consolation in the grim world of the play; it is only with her death imminent that the Old Man realizes (if belatedly) that he did have the possibility of happiness open to him all along: "We had joy and I didn't know it. Come, my precious, take me with you into your night as I hold you" (98).

Despite the glimmer of warmth provided by this scene, it is the absurdity of gratuitous death that triumphs in the play, making a mockery of human pretensions concerning the power of knowledge. As Ionesco said in an interview with Claude Bonnefoy, "The meaning of our existence is that we are here in astonishment and we are made for death" (*ENT* 160).

Macbett

Ionesco's version of *Macbeth* is a darkly comic adaptation of Shakespeare's play. He was inspired to write *Macbett* by Jan Kott's *Shakespeare Our Contemporary,* in which Kott maintains that Shakespeare's goal was to show that power corrupts and that all power is criminal. Ionesco's goal is similar: to show that all politicians are paranoid, that all governments are equally worthless, and that politics always leads to crime. If both Shakespeare and Kott take the character of Macbeth very seriously, however, Ionesco's Macbett is as derisory and grotesque as he is cruel and tyrannical, recalling Jarry's Père Ubu. The play premiered on 3 February 1971, at the Théâtre Rive Gauche in a production directed by Jacques Mauclair; it was well received by mainstream critics[6] and criticized by the left for its antipolitical, antirevolutionary message.

The plot of *Macbett* follows the Shakespearian model, but with some important differences. In Ionesco's play, Banco and Macbett (Banquo and Macbeth) are bachelors, Duncan is a ruthless tyrant, and Lady Duncan conspires with Banco and Macbett to murder her husband. The character of MacDuff is missing, and it is Duncan's son Macol (Malcolm) who kills Macbett; Macol turns out to be even more villainous than either of his predecessors. There are two witches instead of three: one of them turns herself into Lady Duncan and becomes Lady Macbett when she marries her husband's murderer; the other serves as her lady-in-waiting and helps in the onstage costume and makeup changes necessary to carry out the deception. As in *Macbeth,* the prophecies (that Macbett can be killed by no man born of woman, that his army cannot be defeated unless the forest begins to move, and that Banco will be the ancestor of a long line of kings) are fulfilled, but the version in *Macbett* is distorted: the witch delivers her prediction to Macbett in the guise of Lady Duncan, and Macol turns out to be the adopted son of Duncan, the foundling offspring of the union of Banco with a gazelle. Other scenes are distorted as well. In a lengthy speech taken directly from *Macbeth* (act 4, scene 3), Macol vows to "pour the sweet milk of concord into hell"; Malcolm is testing Macduff's integrity in Shakespeare's play, but in Ionesco's, this speech ends the play, presaging absolute evil and doom as Scotland's fate under the next tyrant. Other scenes are deformed with comic effect: in Shakespeare's play, an apparition shows Macbeth the long line of kings (the Stuarts) who will descend from Banquo, whereas in Ionesco's play, the parade of Kings consists of pictures of three popular comic-book characters ("Des Pieds Nickelés") and Ionesco himself, laughing.

An Apocalyptic Vision of History

"Archduke" Duncan, then Macbett, and then Macol are the most vicious and dangerous in a long line of grotesque authority figures populating Ionesco's theater (the Professor in *The Lesson,* the Detective in *Victims of Duty,* Mother Peep in *The Killer,* Brother Tarabas in *Hunger and Thirst,* for example). Although Duncan is portrayed as having the gift of healing (an allusion to King Edward in Shakespeare's *Macbeth*), he is greedy, cowardly, and bloodthirsty. Macbett turns into a ruthless tyrant when he comes to power, murdering his best friend and defying the moral order, while Macol promises to be the most murderous and unprincipled of them all.

The most political of all of Ionesco's plays, *Macbett* is a radical denunciation of every kind of authoritarian government—indeed of all government, since there is no example anywhere in Ionesco's work even of a benign, much less a beneficent, political or social system. All forms of government, all politics are equally oppressive and malignant.

Two factors are at work to produce this unrelievedly dark portrait of authority as evil. One is the deep-rooted fear and resentment of all paternal figures deriving from Ionesco's fear and hatred of his father. Like Ionesco's despised father, each successive ruler in *Macbett* is an unprincipled opportunist. The second—separate, but related to the first—is Ionesco's equally strong conviction that power corrupts absolutely. We have no way of knowing what Duncan's character was like before he rose to power, but both Banco and Macbett express noble and loyal sentiments until they are corrupted by the lure of power.

Underlying and encompassing the play's conviction that any just form of government is impossible is a fundamentally pessimistic view of history itself. In a moment of reflection, Macbett expresses this despair: "History is clever. Everything is beyond our control. We are not the masters of what has been set in motion. . . . Everything that happens is the opposite of what we wanted. It's events that rule man, not man who rules events" (1101). Not only is history a series of events beyond our control, but these events are rushing toward an apocalyptic finish in Ionesco's vision. As he told Bonnefoy, "I've always had an apocalyptic vision of history. . . . We are always living in an apocalyptic age, each moment of history is the apocalypse, but it's more or less obvious, more or less marked. I have the feeling that the world is headed for a catastrophe" (*ENT* 168). This apocalyptic vision is the reason why *Macbett* ends with Macol's speech about "pouring the sweet milk of concord into hell," a crucial distortion of the Shakespearian model, in which peace and order are restored with Macbeth's death. Furthermore, Ionesco added two phantasmagoric scenes of mass slaughter reminiscent of the Holocaust. Early in the play, Macbett describes the horrific battle against the rebel forces: the "dozens and dozens" of soldiers he has killed with his own hand quickly escalate to hundreds killed by firing squad, thousands burned in forests that he set afire, millions dead of fright or suicide, and tens of millions dead of "anger, apoplexy or grief." The amount of blood shed was so enormous that entire armies drowned in it, and the severed limbs and heads of the enemy continued to fight after death (1047–48). As soon as Macbett leaves the stage, Banco enters and repeats the same description word for word, reinforcing the hellish character of the carnage. The same techniques of exaggeration, acceleration, and proliferation are used again in another scene following the battle, during which a large number of guillotines appear on stage and scores of rebel soldiers are decapitated while Duncan, Lady Duncan, Macbett, and Banco calmly drink their tea.

Farce and Metatheater

As always in Ionesco's theater, tragedy and pathos are undercut by farce. Ionesco told Claude Bonnefoy that "the world is nothing but a farce . . . a kind of trick God plays on men" (*ENT* 162–63). In this respect, *Macbett* owes more to Alfred Jarry's scandalous adaptation of Shakespeare (*Ubu Roi*) than to the original, as many critics have pointed out. Like *Ubu*, *Macbett* is a black farce; it derives its humor from comic characters, pastiche and parody, verbal wit, and sly metatheatrical jokes.

Duncan, like Father Ubu, is a cowardly braggart warrior, a stock comic type called in theater the Miles Gloriosus. He is pompous and verbose in the extreme (1057–58), yet so terrified is he of combat that he stays far from any danger and sends the more intrepid Lady Duncan to see how the battle is going; his only thought is of where he might flee if Macbett and Banco are defeated—perhaps to Canada or the United States (1051). Macbett resembles Ubu as well, if to a lesser degree; he exchanges Ubuesque insults with Macol toward the end of the play (1108), and, in the middle of his mock-heroic recital of the carnage of battle, he expresses an incongruous fear that he may have stepped on some of his companions' toes (1048).[7]

While most of the characters in the play come from Shakespeare, they are subject to deformations that often produce a comic effect. The change of one letter in Macbeth's name, for example, produces a name that contains a French word (*bête*) meaning silly or stupid; Banquo becomes Banco, a gambling term used in baccarat. Cawdor becomes Candor— an ironic comment on his duplicity as a traitor and conspirator, and Malcolm becomes Macol, a name that evokes Lady Macbeth's damned spot by its phonetic proximity to *macule* (stain or spot). Other comic deformations of Shakespeare's characters include the incongruous coexistence of the First Witch, Lady Duncan and Lady Macbeth in a single character; this character's strip-tease that ends with Lady Duncan dressed in a bikini and a red and black cape; and the depiction of the line of kings destined to descend from Banco as comic-book characters.

Several kinds of verbal humor appear sporadically to disrupt the establishment of any sustained serious tone. Whereas jokes and playful nonsense are restricted to secondary characters in Shakespeare, all the characters in Ionesco's play are subject to outbursts of verbal silliness. When Banco first encounters the two witches, for example, he delivers this comic threat: "If you didn't look like some kind of women, you would already be gazing at your heads lying at your feet, under your eyes" (1066); Duncan and Lady Duncan engage in a short but intense argument filled with nonsense and distorted clichés (1082–83); responding to Macol's venomous insults at the end of the play, the best that Macbett can muster is "Psychosomatic weakling! Silly idiot! Heroic simpleton! Infatuated imbecile! Incongruous sausage! Spineless fool!" (1108); the incantation of the two witches during the transformation of the First Witch into Lady Duncan consists of a long list of Latin prepositions (1076–77). As elsewhere in Ionesco's theater, lists and strings of words are a source of humor. Expressing his hatred for Duncan at the beginning of the play, for example, Glamiss calls him a "tyrant, usurper, despot, dictator, wrongdoer, ogre, ass, goose—worse than that" (1044); describing the feast to be held in celebration of Macbett's marriage and coronation, two servants enumerate a list of Rabelaisian proportions, including an omelet of 130,000 eggs, 247 blood puddings per inhabitant of the country, and the oil of an entire whale (1094).

The appearance of Ionesco's laughing face in the series of portraits of the kings to come is but one of several metatheatrical winks at the audience, underscoring the play's status as self-conscious artifice. In addition to the obvious borrowings from Shakespeare, the play contains more subtle allusions to Ionesco's archenemy Brecht. The scene between a traveling vendor and a brutal soldier, for example, carries strong echoes of *Mother Courage,* as do several mimed scenes portraying the victimization of common people by war. Other distancing (deliberately nonnaturalistic) effects include the technique of having some passages of dialogue sung rather than spoken (as used previously in *The Killing Game* and *A Stroll in the Air,* for example) and the use of large puppets to represent some of the guests at the banquet scene. Finally, deliberate anachronisms (the sound of an airplane when the witches take off, allusions to the United States and Canada, and the appearance of Lady Duncan in a bikini, for example) serve to break the frame of the play by reminding the audience of the contemporary moment.

Systematic doubling and repetition also reinforce a nonnaturalistic tone that sometimes borders on that of a fairy tale (complete with witches and ghosts). Banco and Macbett are mirror images of each other. The stage directions specify that they are to wear the same costume and the same beard, and their identities are unstable. Lady Duncan mistakes Banco for Macbett, and when she does meet Macbett, she remarks that he doesn't resemble himself very much; he replies that he is often taken for his own double, or for Banco's double, when he is tired (1056). They are both virtuous and loyal servants of Duncan in the beginning who are corrupted by the lure of power. At one point, they deliver in succession lengthy, identical monologues describing the horrific battle they have waged against the rebels Candor and Glamiss (1047–50). Later, as they ponder in turn the meaning of the witches' predictions, they again repeat several lines of dialogue word-for-word (1069–70).

Misogyny and the Role of Women

The strongly misogynistic bent that pervades Ionesco's theater is quite evident in this play. In it, women are portrayed as witches who enthrall and seduce men into succumbing to evil, only then to abandon them to suffer at the hands of fate. The work of seduction on Macbett begins even before the appearance of the two witches, as Lady Duncan flirts with him during the execution scene (1061–63). Later, when the two witches fail to persuade Macbett to murder Duncan by appealing to his ambition, the First Witch turns into Lady Duncan and seduces him in flagrantly sexual fashion. Dressed in a "shiny bikini," she gives him a dagger and says (in a siren's voice), "Take it if you want it, if you want *me*. . . . It's with this dagger that you will kill Duncan. You will take his place next to me. I will be your mistress" (1078). The scene ends with Macbett rolling at Lady Duncan's feet: the only thing visible on stage is Lady Duncan in her "resplendent nudity," while the lady in waiting sums it up with an ironic "Omnia vincit amor" (Love conquers all) (1079). This is a significant change from Shakespeare's play, in which Lady Macbeth urged her husband to seize power; in Ionesco's play, the lure of feminine sexuality, rather than political ambition, is the driving force behind Macbett's actions.

That women are fundamentally evil and dangerous is implied in several other ways. Even before the transformation, Lady Duncan is shown to be cruel and heartless. Annoyed by the moans of a mortally wounded soldier, she is going to stab him to shut him up; her only remark when he stumbles offstage to die, thus sparing her the trouble of killing him, is "Well, at least he's polite" (1053). During the mass execution scene, she is the most attentive of the spectators, counting twenty thousand deaths before she is dragged away protesting that she wants to see the rest (1063). Classical and Christian allusions link the two witches (and, by extension, women) to evil. The transformation of the First Witch into Lady Duncan is completed with all three characters, chanting "Video meliora, deteriora sequor" (1077). Unlike the nonsense Latin that precedes this moment, these words ("I see the better way and choose the lesser one") are a citation from Ovid's *Metamorphoses* (book 7) spoken by Medea, classical symbol of unnatural evil and witchcraft. As the two witches revert to their preferred ugly appearance ("ugly with the ugliness of all the vices," [1075]) after the wedding ceremony, "Lady Macbett" (the First Witch) relates how difficult it was for her to endure the presence of Christian symbols: the cross and the white wedding dress burned her, the communion wafer burned her throat and almost choked her, and she nearly fainted at the sight of holy icons (1098). With Macbett's doom sealed, the two witches then ride away on a flying suitcase, laughing with glee at having accomplished their mission. As they leave, they comment that "the boss" (the Devil) will be pleased and that he's waiting to assign them their next mission (1099). If it is the inevitable downward spiral of history that dooms man in the play, it is women who are the agents acting (even if at the Devil's behest) to bring that doom about.

Notes

1. Ionesco finished the play in 1964, and it was premiered (in German) at Dusseldorf in December of that year. The Parisian premiere at the Comédie française caused something of a scandal; the brainwashing scene in the last episode was greeted with boos and catcalls, and the performance was disrupted for ten minutes. Recalling this premiere in *La Quête intermittente,* Ionesco remembers that Tom "Bishof" [*sic*] was so bored that he thought the play would never end and that many people (including Samuel Beckett) came backstage to congratulate him (*Quête* 56–57).

2. In 1966 Ionesco decided to add a fourth episode entitled "Le Pied du mur" (The Foot of the Wall) to the play. It was premiered separately later in 1966; like the other three episodes, it is self-contained.

3. This is my translation of the original French. The English translation is inadequate: "Though I can almost feel her presence, behind that there's a void" (43).

4. This is a reference to a concept from the work of Carl Jung, whose terminology and thought have influenced Ionesco. For Jung, the anima is "the autonomous psychic content in the male personality which can be described as an inner woman" (*Collected Works,* trans. R. F. C. Hull, vol. 11 [New York: Pantheon Books, 1963]: 149).

5. See also the stage directions on p. 70: "Second and Third Women and Young Man could continue to cry for help at their window or they might arbitrarily appear separately in windows one, two, and three, jerking their arms and bobbing about like puppets."

6. The critic for the *New York Times* called the play a "literary cabaret," and Poirot-Delpech (not always a fan) praised the play for its "unparalleled inventive freedom."

7. This remark is an allusion to a scene in Jarry's play in which Ubu steps on the king's toes to signal to the conspirators to fall upon the king.

CHAPTER SEVEN

Dream Work: *A Hell of a Mess!*, *Man With Bags*, and *Journeys Among the Dead*

Ionesco's last three plays move progressively away from his obsessions with social and political evil toward intensely oneiric, personalized, and hermetic psychodrama. In each play, a solitary man grapples with alienation and conflict, with family or society or both; with each play, the solitary man becomes more and more clearly autobiographical, and the subject matter becomes increasingly close to Ionesco's efforts to deal with the personal relationships in his own past. These plays rely to a larger extent than earlier ones on the written text, despite Ionesco's professed desire to recreate on the stage (in the last two, at any rate) the incoherent logic and suprareal atmosphere of a dream. The repetition of thematic material familiar to any reader of Ionesco's journals, along with the (sometimes) hermetic psychoanalytic content of the dream plays, can make them difficult to stage effectively. (They are, in this sense, similar to both symbolist and surrealist theater.) Some striking images do appear, however: in a reverse image of the end of *Exit the King*, the protagonist of *A Hell of a Mess!* confronts an ontological abyss represented by brilliant light that swallows up the stage, and the final tableau of *Man With Bags*, with its proliferating suitcases and mute ballet, is an effective use of scenic language reminiscent of *The Chairs* or *The New Tenant*.

A Hell of a Mess!

Ce Formidable Bordel! (*A Hell of a Mess!*) is, like the two previous plays, an adaptation. Based on Ionesco's only novel, *Le Solitaire* (*The Hermit,* published in 1973), it premiered on

14 November of that same year in a production starring and directed by Jacques Mauclair at the Théâtre moderne. The apocalyptic vision of history that marked *The Killing Game* and *Macbett* so profoundly are carried over into both novel and play; this vision has become more personalized, however, announcing the later dream plays.

Both the play and the novel rework familiar themes and obsessions—claustration and the symbolism of space and habitations, nostalgia for a lost paradise, metaphysical angst in the face of death, the futility of politics (specifically, here, of revolution), the unbearably quick passage of time, and a certain fear and loathing of women. Viewed in retrospect, both works represent, in a sense, the author's final retreat from the social or political dimension of human existence; the last two plays are intensely personal oneiric psychodramas.

The Hermit is a first-person novel narrated by a Bérenger-type character who receives an inheritance and quits his job at age thirty-five. A creature above all of habit, he is an unremarkable, inexpressive, and indolent man with a drinking problem and no ambition. The events he recounts are few: he moves into his own apartment, dines regularly at a nearby restaurant, lives with a waitress from the restaurant until she tires of his passivity and moves out, barricades himself in his room while a revolution rages outside, and finally sees a mystical vision of a paradisiacal garden, whose radiance remains with him after it disappears. The bulk of the novel, presented in the form of a journal, consists of the narrator's philosophical musings on the human existential condition: "In *The Hermit,* I created a narrator who is in conflict with history, or who rather lives in parallel to history. History and politics try futilely to solve or to mask the fundamental problem of our condition, because they cannot answer these questions: What am I doing here? Why am I here? What is this world that surrounds me?" (*ENT* 195). Using the unmasked first person for the first time outside his journals, Ionesco was trying, he said, to "say everything" that could not be said in the theater, because the words of a dramatic character are always an implicit third person.

The adaptation of this first-person narrative for the stage presents an even greater challenge than the earlier adaptations of short stories written in the third person. Ionesco's solution was to use both visual and verbal condensation and displacement in the play to create a much more dramatic and nightmarish world than the highly discursive world of the novel (even though the play treats roughly the same events as the novel). The curtain rises on a scene very reminiscent of the beginning of the second act of *Rhinoceros*—in a nondescript office, a group of clerks (including a pretty young girl, a militant leftist, and a dull but overbearing boss, as in *Rhinoceros*) are discussing their absent colleague. He has just resigned, causing them intense envy that takes the form of anger and vituperation. As soon as he appears, their anger changes to extreme, even obsequious, cordiality. In a series of fifteen rapid scenes (fourteen, if the production contains an intermission), the Character's former colleagues bid him farewell in a neighborhood bistro; the Character then finds an apartment and meets three of his neighbors and his concierge, becomes a regular customer at a local restaurant in one visit, witnesses the collapse of society and everyday life caused by the outbreak of a revolution, lives with a waitress who leaves him, and ages rapidly until the vision of an Edenic scene at the end of the play causes him to realize that the "whole thing" (his life and the world he had lived in) was nothing but an enormous joke or trick played by God ("that rascal").

From Novel to Play

The Character, like the narrator of the novel, is anonymous, but, unlike the Hermit, he is almost totally mute—he speaks only six times during the entire first act, and his longest utterance is barely ten words. The Hermit's words are displaced, either given to other characters in the play or subsumed in the dramatic action, and most of the explicitly philosophical musings are absent. More than just a technical trick (how to transform a private journal into a play), this change makes of the main character an observer of and receptacle for the solitude of all the other characters. As Ionesco told Bonnefoy, "This time it wasn't just the solitude of the character that I tried to emphasize, but also the solitude of the characters around him. . . .

183

My main character is there to listen to the others' monologues and, in doing that, he receives their solitude" (*ENT* 109). Thus Lucienne (the pretty former girlfriend from the office) and Agnes (the waitress who moves in with the Character, named Yvonne in the novel) supply the Character's side of their conversations and deliver the lyrical paeans to the power of love that belong to the Hermit in the novel; Jacques (the militant leftist), the Concierge in the Character's new apartment, and the Character's neighbors give voice to the conflicting views of politics and society found in the Hermit's narrative; and ghost-like figures from the past appear at the end of the play to speak to the Character of their love for him, replacing the Hermit's own reminiscences.

The iterative of the novel is replaced by the singulative in the play as time, events, and characters are compressed and condensed. One long scene in the restaurant replaces a series of visits in the novel; all the events of the revolution happen at once; the Character has just two former girlfriends (Lucienne and Janine), whereas the Hermit had three (Lucienne, Janine, and an additional one named Jacqueline). Time accelerates rapidly and concretely, especially at the end: in the course of one scene between Agnes and the Character four years pass (one year just during the time it takes Agnes to say good-bye); and time accelerates even more rapidly in the final scene, during which all the characters from earlier in the play grow up, have children of their own, and die.

The violent events surrounding the revolution dominate the play much more than the novel, so that the play has a more bitterly satiric and despairing tone.

The greatest difference between the two is the ending. The novel ends with a hopeful vision of paradise; the end of the play, on the contrary, is full of derisive, ironic laughter. Commenting on his decision to end the play differently from the novel, Ionesco has said,

> Despite my apocalyptic vision of history, I think I've never completely abandoned my humor. Still, I do have the feeling that history, as it is—that is, terrible, tragic, unacceptable—is a sort of practical joke

that God is playing on man. . . . During the whole
performance, just as throughout the book, the hermit is uneasy; the others speak to him, he meets
them, invites them over, tries to understand what
they tell him, what's happening around him, and
nothing is clear, everything causes him anguish. At
the end he starts to laugh and he says, "You rascal,
I've understood you." . . . The hermit understands
that this magnificent, awful world is a mirage, a joke
God is playing on man; like my character, the world
joins in the game and since it's a farce, let's accept it
with good humor. (*ENT* 163)

One key to understanding the great difference between the
two endings can be found in the progressive disappearance in
the play of the transforming power of light. In the play, light
does initially have the power to transform the world. During
the Character's first meal at the neighborhood bistro, a sunbeam suddenly illuminates the tablecloth, transforming the
entire scene; just as Bérenger does in *The Killer,* the Character exclaims, "It changes everything . . . it's strange . . . strange
. . . brand-new" (71). While the sunbeam remains, all the characters' movements become dancelike, the dialogue is sung, and
all the sound effects become melodious. With its disappearance, the melodies and joy also disappear, returning the restaurant patrons to their ordinary state of dull gloominess.
Later Agnes, the waitress, tries to draw the Character out
of his torpor and despair by describing in a long monologue a
mystical voyage to a splendid country where everything is
peaceful, calm, and luminous.[1] To get to that land, they will
sail "on a beautiful white boat, between the sky and sea." They
will spend "long days on the boat, on the bow of the boat, in
the sun. We'll be all tanned. The white boat, the blue sky, and
water, and then two handsome crewmen, two captains in white
uniforms in the southern seas" (120). When the Character asks
her what color eyes the people who live there have, she tells
him they are the color of light. Unlike the scene in the restaurant, however, this one offers no visual correlatives of this light,
and the Character is left unmoved by Agnes's vision: he has

lost the capacity to experience the euphoric lightness that Ionesco has so often recounted in his journals and plays.

The novel ends with the Hermit's description of an Edenic garden with a beautiful white, flower-covered tree and a silver ladder leading up to the blue sky: "The garden approached me, surrounded me, I was part of it, I was in the middle of it." He goes on to say that, although the vision disappeared after a timeless moment, "Something of the light that had penetrated me remained. I took that as a sign" (191). The ending of the play is radically different, however. The stage is flooded with a brilliant light, and all other elements of decor except the Character's chair disappear; in the empty space, a large tree appears. This character, unlike all the previous incarnations of Bérenger, has lost his capacity to see the world anew, to be astonished: "I don't understand what's going on and there's no point trying. No one could understand. And yet somehow I'm not surprised. In fact it's surprising that I'm not surprised. Very surprising" (151). Realizing that he has been the victim of a terrible metaphysical joke, the Character can do nothing but laugh derisively, signaling the end of an era in Ionesco's theater.

Despite the significant differences between the play and the novel, both return frequently to themes that run throughout Ionesco's work.

Spatial Symbolism

Many of the images and themes that dominated *Hunger and Thirst* return in *A Hell of a Mess!*. Oppositions outlined in the discussion of the earlier play—inside versus outside; home as prison or womb; ascension toward heaven versus sinking into the earth—recur in *A Hell of a Mess!* in sharpened, more concise form.

In both the play and the novel, the Character's new apartment represents a significant move upward, both socially and spatially. In the novel, the Hermit describes the apartment where he had lived prior to his inheritance: small, sad, and damp, it was dark and crammed full of his dead mother's furnishings. The new apartment, by contrast, is on the third floor and has views out of several windows; there is plenty of light, and the furniture is all new. Since the Character in the play is mute, it is the old lady selling him the apartment who talks at length about the virtues of the apartment's solid construction: "Real estate is the best investment, we all know that, and that's what I've always done, but in good real estate, good solid buildings,[2] not stuff made out of hollow bricks and compressed paper" (31). The building is one hundred years old; its age signifies enduring security. Located in the "southern suburbs," the neighborhood is blessed with warm weather, abundant sunshine, blue skies, and masses of colorful flowers. The Character is able to look down on the world below in three different directions—onto the crowded, noisy city street to the left; onto a quiet, peaceful side street in the direction of the audience; and onto an interior courtyard at the rear of the stage. While the apartment (initially, at least) represents comfort, security, and success for the Character, each of the three exterior spaces has its own significance. In the words of the Old Lady, "On one side, you have the big city, and on the other, the small town" (33–34). The big city is dominated by noisy buses and trucks, and, later, by the sound of gunfire during the revolution; it increasingly represents a threat to human life, a deadly battlefield. The small town, on the other hand, is described solely in terms of the people who live there; it is quiet and peaceful. When the revolution begins, it is the quiet residents of this street who perish first. Finally, the space of the interior courtyard, protected as it is from the turmoil outside, becomes the site of the miraculous tree and garden that appear at the end of both play and novel.

As the outside space becomes more and more dangerous with the spread of the revolution, the interior of the apartment becomes less a refuge than a claustrated prison. From the middle of scene 13 on, all the windows in the apartment are blocked with mattresses, becoming barricades against the outside rather than means of access to it—a concrete correlative of the Character's stubborn refusal to speak. With the telephone lines cut, the Concierge is the only link with the outside; she appears at increasingly frequent intervals with meals for the Character and (for a time) Agnes. That the outside poses a mortal threat is made concrete by the constant sound of gun-fire coming from the street and by a bloody hole made instantly in the white flag that the Character tentatively pokes out through the mattresses in the penultimate scene. This isolated life of a prisoner soon proves too much for Agnes, who leaves after "four years" (represented by one scene); the Character remains shut up in this space for the rest of the play (and of the novel).

The play has no exterior scenes (unlike the novel, in which the Hermit stumbles into several scenes of mob violence), but there are some social spaces that mediate between the private isolation of the Character's apartment and the public interac-tion and conflict of the outside world. The office in the first scene and especially the two restaurants offer the Character a relatively secure framework that can both shelter him from and expose him to society. It is at the first restaurant that Lucienne delivers her long address on the subject of love, and it is in the second that the Character meets and attracts Agnes. Both the Hermit and the Character are attached to routine and order, and taking meals at a particular place and particu-lar time is a very important part of this routine. These semipublic places are not closed off to the outside, however; revolutionaries and then the revolution itself breach the walls of the second restaurant shortly after the Character becomes a regular customer there, driving him back into the cloistered confines of his apartment.

In his apartment the Character constructs the barricades that will separate him from the outer world—including, ulti-mately, other people. As in *Hunger and Thirst*, one aspect of this enclosure is the womblike security it offers, but the other aspect is stifling, confining imprisonment. That there is no exit from this prison is underscored by the Character's refusal to find any hope in the vision of the tree and silver ladder that appears at the end of the play; for him, this image is nothing but another bad joke.

Love, Redemption, and Paradise Lost

Although the Character in the play has lost any hope of es-caping this "hell of a mess," the nostalgia for paradise lost and longing for a redemptive love that marked Ionesco's earlier work are not absent from the play. Rather than being formulated by the narrator (as in the novel), these themes are present in the speeches of two of the Character's lovers. Early in the play, Lucienne delivers a long paean to the power of love (words belonging to the Hermit in the novel): "If you had really loved me . . . well you know they say that love can move mountains. Love bends iron, love breaks through shackles. Nothing is stronger than love. . . . Who knows, if things had been different, it might have worked out for us. Perhaps a bright flame was hidden under the ashes of our love. But all I could make out then in the grayness of the ashes, was more ashes. Perhaps it could have turned into a temple of love once, with white columns and a shining altar" (16).[3] Later Agnes tries to wrest him from his torpor with the glowing vision of an idyllic cruise in the southern seas to a miraculous land of blue skies, brilliant flowers, sunny days, and starry nights, complete with silver ladders ascending to heaven on every street corner (121).

At the end of the play, many persons from the Character's past (his mother, his schoolteacher, Lucienne, Agnes's daughter, Jacques's son, even anonymous figures) appear to tell him how much they loved him. Significantly, the Character rejects them all with derisive laughter; what good is the power of love in the face of the inevitability of death?

Misogyny

Women play a very prominent role in *A Hell of a Mess!*. The Character is infantile, silent and passive. Women feed him (the two waitresses and the Concierge) and even speak for him (Lucienne, the Concierge, Agnes). In contrast to the Character's silence, the women in the play talk excessively, recalling the logorrhea of the concierge in *The New Tenant*. The same ambivalence toward women as nurturing but confining maternal figures seen in earlier works (*The Chairs, Victims of Duty,* and *Hunger and Thirst,* for example) marks this character's attitudes toward the women in his life. While they feed and sustain him, they also exert constant pressure on him to do or be something, a pressure that he steadfastly resists. Like the

Old Woman in *The Chairs,* the Character's mother (appearing briefly at the end of the play) had been full of ambition for her son: "I told you, my son, I told you to work hard. I told you that, ever since you were a little boy. I would've liked you to have another kind of life. Ah, if only you had done well in school as I told you to, you could have become an army captain with a beautiful uniform and decorations, lots of decorations. I suffered so much for you. I loved you so much. My poor little boy, poor little boy" (148).

Like his mother, Agnes wishes that the Character would have "another kind of life": "What are you waiting for? You have everything within your reach. I'm here and you won't touch me and you're afraid. Yes, you seem as though you're afraid. Oh, if only you wanted, if only you'd dare. What are you waiting for?" (131–32). It is true that the Character is afraid of and repelled by women. He has no physical relations with women in the play, so repelled is he by their "gaping wound"— their sexuality: when he contemplates the sleeping Agnes, an expression of fright comes over his face as he says, "What a wound, what a deep bloody wound you carry around with you, you poor creature" (133).

Futility of Politics

Just as *Macbett* satirized and denounced the evil of tyrants, *A Hell of a Mess!* targets the demagoguery and futility of revolution and mob violence. The revolutionaries in the play are bloodthirsty butchers: "We've got to draw blood. Justice will be served by our lust for blood" (79). (It is no coincidence that the most bloodthirsty rebel is a woman.) Their primary goal, enunciated (significantly) by the single woman rebel, is "Revolution for the pleasure of it" (82). Mindless and violent, these rebels are given to shouting either clichés—"Here's to the class struggle"—or self-contradicting nonsense—"To dictatorship but with liberty for all" (80). Claiming that they want to transform society in the name of fraternity and equality, they destroy the bar-restaurant whose owner-proprietor had offered them food and drink. The police are no less brutal and bloodthirsty than the revolutionaries.

190

Constant allusions in the play to past revolutions, historical and fictional, underscore Ionesco's conviction that history offers no possibility of melioration of the human condition; on the contrary, the history of society and politics is seen as an accelerating descending spiral leading to the apocalypse. In the play, this apocalyptic view of history is espoused by the Concierge: "Let them blow themselves up. Let them massacre themselves. Let things rip, explode, burn up and then that's that. The human adventure has lasted long enough. Let it be over with and not worry us any longer. The creator put his foot in it with this one" (113). Like the narrator in the novel and Ionesco in his journals and essays, the Concierge views politics and social upheaval as futile and beside the point: "You make revolutions because there are no more metaphysical theories to hang on to. You don't realize it, but it's the existential condition which is in bad shape. . . . There is no 'good' society. Tyranny, dictatorship, liberalism, capitalism, all are no good" (108–9).

Man With Bags

L'Homme aux valises (*Man With Bags*) premiered in 1975 at the Théâtre de l'Atelier. Like *A Hell of a Mess!*, it starred and was directed by Jacques Mauclair. It is more personal and oneiric than the previous play, a transposition to dramatic form of dreams, memories, and musings already published in *Fragments of a Journal* (1967) and *Past Present Present Past* (1968). As he told Claude Bonnefoy, Ionesco was trying to recreate here more authentically than in earlier plays the true atmosphere of a dream; in plays like *Amédée, The Killer, A Stroll in the Air,* and *Hunger and Thirst,* oneiric images abound, but "the language that accompanied them had none of the incoherence or incoherent coherence of dreams. In *Man With Bags,* I tried to adapt language—the spoken language, the dialogue—to the oneiric images" (*ENT* 73). That he was only partially successful may be due to his continued struggle to find words to accompany those images rather than letting the images speak for themselves; the play's most effective elements are precisely those which are nonverbal—the oppressively heavy suitcases

191

that the man must drag with him everywhere, and the final scene. Ionesco's goal in writing the play, he said, was to find his origins and his identity; it is also a nightmarish version of the totalitarian society he found in Romania during his adolescence.

The play's structure is deliberately fragmented; in nineteen scenes, dreams embedded within other dreams are grouped thematically rather than chronologically. Despite this fragmentation, the play does take the form of a journey (both into the past and into an alien land) with a beginning and an end. Also serving to unify the play are the constant presence of the protagonist (First Man), witness to and actor in his own nightmares, and the recurring appearance of two heavy suitcases.

The curtain rises on a dimly-lit stage; barely visible is the First Man with his two suitcases. A painter tells him that they are in Paris in 1938, or perhaps 1950. From across the Seine come the sounds of crowds shouting and trumpets blaring—the political and social upheaval that dominated so much of *A Hell of a Mess!* has receded to the other side of the river. A boatman appears, offering to take the man to his hotel, and thus the man's journey into his past begins. The next five scenes are organized around the man's search for his origins among various dead family members. After the man fails a test of riddles administered by "the Sphinx" (scene 7), the boatman reappears, and the man embarks on the next stage of his journey. After much difficulty, he finally arrives in a mysterious country where he apparently was born, but whose language, geography, and customs are completely unknown to him. A series of tragicomic vignettes (scenes 9–14) depicting the man's alienation from the totalitarian bureaucracy culminates in a Kafkaesque trial in which the man is accused of not eating his vegetables (scene 15). Following an interlude in which an idyllic vision reminiscent of Ionesco's boyhood in La Chapelle-Anthenaise is combined with a comical Proustian intertext, the man overcomes several obstacles—for example, inability to find transportation, and the tempting offer of sex from a beautiful young woman (scene 17)—and finally arrives at his destination. In a port named Kinichev, he finds waiting for him his now aged wife, whom he had left many years previously. The final scene (scene 19) is a mute ballet in which travelers and suitcases proliferate.[4]

A Search for Origins and Identity

Running through the entire play is the man's search for his identity, which is fluid; he is father, husband, son, friend, foreigner, tourist, "other," writer. He is at home in none of these identities, however, and is thus always an exile, defined negatively as who, what, and where he is *not*. As Ionesco told Bonnefoy, "This character doesn't really belong to any particular group; everywhere he goes, he feels totally foreign" (*ENT* 173).

As Rosette Lamont has pointed out in her excellent essay on the play, the wandering man is involved in a search for his origins that recalls the plight of the wandering Jew, victim of the Diaspora and the Holocaust, "the symbol of universal persecution, the essence of human suffering" (260–61). A scene early in the play (scene 5) establishes the importance of mothers and names in this search. In their old home town, the man encounters his maternal grandparents. After the elderly grandfather goes offstage to die, the man asks the grandmother if she is dead as well, and she responds by shedding all signs of old age and rising up rejuvenated before him. The man then declares to a clerk from city hall that he has come to learn his grandmother's maiden name—the real name of his great grandmother; his grandmother always kept her maiden name a secret. Significantly, the key to this man's identity is thus defined matrilineally—just as Jewishness is—even though family names are passed down through the father. Perhaps, the clerk suggests, she belonged to a persecuted ethnic group or a "condemned race"; he warns the man that it might be dangerous to persist in his search. The man insists that he wants to know about his origins, no matter what the cost. Then, when the man exclaims at how young and lovely his grandmother looks, the same clerk tells him that she was rejuvenated "because she changed her name, which was keeping her apart from other people and sinking her into old age" (1217). The man is immediately struck with misgivings, wondering whether his grandmother had the right to change her name.

Uncertainty about names and identities continues throughout the play. In scene 6, the man believes that his wife is his mother, and he is unable to remember or recognize a son and a daughter. When he arrives in a foreign country in scene 10, he has forgotten what his name is: on his business card, his name is Filard; but the name on his identity card might be Marty, Marly, Vardy, Mofty, or Cofty. The man's real name is on his passport, he says, but he doesn't have it with him. In the meantime, one of the policeman interrogating him claims that he is a childhood friend named Koriakides. Confronted by some menacing police a short time later, the man puts on a ridiculous disguise and tells them, "Look, you can see it's not me. . . . You can see that I'm someone else" (1252). When he finally arrives at the consulate to obtain a new passport, he cannot remember his father's name, his age, his profession (he claims to be a "specialist in existence"), or his mother's name (it might have been Ursula, Elise, Mariette, or Blanche) (1255–56).

The First Man is not the only character in the play to lack a stable identity. Upon his arrival in the foreign country, for example (scene 10), the man recognizes two passersby as old friends named César and Marius (characters in the well-known Marcel Pagnol novels). He is corrected immediately, however, by the two policemen: these men are named Philip and Paul. Later, after the man leaves the consulate, the Consul himself questions whether any of us can know our true identity, since it is only through our function in society that we have one. Immediately, a policeman arrives to announce that he no longer has any function, and thus, no identity. "So what?" is the Consul's reaction. "That way, no one can blame us for anything" (1257).

Closely linked to the man's identity are the suitcases. According to Ionesco, the suitcases in the play symbolize the unconscious, the subterranean and unknowable stratum of our identity. Filled with the dead weight of guilt and unacknowledged dread, the suitcases are a heavy encumbrance that constantly interfere with the man's journey toward self-knowledge: they cause him to miss a train, he must book a hotel room just to have a place to keep them, and he is frequently delayed by the necessity of finding someone to watch them for him. As the play progresses, it becomes apparent that the man does not really know what is in the suitcases any more than he knows who he is. In scene 12 he takes the silly Groucho Marx look-alike disguise out of one of the suitcases; later, in scene 15, he is surprised to find the suitcases filled with the beets and potatoes he is being accused of buying but not eating, along with socks and cement. In the following scene, he tells three policemen that his suitcases contain nothing but cement; when the men open them, they find a doll and some dirty laundry, and yet they confirm that they do indeed contain cement. Just as psychotherapy aims to lighten the burden of neurosis by offering the patient some insights into the secrets buried in the unconscious, it is only when the suitcases are opened and the contents examined that they become light and the man is able to lift them easily. Thus after the police open the suitcases and give them back to him, the man exclaims, "They've lifted the weight from my heart" (1276).

One sign that the man's search for his identity and origins is destined to be fruitless is the absence of a third suitcase. When the boatman from the first scene delivers him to his destination in scene 8, the man insists that he had embarked with three suitcases, not two. At the end of the play he again refers to the lost suitcase: "Since I lost the other one, I don't have my third dimension any more. I'm missing something, on the inside" (1282). Significantly, the missing suitcase is the most important one, the one containing his "manuscript": "What about my manuscript? I'll have to reconstruct it, start it all over again from the first line to the last. I can't remember anymore what I wrote—that manuscript was my only treasure!" (1225–26). This man has thus suffered a double loss; a writer (like Ionesco), he has lost the key to his profession, and he has also lost the entire story of his life—the manuscript of his past. He spends a great deal of time and energy trying to obtain the documents necessary to "reconstitute" this manuscript—the passport and pass that will give him entry to the past, and the driver's license ("permis de conduire") and construction permit ("permis de construire") that will allow him to reconstruct and control his life. He never does succeed in obtaining any of them, however. Even at the consulate, the papers he gets are a false pass and a bogus "medical certificate."

Like the contents of the man's suitcases, the contents of
the unconscious are closed to us except for the displaced, condensed images of our dreams. Thus it is only in dreaming that
knowledge is possible. Speaking of the play, Ionesco told
Bonnefoy, "These dreams are true, because they are linked
directly to lived experience, either through obsession or
memory." They are "more real" than conscious, rational
thought because they are "more incisive, more agonizing" (*ENT*
172). Within the play itself, there are several references to
the special insight available only to dreamers. In scene 6, for
example, the fact that the man is dreaming is made explicit
when his grandmother tells him that all his loved ones are dead:

> First Man. And to think I didn't know it!
> Old Woman. And look, a few minutes of dreaming
> and you've learned everything.
> Man. How could I have been so unaware? How could
> I have not suffered from these absences? To be lu-
> cid, I'd have to spend my life dreaming. (1220)

Near the end of the play, the man experiences an epiphany in
which he finally recognizes his wife and understands his journey. When his wife says that he has awakened into a life in
which he has done almost nothing but sleep, he corrects her:
"I'm waking up in a dream. I won't fall asleep again in my
dream" (1284).

The Oedipal Drama

In her essay on this play, Rosette Lamont calls the man another of Ionesco's "Oedipes manqués" (260). Deborah Gaensbauer
expands upon this theme in another excellent article on the
play. Like Oedipus, the protagonist is a wandering stranger;
in one scene, a Sphinx demands that he answer a series of
comical or nonsensical riddles; and, as Gaensbauer rightly
points out, "his adventures center around a search for mother
and a rejection of father figures" (391). As always in Ionesco's
theater, women are ambiguous maternal figures and men are
menacing, repressive authority figures.

The positive qualities associated with women in the play are those of the nurturing good mother. Like the waitresses in *The Hermit* and *A Hell of a Mess!,* a waitress appears near the end of *Man With Bags* to tell the man, "I'm here to serve you" (1279); immediately afterward, a beautiful young woman offers him sex and a ride to the train station; and, at the end of his journey, the man finds his long-suffering and faithful wife waiting patiently at the destination she knew about because of her "antennae." Here as elsewhere in Ionesco's theater, the mother represents the possibility for ego-fusion, that blissful union of identity possible only between mother and infant before the painful onset of individuation.[5] The dreaming man's longing for this prelapsarian state of grace is sublimated in the play in several different ways.

A typical mechanism by which repressed desires may surface in dreams is displacement; taboo or frightening wishes (in this case, the son's desire for union with his mother) are modified and/or attributed to other figures in the dream. There are two scenes in which the longing for union is displaced onto a daughter figure. Scene 4 is a touching encounter between a very elderly woman in a wheelchair (the daughter) and a young, beautiful woman (the mother who had abandoned her many years earlier, either through death or through desertion). In a very emotional exchange, the young mother vows that they will never be separated again, and the old woman exclaims how happy she is as her mother pushes her wheelchair off the stage. This intense desire for union is echoed in scene 12, in which a young woman is pleading with her dear friend, her "twin," to see her; otherwise she will surely die, she says: "I looked at your picture constantly. I stared at your eyes, I kissed your picture, I caressed your hair, your face. When I closed my eyes, I could still see your face. . . . There's nothing but you, my flower, my icon" (1245). She says that she feels "cut in two" without this woman, and she does in fact collapse and die when the other rejects her. Significantly, the friend refuses to see her because she has a new husband—the infant's place has been usurped by the father.

Another sort of displacement is a desire for sexual union wherein the mother is replaced by the wife or the seductress.

Several times in the play the man is unable to differentiate between his wife and his mother. In scene 6, for example, the man tells his wife that he always thought that she was his mother. When he realizes that his mother has been dead for twenty years, he breaks down in tears:

> Man. I've been all alone for so long, without my poor dear little mother! How did I go on living without her?
> Wife. You didn't notice she was gone. . . . I was there. I took her place. (1219)

The man remembers how happy his mother had been at their wedding, recalling an earlier scene in the play (scene 2) in which the man, accompanied by his wife and son, visits the house where he was born and where his mother died. The elderly mother comes out of the house and hands her son over to his wife: "I'm entrusting him to you. Now you're the one who's going to take care of him" (1210). Later in the play another version of the mother—mother as temptress, forbidden seductress—appears in the form of the sexy young blond dressed in skimpy underclothes and white gloves. She offers to have sex with him, but they can find no place hidden from the view of her very cooperative husband (a father figure who is watching over the man's suitcases) and all the party guests (society).

The dark side of this maternal love inspires fear and multifaceted, pervasive guilt. The appearance of maternal figures in the play is frequently associated with images of buildings sinking into the ground, dampness, and destruction by fire. Familiar symbols in Ionesco's theater of metaphysical angst, they also represent an infantile fear of engulfment and desire for freedom that arise with recognition of the mother's enormous power. Cronelike old women abound in the play, including the old vendor who, in the trial scene, charges the man with buying vegetables he had no intention of eating. Like a witch, this old woman seems to have magical powers, causing the potatoes and beets in question to appear both on a table before the judges and in the man's suitcases: "It's magic!" he exclaims. "That'll teach me to go to market!" (1271). The malefic nurse who accompanies the murderous doctor is an apt symbol for the conflict and tension between the good and bad mother. Dressed in a uniform symbolic of nurturing care for others, she carries a huge pair of scissors in scene 12 (the threat of emasculation), and it is she who delivers the fatal injection that kills the old woman with a tree inside her in scene 14.

Inseparable from the fear these maternal figures inspire is guilt. Repeatedly in the play, the man dreams of being a bad son: he can't remember whether his mother is alive or dead, whether she ever wrote him any letters, whether or not he answered them, and so forth (see, for example, scene 10). In scene 3 a young man is not sure whether the old woman with him is his mother. When he tries to leave, she heaps abuse on him, accusing him of trying to kill her. The son then frantically tries to prevent her from committing suicide. On one level, this scene recalls the episode from Ionesco's own childhood in which he witnessed his mother's half-hearted suicide attempt. At a deeper psychological level, however, the dream also represents the son's sublimated wish to kill the mother; this kind of sublimation is another form of displacement by which our most frightening and deeply suppressed wishes can be fulfilled in our dreams. The wish to kill the mother becomes overt in the hospital scene (scene 14), in which the man agrees to assist in the execution of an old woman with a tree growing inside of her in order to obtain the visa he needs. The burden of guilt the man carries (the heavy load of cement that he must drag around in his suitcases) arises in large measure from these frightening, forbidden desires. The man's own guilty feelings are also one component of the repeated instances during the play when he is interrogated, accused, and put on trial for mysterious transgressions of which he remains ignorant.

As always in Ionesco, men are most often fearsome authority figures. The numerous guards, policemen, soldiers, and judges in the play are judgmental, disapproving father figures who reflect Ionesco's own relationships with the father he loathed. Perhaps the most menacing of these is the doctor-mayor-prison guard of scene 14 who terrorizes the elderly hospital prisoners and shoots the already dead old woman in the head, displaying an excessive brutality reminiscent of Ionesco's recollection of his own father beating an elderly Jewish man. Like the Consul, from whom the man tries to obtain a passport, this doctor promises to help the man (he will get a visa for him, he says, if he helps to murder the old woman), but he only lets him down—failing him, just as Ionesco's father failed to stand by his son. Denunciation of authoritarian regimes (a theme sounded in numerous earlier plays) is more effective here, for two reasons. First, the multiple figures of totalitarian oppression are integral to the action of this play, not nightmarish aberrations (as they were in *A Stroll in the Air,* for example). More importantly, however, the protagonist's rebellion is personalized as a function of Ionesco's own Oedipal drama (coupled with the specific circumstances of his father's role in the rise of fascism in Romania) rather than the detached observations of an ironist (as in *The Killing Game, Macbett, The Hermit,* and *A Hell of a Mess!*). The alien country whose language and geography the man has forgotten is a clear allusion to Ionesco's forced return to the country of his birth, Romania, where he had to live with the despised family of the father who had deserted him.

Nevertheless, hatred of the father is subtended by the man's yearning for a good father who will be a guide and mentor (the painter, the boatman, the Consul, the guard who remembers him as Koriakides and helps him, the complacent husband who watches over his bags), the father whose love the abandoned son wishes so much to win. This aspect of the Oedipal drama (admiration and yearning) surfaces in a brief, otherwise cryptic transitional scene (scene 9) in which, against a backdrop of bright colors and gay music, the man joyously hails a passing character named Shafer, calling out, "You're the king"—a clear reference to hero worship of the all-powerful father. Immediately afterward, Shafer reappears, this time in the company of his new bride (the mother), who throws her bridal bouquet to the man (her son). Another man enters to take the flowers away, telling the man he has no right to them, an allusion to the fact that the father, not the son, has the right to the coveted place alongside the mother. The man's response to this accusation of usurpation is that it wasn't his fault—the gesture (the seduction) was initiated by the mother.

Language and Humor

Despite the play's grim atmosphere, it contains a kind of nightmarish humor, much of it grounded in language. The language in the play can either fail to communicate on a rational level or betray the speaker by communicating too much. When the man arrives in the mysterious foreign country, for example, he is suddenly unable to understand the questions of a policeman, and so the second policeman "translates" for him; roughly half of the translations are, however, exactly the opposite of what the man has said. These mistranslations produce a comic effect reminiscent of certain sketches from *Monty Python's Flying Circus,* Woody Allen movies, or *Saturday Night Live,* but they also represent the split between the conscious (or surface) meaning of what the man says and the unconscious truth behind his words and actions. When asked why he has come to the country, for example, he says that he has come only as a tourist; according to the translation, however, he has come looking for hidden secrets, hoping to use "old friends and relations" as sources of information. At the psychological level, in other words, the man can never really be an innocent tourist in this country. This supposedly innocent journey into the world of dreams is in fact an attempt to unearth the secrets buried in the man's past and in his unconscious. The man claims that he has no interest in politics and is no enemy of authority; the translator says that he hates authority but has been hiding his feelings and that his politics are opposed to those of the country he is visiting. Here the function of the translation is to unmask the man's lies, since it is clear that he does in fact despise authority and can't wait to escape the repressive regime of this totalitarian country.

Not all the language games in the play are so densely charged; as one might well expect from Ionesco, there are several instances of comic wordplay: a sphinx subjects the man to a test in which he must solve a series of clever punning riddles; the police release the man from custody after he gives an inventively mistranslated definition of the word cormorant, and, in the courtroom scene, the witnesses swear their oath by "the Tsar, the court and the little Crown Prince." Finally, the incongruous appearance of several characters from *Swann's Way* in scene 16 adds a light and humorous touch to this idyllic interlude in which Proust's famous hawthorns come in fanciful blue and green as well as pink and white, and Combray lies adjacent to La Chapelle-Anthenaise.

Journeys Among the Dead

Ionesco's last full-length play represents his final attempt to create on the stage the unmediated dream state, as well as his most exhaustive and autobiographical exploration of his painful, conflicted relationships with his parents, ancestors, wife, and friends. If *Man with Bags* is primarily a search for the mother, *Voyages chez les Morts* (*Journeys Among the Dead*) focuses on the protagonist's relationships with his father, the father's second family, and the protagonist's other male ancestors. In the earlier play, the man is searching for his origins and identity; here, the main character (Jean) has a fairly stable identity and is now seeking to settle the score with his father. Where male authority figures were largely displaced into the realm of social and political forces in the earlier play, they take center stage in *Journeys Among the Dead,* despite Jean's repeated assertions that the goal of his quest is still to find his mother.

Although this play was not performed until 22 September 1980, at the Guggenheim Museum in New York, Ionesco was apparently already working on it in January 1977, when he told Bonnefoy that he was trying in a new play not to change anything that he saw, heard, or said in his dreams (*ENT* 73). Like *Man With Bags,* it is composed of a series of dream scenes (eighteen of them); again, the theme of travel announced in the title serves to organize, however loosely, an intensely personal psychodrama that stages material easily recognizable for readers of Ionesco's journals and essays but more cryptic for spectators unfamiliar with his personal history and obsessions. Beginning with his maternal grandfather and great uncle, the protagonist encounters his dead family members and reenacts various episodes from different moments in the past, including his arrival in Bucharest, his strained relations with his father and members of his stepmother's family, and his recollections of the different places he has lived (la Chapelle-Anthenaise, rue Claude Terrasse, Cerisy-la-Salle). The play ends with two long scenes. The first (scene 17) is a magical, apocalyptic judgment scene in which an old woman (mother, grandmother, and great-grandmother) exacts revenge on the father, stepmother, and the stepmother's family before being transformed into a young and beautiful singer. The final scene consists of an extended monologue delivered by a solitary character seated alone on a bare and brightly lit stage. A rambling string of free association and surrealistic images, it is a meditation on knowledge and language that takes the form of theme and variations.

Many characters and situations from *Man With Bags* reappear in *Journeys,* albeit in somewhat altered form. Several important characters who were anonymous in the earlier play are now named: the protagonist is Jean (although his great-uncle calls him Victor), his maternal grandfather is named Leon, the great uncle is Ernest, his wife is Arlette (often confused with his sister Lydia), a childhood friend is named Georges, and his stepmother's brothers are named Paul and Peter. The names serve to make these characters specific individuals in Jean's (Ionesco's) personal psychodrama, whereas the earlier figures remained universal types or archetypes. Situations, events, and themes taken from the earlier play include Jean's desire to find his mother; his confusion about whether a woman is his wife, mother, or sister; his inability to speak the language of the country (here identified as Romania); the tremendous difficulties he encounters in traveling; the pervasive guilt he suffers; and the transformation of an old woman (the mother) into a beautiful young one. Finally, the difference between the two titles also illustrates a shift of focus. In the first play, the journey has no specific destination, and the play revolves around questions of the man's identity and the content of his suitcases; in the second, the goal of Jean's Orphic journey is specific—his quest for knowledge in the kingdom of the dead, among all those members of his family now deceased.

Travel versus Home

As in *Hunger and Thirst,* travel in this play represents the possibility for adventure, escape from the stifling confines of routine, and the anguished wandering of a lost soul in search of a "real home." The ambivalence surrounding the idea of the home is summed up in a conversation between Jean and his friend Alexandre in the fifteenth scene of the play. Alexandre evokes the comforting habits of living "in a cage": "The truth is, we love retracing our own steps. The same little glass of wine each morning, the first cigarette. A new day dawns. We love the habits we've acquired, however uncomfortable they are" (1344). Travel, on the other hand, offers both the temptation of escape from the cage and the threat of leaping out into a "bottomless abyss of adventure" (1346).

Evocations of two mythical lands named Bogandi and Aluminia recall the euphoria experienced by Bérenger in the Radiant City in *The Killer* and by the young Ionesco in the luminous landscape of La Chapelle-Anthenaise. For Jean, Bogandi's most attractive feature is the sensation of harmony and balance prevailing there: the houses are "well-proportioned, neither too high or too low" and people don't often go outside, "probably because they feel good at home—they have everything they need there" (1293). In Aluminia, Jean recalls during a conversation with his sister (and Ionesco's sister was with him at La Chapelle-Anthenaise), the light had a special quality that "puts your heart back in the right place": "It was so beautiful that I thought I was dreaming" (1339). These paradisiacal landscapes represent an idealized space where Jean's soul might feel truly at home. Necessarily inaccessible, they retain their magical power precisely because they remain always elsewhere.

Travel, often as difficult in this play as in *Man With Bags,* signifies a search for a real home (both "fatherland" and "mother") as well as a desire to escape from home. Various feelings toward home are associated with the different kinds of dwellings depicted and evoked in the play. The small, dark rooms with low ceilings in which many of the scenes take place make of the home both womb *and* grave. Repeating his birth in scene 3, albeit in reverse, Jean crawls on his belly through a very small door into the small, dark room where his mother and grandmother live. Conversely, the rooms in which Jean meets his grandfather and uncle resemble graves: they are in "low houses with low ceilings and the dirty white walls" favored by the family (1291). Likewise, at a kind of reunion of all the now dead members of his immediate family (scene 11), Jean's sister tells him that his room is right next to hers; it is long, dark, and uncomfortable—clearly, a coffin. Dripping with humidity, these houses are sinking into the ground—a familiar symbol in Ionesco's theater for the depressive pole of those bipolar affective states that afflict so many of his characters.

"Home" finally signifies the ultimate cessation of travel, indeed of all motion. The apartment on rue Claude Terrasse, the mill at La Chapelle-Anthenaise, and the chateau at Cerisy-la-Salle are "mental decors" in which Jean felt "at home." In scene 8, while the decor in the background is transformed successively to represent those three dwellings, Jean describes his life as a journey: "For nearly a century, I didn't know where I was coming from, where I was going, or where I was" (1318). Now, at the end of his life, he has arrived in "another place," described by the woman who owns it as "the antechamber of motionless truth" in which he can already smell the "pure air of absolute truth" (1320). Contrary to his fears and expectations, his entrance into death's antechamber has been as effortless as walking through a door; he has taken his greatest trip, he says, without even knowing it.

The dichotomy between home and travel is resolved in the image of travel as living in a house "big enough to change bedrooms every night" (1335). Thus imagined, the home itself becomes the site for expansive joy, a welcoming, nurturing "chez soi." In scene 7 and again in scene 17, Jean describes a fantastic palace that he owns in the country; it has countless rooms, a full-sized theater, soundstages and film studios, and an attic so vast that it contains lakes, fields, trees, castles, and ruins.

Houses big enough to allow their occupants to sleep in a different bed every night are the perfect setting for dreaming—the means of travel that gives the play whatever structural coherence it has. Travel through dreams represents

Jean's quest for the truth, since people and places remain factitious for him if they are not dreamed. As he tells his friend at the beginning of the penultimate scene, "Real houses are the ones you remember, but they are also and above all the ones you remember in your dreams, the ones you find again and walk into in your dreams." It is in their dreams, not in this "false reality," that these two friends have met most often to discuss "the one and the many" (1349). Beginning with the title, the play is clearly a series of dreams in which Jean relives his past and visits dead relations. Jean is, moreover, a very self-conscious dreamer. As he tells a filmmaker for whom he wishes to write a scenario (in scene 7), he is still full of interesting ideas because, "as long as you're dreaming, you stay young" (1313). Encountering his father in scene 4, he wonders aloud why he has resumed dreaming about him after a period of many years when the father and his second family were absent from his dreams. The answer, he concludes, is that he is now close to death himself, and his bitterness has lessened enough to permit him to try to come to terms with his old anger and hatred before joining his parents in death.

Guilt, Debt, and Retribution

Coming to terms with the past is difficult and bloody work in the play, marked by guilt, recrimination, and retribution rather than reconciliation. Jean's relations with the father in the play are explicitly autobiographical; the dialogue frequently echoes Ionesco's journal entries about his own family drama. Father and son both recognize that Jean had always defined himself in opposition to his father, rejecting his profession, his politics, his language, and his new family. Jean reproaches the father for his desertion of his mother, for his violent temper and frequent beatings of servants and his own son, for his chameleonlike lack of political principles. Just as the father refuses to acknowledge his debt to Jean's mother and sister, he refuses to recognize Jean's success as an author: "He's good for nothing; he'll never have a brilliant career, he'll never be a lawyer like me" (1329). Faced with such rejection, Jean remains an unhappy little boy seeking his father's praise. Twice in the

206

play (scenes 4 and 6), the father asks to see what his son has spent his life writing. (Ionesco's own father died before he became successful and never did read any of his son's work.) In scene 4, all that Jean finds to show his father is a mass of scribbled papers and notebooks, causing his father to comment, "There's nothing there, son—you haven't left any messages at all. You've done nothing but mutter and mumble, pieces of words, fake words, and you tried to pass yourself off as some kind of prophet, a witness, an analyst of the situation!" (1301). In a mirror situation two scenes later, the father again asks to see the son's work; this time, however, it is so that he can appreciate how soundly he has been defeated: "Show me what you've done so that I may be even more destroyed in defeat and so that I can appreciate your fame and admire you all the more" (1311). Once again, what Jean pulls out of his desk is worthless junk—scraps of yellowed paper, rusted bits of wire, a cookbook, dirty rags, pencil stubs, and a bottle of black ink that he spills over everything. Still persisting, he opens yet another drawer and finds in it nothing but handfuls of dust.

Thus, while Jean desires vindication and admiration from his father, it is apparent that the source of his unhappiness is not only the judgment he fears from others but also the internalized conviction that he and his work are worthless. Furthermore, he feels guilty himself for having abandoned his mother and sister and having allowed his mother to support the family while he "wasted" years in his fruitless literary endeavors. The chorus of reproach and blame reaches a crescendo in scene 11, in which the father, grandmother, and sister all join in condemning Jean for failing to support his elderly, hardworking mother. The scene ends with a triple dose of blame and guilt:

> Grandmother. He feels guilty, but that doesn't help matters at all.
> Sister. You're made to sponge off of others.
> Father. You can keep him! (1329)

While the main focus of this play is on Jean's settling his accounts with his father, guilt about his conduct toward his mother (the focus of *Man With Bags*) surfaces as well. As in the earlier play, Jean is never sure whether he has received letters from his mother or sent any to her. She reproaches him on two occasions for eating too much, and in one scene he dumps a large bag of groceries on her floor, a vain attempt to atone for all the years when it was her hard work that supplied him with food.

The most important symbol for guilt and atonement is money. Jean and all the other characters are obsessed with money; this preoccupation reflects both the poverty of Ionesco's youth after his father's desertion and the father's alternating generosity and miserliness during Ionesco's years in Romania. Throughout the play Jean is either giving large sums of money to people, asking for money, or looking for money to "rescue" his uncle, his mother, or his grandparents. In the first scene, for example, Jean gives a lot of money to his Uncle Ernest, after being reminded of how generous Ernest had always been. Ernest tells him that it's not enough, however. He then tells Leon (the maternal grandfather) that Jean has paid back part of what he "owes," but Leon points out that the money is "no good" (1291–92). Reminded by his sister (in scene 13) that he always used to be able to find money on the ground when they needed it, Jean finds many coins, but they are all worthless old pennies withdrawn from circulation (1338). Much of Jean's resentment toward Madame Simpson (also called Helen), his father's second wife, revolves around what he perceives to be her desire to rob him, his sister, and his mother of their rightful inheritance. Flanked by her two brothers, she is a classic evil stepmother straight out of a fairy tale. The penultimate scene in the play (scene 17) is a cathartic climax in which the elderly mother/grandmother figure sets up a tribunal and plays the dual roles of Justice and Vengeance. She exacts bloody revenge on the father, Mme Simpson, and the latter's two brothers before being transformed into a beautiful young woman who sings in triumph. Thus are the wayward father and his second family paid back for their wrongdoings toward Jean and his mother.

Language

Ionesco's theater ends as it began—in torrent of words that both interrogate and play with language. In marked contrast to the mutism of the anonymous characters of the previous two plays, Jean is extremely voluble: his speech echoes the verbosity and the concerns of the narrator of *The Hermit* (or of Ionesco himself, writing in his journals and essays). What is missing, however, is the coherence and rationality of either one, the poetic, articulate diction that marked the classic plays of Ionesco's middle period. One reason for this difference is Ionesco's expressed desire to reproduce more closely than ever before the incoherent language of dreams. As he told Bonnefoy about his use of dreams in earlier plays (specifically, in *A Stroll in the Air* and *Hunger and Thirst*), "In the plays I've just cited, I used oneiric images. Although I used them, however, I didn't probe them deeply enough. That is, those images were in fact remembered dreams, but the language accompanying them didn't have the incoherence—or the incoherent coherence—of dreams" (*ENT* 73). As he went on to tell Bonnefoy, he was trying at the time of the interview (1977) to transcribe directly what he saw, heard, and said in his dreams in the play he was writing (*Journeys Among the Dead*).

Certain passages of dialogue in the play revert to the automatized, frenetic wordplay of language gone wild that characterized Ionesco's earliest work. At the end of scene 6, for example, after Jean's second effort to impress his father with the brilliance of his life's work fails (when he has nothing but handfuls of dust to show), he delivers a nonsensical punning speech about "the defense of the Occident," thus confirming his father's earlier negative judgment that his work was nothing but meaningless mumbling. All of scene 10, in which Jean and six other characters are waiting for a bus, is a string of cliché-ridden non sequiturs and puns that sound as though they belonged in *The Bald Soprano,* with a similarly unnerving comic effect. What Ionesco said about the earlier play would be equally apt applied to this scene: "I ended up writing a comic play even though the feelings I was trying to convey were not comic at all. Several factors coalesced around this starting point: a feeling of the strangeness of the world, of people speaking a language I no longer knew, of ideas being emptied of their content, of gestures losing their meaning" (*ENT* 74). As in *Man With Bags,* the strangeness of language is also grounded in Ionesco's own experience of having to relearn Romanian, which appears in the play in the form of the books that Jean is unable to read and the father's language that he cannot understand.

In the climactic revenge scene (scene 17), Jean lays to rest the issues arising from his past through a ritual farewell to his family—the murder and banishment of the father and his second family, the triumphant apotheosis of the mother figure. The denouement that follows this resolution of a personalized psychodrama is a lengthy tirade delivered by a solitary character (either Jean or his representative). In many ways reminiscent of Lucky's manic soliloquy from Samuel Beckett's *Waiting for Godot,* this last outpouring is a meditation on the impossibility both of knowledge and expression through language. The speech begins and ends with "I don't know," a final admission of the futility of the search for truth and knowledge that had provided the structure for the last two plays. The speech is composed largely of striking images and distorted words that recall both the free association and automatic writing practiced by surrealists like André Breton and Philippe Soupault, and the disintegrating language of *The Bald Soprano.* Surfacing repeatedly and organizing this logorrhea is the paradoxical assertion of the ultimate failure of language to represent or to express: "None of this has anything to do with what I see. I don't have my language anymore. The more I say, the less I speak. The more I speak, the less I say" (1357–58); "While talking, I realize that words say things, but do things say words?" (1360).

The final "I don't know" of this play represents, in a sense, Ionesco's retreat from his thirty-year struggle with language (see chapter 1). His theater has come full circle since the initial assault on language's failure to signify in *The Bald Soprano*—through the faith in language evident in the plays of the middle period, ending finally with the playwright's withdrawal from the battlefield.

Notes

1. This splendid country resembles nothing so much as the ideal land described in Baudelaire's "L'Invitation au voyage," where "tout n'est qu'ordre et beauté,/ Luxe, calme et volupté" (there is nothing but order and beauty, luxury, calm and pleasure). Ionesco did undertake a doctoral thesis on Baudelaire.

2. The French text is more specific; it gives "good stone, real stone."

3. The French text gives "radiant columns and a burning altar."

4. In a review of the American premiere, one reviewer gave a vivid description of the effect of this invasive proliferation and acceleration: "As the suitcases accumulated, the floor became a mass of trapped dreams and debris from dreams—moving in squares, circles, accompanied by a sound track of horns blowing in a traffic jam." See *Educational Theater Journal* (March 1978): 122.

5. For an expanded discussion of this point, applied to Ionesco's work as a whole, see my article "Expressing the Inexpressible: Ionesco and the Struggle with Language."

CHAPTER EIGHT

Other Works and Conclusion

Ionesco's career has been even more Protean than the preceding seven chapters indicate. He is the author of many shorter sketches and radio plays, several film scenarios produced for both cinema and television, an opera libretto, several ballet scenarios, and a series of dialogues for an American textbook (*Mise en Train*).

Selected Shorter Plays

Ionesco has written many brief sketches for the theater. Following the relative success of *The Chairs* in 1952, Jacques Poliéri produced an evening of seven short sketches at the Théâtre de la Huchette in September 1953. Included in this evening were *Le Salon de l'automobile* (*The Motor Show*), first broadcast over radio in 1952, *Le Maître* (*The Leader*), and *La Jeune fille à marier* (*Maid to Marry*), along with four unpublished sketches. *The Motor Show* is an absurdist parody of the clichés, tactics, and language involved in purchasing an automobile, full of incongruous, comically deformed phrases and puns. In *Maid to Marry,* a man and woman exchange empty platitudes about modern life, after which the woman's daughter appears on stage; she is a virile looking man (played by Jacques Poliéri in the original production) who appears to be in her thirties. The mother says that she is ninety-three but that, since she owes them eighty years, she's only thirteen. *The Leader* resembles a very short, burlesque version of Beckett's *Waiting for Godot* (1953) in which the long-awaited character does appear; when he finally enters, he has no head.

This sketch anticipates the denunciation of fanaticism and mob tyranny that appeared later in plays like *The Killer* and *Rhinoceros*.

As Ionesco's fame and public acceptance grew, his work began to be commissioned: *Scene à quatre (Foursome)* was premiered at Gian Carlo Menotti's Spoleto Festival in Italy in 1959, and *Délire à deux (Frenzy for Two, or More)* premiered in 1962 as part of an evening of one-act plays under the collective title *Chemises de nuit* (Nightshirts). The former piece is a metatheatrical burlesque farce full of absurdist word play and barely contained violence. Three quarreling men end up fighting over a pretty woman, undressing and then dismembering her as she turns toward the audience to say that she agrees completely with them that the sketch is totally stupid. The violence of *Foursome* reappears in *Frenzy for Two,* in which a pair of lovers have an absurd, violent quarrel (over whether a tortoise and a snail are the same animal or not) in the midst of the escalating chaos and destruction of a civil war.

The year 1966 saw no fewer than five major productions of works by Ionesco in Paris. In addition to the premiere of *Hunger and Thirst* at the Comédie française, there was a reprise of *Frenzy for Two* in March, on a double bill with a one-act play entitled *La Lacune (The Oversight)* that had premiered the previous year at a regional theater, le Centre dramatique du sud-est. Jean-Louis Barrault, who had played the role of Bérenger in the original production of *Rhinoceros* and had become the director of the national theater at the Odéon, was the director. *The Oversight* is a light, amusing piece that portrays a famous, well-respected university professor who discovers late in his career that all his prestigious degrees and achievements are invalid because he never graduated from secondary school. In May, Antoine Bourseiller directed the premiere of *Le pied du mur (The Foot of the Wall)* at the Théâtre de poche-Montparnasse, on a bill with *Maid to Marry* and two works by Arrabal. This was the fourth episode that Ionesco had composed for *Hunger and Thirst* after the work premiered at the Comédie française; when performed with the rest of *Hunger and Thirst,* it becomes the third of four acts. In July, Bourseiller directed a series of amusing sketches entitled

Leçons de français pour Américains (French Lessons for Americans) at the Théâtre de poche-Montparnasse. These were seven of the dialogues that Ionesco had composed for Michel Benamou's introductory textbook *Mise en train,* performed by American students. These sketches were later expanded and published as *Exercices de conversation et de diction françaises pour étudiants américains* (Exercises in French conversation and diction for American students). In November Georges Vitaly directed another evening of ten short sketches under the collective title *Mêlées et démêlées.* Four of the dialogues from *Mise en train* were reprised, along with four previously performed sketches, an unpublished sketch entitled *Chocs,* and *Pour préparer un oeuf dur* (How to Cook a Hard-Boiled Egg), a monologue whose title is completely self-explanatory. The year ended with an acclaimed reprise of *Exit the King,* directed by Jacques Mauclair at the Théâtre de l'Athénée.

Scène is a highly polemical dialogue that reiterates Ionesco's lifelong commitment to the value of individual freedom and the horror of political repression. Like Samuel Beckett's *Catastrophe,* it was written for and performed at the 1982 Avignon Theater Festival in honor of then-jailed dissident playwright Vaçlav Havel, who was later to become president of Czechoslovakia. As Rosette Lamont notes in her translator's preface to *Scène,* this sketch proves that Ionesco "is not, as he claimed to be, an apolitical playwright but on the contrary a profoundly committed political thinker" (105).

Films

Ionesco has written a number of film scenarios. *L'Oeuf dur* (*The Hard-Boiled Egg*) is a pseudodocumentary about making hard-boiled eggs that frequently dissolves images of a young woman performing this task in her kitchen into surrealistic visions of hourglasses turning into women, white birds being shot out of the sky, and eyes that turn into blue sky. *La Colère* (*Anger*) was one of seven episodes in the 1962 film *Les Sept péchés capitaux* (The Seven Deadly Sins); in it, a meaningless argument between a young married couple escalates into the total destruction of the entire planet by floods, earthquakes, and atomic explosions. *La Vase* (*The Mire*) is a scenario produced for German television in 1970 by H. von Cramer; Ionesco himself played the only role. Narrated entirely in voice-over, *The Mire* portrays the contrast between light, joy, and evanescence and darkness, heaviness, and despair that recurs so often in Ionesco's theater. Filled with images reminiscent of those in *Victims of Duty, Hunger and Thirst,* and *Exit the King,* it ends with the character sinking and disappearing into the mud of a swamp. Ionesco also wrote the narration for an animated Polish film entitled *Monsieur Tête,* produced in 1959 by Jan Lenica; the film won the critics' prize at the Tours film festival that year.

Other Works

Given the number of plays in which passages of dialogue are designated to be sung rather than spoken, it is not surprising that Ionesco has written a libretto for an opera. *Maximilien Kolbe* is based on the same episode that inspired Rolf Hochhuth's *The Deputy*—the self-sacrifice of a Polish priest at Auschwitz in 1941. He has also written several ballet scenarios. *Apprendre à marcher* (*Learning How to Walk*) was performed in April 1960, by the Ballets modernes de Paris at the Théâtre de l'Etoile. It is an allegory based on rehabilitation of motor skills that includes a sun-drenched garden and a ladder leading off into infinity—symbols familiar to Ionescophiles. Other ballet scenarios include an adaptation of *The Lesson,* produced for television in 1962, *Le Jeune homme à marier* (The Young Man to Marry) (1965), and *Le Triomphe de la Mort* (The Triumph of Death) (1971). Ionesco's gift for humor and satire appear as well in the mock-epic parody of Victor Hugo entitled *Hugoliade* (1982), in his delightful series of four *Contes pour enfants* (Stories for Children) (1969–75), and in the volume of satiric essays published during his youth in Romania entitled *Nu* (No), published in Romanian in 1934 and in French in 1986.

It remains to be seen how Ionesco will be viewed by posterity. His career began in 1950, the start of a period of intense activity and exciting innovations in Parisian theater. Along with Arthur Adamov, Samuel Beckett, Jean Genet, and others, he helped launch the new theater that came to be known as Theater of the Absurd. Precisely because of his estrangement from and antipathy toward conventional theatrical forms and style, he brought a fresh, subversive talent that helped to revolutionize and invigorate theater during the 1950s. Notable among his contributions are the use of proliferating objects that displace the human domain; wickedly inventive assaults on the rigid, empty forms of language; and a performance style that confronts and provokes the audience directly. His best early plays have all the spontaneity, humor, and energy of Alfred Jarry, Dada, and surrealism.

Considered in the beginning an avant-garde iconoclast, thus reviled by critics on the right and praised by those on the left, he was later embraced by the establishment for his humanistic defense of the individual and rejected by the left for his stubborn refusal of ideology and his unwillingness to admit that his passionate defense of individual freedoms was itself an ideology. The mature works of the Bérenger cycle reflect both Ionesco's acceptance of "establishment" theater (these plays contain fully humanized characters; coherent plot and structure; and eloquent, literary language) and mainstream theater's acceptance of him. By the mid- to late-1960s, Ionesco could no longer be considered an innovator or a member of the avant-garde. Whereas his famous contemporary Beckett had continued to pursue experimentation in the direction of minimalist theater and elaboration of an Artaudian "concrete language of the stage," Ionesco was writing complex, literary pieces that relied more and more on elaborate staging and special effects. The near-revolution of May 1968 ("les évènements de mai") triggered an explosion of experimentation in French theater; the Living Theater disrupted the Avignon Theater Festival that year with its controversial *Paradise Now!*, and Ariane Mnouchkine had begun her work with the Théâtre du soleil. The theatrical avant-garde had become communal and collaborative, and Ionesco was definitively left behind as an innovator.

He is, of course, now firmly ensconced as one of the "Immortals" (the title awarded informally to the forty members of the Académie) by the fact of his election to the Académie française; and the many international prizes and awards he has won for his work, both in and outside of theater, confirm his importance. As of this writing, *The Bald Soprano* continues its run in Paris; along with *The Chairs, Rhinoceros,* and *Exit the King,* it has certainly achieved the status of a classic, destined to be performed and studied long into the future.

The startling political upheavals that have marked the 1990s, with the disintegration of the Soviet Union and the overthrow of one totalitarian regime after another in Eastern Europe, may indeed make Ionesco's militant denunciation of Marxist-Leninist thought sound prophetic. Yet the current dismal state of world affairs, in which fratricidal ethnic and nationalistic conflict seems to be the rule rather than the exception, offers little hope that any kind of permanent solution to the enduring problems facing humanity will ever come from political change. This condition seemingly confirms the apocalyptic vision that marks so much of Ionesco's work. As Ionesco told Bonnefoy, "History and politics try futilely to solve or to mask the fundamental problem of our condition, because they cannot answer these questions: What am I doing here? Why am I here? What is this world that surrounds me?" (*ENT* 195). Or, in the words of the Concierge from *A Hell of a Mess!,* "There is no 'good' society. Tyranny, dictatorship, liberalism, capitalism, all are no good" (109); "The era of revolutions is over, don't they know that? . . . They still make revolutions, but they don't serve any purpose. . . . It's the existential condition which is bad, very bad. . . . Let them blow themselves up. Let them massacre themselves. The human adventure has lasted long enough. Let it be over with and not worry us any longer" (112–13).

SELECT BIBLIOGRAPHY

Because publications by and about Ionesco number into the thousands, the following bibliography is highly selective, listing references only to major works. Reviews and interviews are, for the most part, omitted. Books written in languages other than English are omitted unless of special interest or value. With one exception, all articles listed are written in English. Readers interested in pursuing further research are referred to the bibliographies listed in part B.

A. Works by Eugène Ionesco

PLAYS (FRENCH EDITIONS)

Théâtre complet. Ed. Emmanuel Jacquart. Paris: Gallimard (Edition de la Pléiade), 1991. This is the definitive French edition of Ionesco's theater, with an exhaustive critical apparatus. In addition to all the plays previously published in the editions listed below, the volume contains two previously unpublished sketches (*La Nièce-Epouse* and *Le Vicomte*). Missing, however, are all the film scenarios, *Maximilien Kolbe* (an opera libretto), and the short piece *Scène*.
Théâtre I. Paris: Gallimard, 1954. (*La Cantatrice chauve; La Leçon; Jacques, ou la Soumission; Les Chaises; Victimes du devoir; Amédée, ou Comment s'en débarrasser.*)
Théâtre II. Paris: Gallimard, 1958. (*L'Impromptu de l'Alma, ou le Caméléon du berger; Tueur sans gages; Le Nouveau Locataire; L'Avenir est dans les oeufs, ou Il faut tout pour faire un monde; Le Maître; La Jeune Fille à marier.*)

Théâtre III. Paris: Gallimard, 1963. (*Rhinocéros; Le Piéton de l'air; Délire à deux; Le Tableau; Scene à quatre; Les Salutations; La Colère.*)

Théâtre IV. Paris: Gallimard, 1966. (*Le Roi se meurt; La Soif et la Faim; La Lacune; Le Salon de l'automobile; L'Oeuf dur; Pour préparer un oeuf dur; Le Jeune Homme à marier; Apprendre à marcher.*)

Théâtre V. Paris: Gallimard, 1974. (*Jeux de massacre; Macbett; La Vase; Exercices de conversation et de diction françaises pour étudiants américains.*)

L'Homme aux valises, suivi de Ce Formidable Bordel!. Paris: Gallimard, 1975.

Voyages chez les morts, ou Thèmes et variations. Théâtre VII. Paris: Gallimard, 1981.

PLAYS (ENGLISH EDITIONS)

Four Plays. Trans. Donald M. Allen. New York: Grove, 1958. (*Plays 1.* Trans. Donald Watson. London: Calder, 1958.) (*The Bald Soprano; The Lesson; Jack, or the Submission; The Chairs.*)

Amédée, The New Tenant, Victims of Duty. Trans. Donald Watson. New York: Grove, 1958. (*Plays 2.* London: Calder, 1958.)

The Killer and Other Plays. Trans. Donald Watson. New York: Grove, 1960. (*Plays 3.* London: Calder, 1960.) (*The Killer; Improvisation, or The Shepherd's Chameleon; Maid to Marry.*)

Rhinoceros and Other Plays. Trans. Derek Prouse. New York: Grove, 1960. (*Plays 4.* London: Calder, 1960.) (*Rhinoceros; The Leader; The Future is in Eggs, or It Takes All Sorts to Make a World.*)

Exit the King. Trans. Donald Watson. New York: Grove, 1963. (London: Calder, 1963). (*Plays 5.* Trans. Donald Watson. London: Calder, 1963). (*Exit the King, Foursome, The Motor Show.*)

A Stroll in the Air and Frenzy for Two, or More. Trans. Donald Watson. New York: Grove, 1965. (*Plays 6.* Trans. Donald Watson. London: Calder, 1965.)

Hunger and Thirst and Other Plays. Trans. Donald Watson. New York: Grove, 1969. (*Plays 7.* Trans. Donald Watson. London: Calder, 1968.) (*Hunger and Thirst, The Picture, Anger, Salutations.*)

Killing Game. Trans. Helen Gary Bishop. New York: Grove, 1974. (*Plays 8.* Trans. Donald Watson. London: Calder and Boyers, 1971.) (*Here Comes a Chopper, The Oversight, The Foot of the Wall.*)

Macbett. Trans. Charles Marowitz. New York: Grove, 1973. (*Plays 9*. Trans. Donald Watson. London: Calder and Boyers, 1973.) (*Macbett, The Mire, Learning How to Walk.*)

A Hell of a Mess!. Trans. Helen Gary Bishop. New York: Grove, 1975. (*Plays 10*. Trans. Donald Watson. London: Calder, 1976.) (*Oh What a Bloody Circus, The Hard-Boiled Egg.*)

Man With Bags. Trans. M.-F. Ionesco, adapted by Israel Horovitz. New York: Grove, 1977.

The Man with the Luggage, The Duel, Double Act. (*Plays 11*) Trans. Donald Watson and Clifford Williams. London: Calder, 1979.

Scene. Trans. (with introduction) Rosette Lamont. *Performing Arts Journal* 24 (1984): 105–12.

Journeys Among the Dead: Themes and Variations. (*Plays 12*) Trans. Barbara Wright. London: Calder (New York: Riverrun), 1985.

OTHER WORKS (FRENCH EDITIONS)

La Photo du Colonel. Paris: Gallimard, 1962. Short stories. ("Oriflamme," "Le Piéton de l'air," "Une victime du devoir," "Rhinocéros," "La Vase," "La Photo du Colonel," "Printemps 1939.")

Notes et Contre-notes. Paris: Gallimard, 1962. Rev. ed. 1966. (essays)

Entretiens avec Claude Bonnefoy. Paris: Belfond, 1966. An expanded, updated edition, with new interviews, was published in 1977 with the new title *Entre la Vie et le Rêve* (Paris: Belfond).

Journal en miettes. Paris: Mercure de France, 1967. (journal)

Présent passé. Passé présent. Paris: Mercure de France, 1968. (journal)

Découvertes. Geneva: Albert Skira, 1969. (essays and drawings)

Discours de réception d'Eugène Ionesco à l'Académie française et réponse de Jean Delay. Paris: Gallimard, 1971. (acceptance speech)

Le Solitaire. Paris: Mercure de France, 1973. (novel) (Citations in my text are taken from the excellent edition with introduction and notes by H. F. Brookes and C. E. Fraenkel [London: Heinemann, 1977].)

Antidotes. Paris: Gallimard, 1977. (essays)

Un Homme en question. Paris: Gallimard, 1979. (essays)

Le Noir et le blanc. St. Gall: Erker, 1981. (essays and drawings) Rpt. as *Le Blanc et le noir.* Paris: Gallimard, 1985.

Hugoliade. Trans. (from Romanian) D. Costineanu and M.-F. Ionesco. Paris: Gallimard, 1982.

Non. Trans. (from Romanian) M.-F. Ionesco. Paris: Gallimard, 1986. (essays) (*Nu* Bucharest: Vremea, 1934.)

La Quête intermittente. Paris: Gallimard, 1987. (journal)

OTHER WORKS (ENGLISH EDITIONS)

Notes and Counter Notes. Trans. Donald Watson. New York: Grove, 1964.

The Colonel's Photograph and Other Stories. Trans. Jean Stewart and John Russell. New York: Grove, 1967. ("Oriflamme," "The Colonel's Photograph," "The Stroller in the Air," "A Victim of Duty," "Rhinoceros," "The Slough," "Spring, 1939.")

Fragments of a Journal. Trans. Jean Stewart. London: Faber, 1968 (New York: Grove, 1968).

With Michel Benamou, *Mise en train.* New York and London: Macmillan, 1969. (A French language textbook for which Ionesco wrote the dialogues.)

Conversations with Eugène Ionesco. Trans. Jan Dawson. London: Faber, 1970.

Present Past Past Present: A Personal Memoir. Trans. Helen R. Lane. New York: Grove, 1971 (London: Calder and Boyers, 1972).

The Hermit. Trans. Richard Seaver. New York: Viking, 1974.

Maximilian Kolbe. Trans. (with introduction and notes) Rosette Lamont. *Performing Arts Journal* 17 (1982): 29–36. (opera libretto)

Hugoliad. Trans. (from French) Yara Milos. New York: Grove, 1987.

UNTRANSLATED FROM ROMANIAN

Elegii pentru fiinte mici. Craiova: Cercul Ananelora române, Scrisul Românesc, 1931. (poetry)

B. Bibliographies

Cabeen, David Clark, ed. *A Critical Bibliography of French Literature.* Vol. 6: *The Twentieth Century.* Ed. Douglas W. Alden and Richard A. Brooks. Syracuse: Syracuse UP, 1980. 3 vols. Vol. 3, chap. 38: 1837–64. Highly selective, evaluative, annotated by specialists on Ionesco. Cutoff date is 1977.

French XX Bibliography. Critical and Bibliographical References for the Study of French Literature since 1885. Vol. 5–. (no. 21–). New York: French Institute/Alliance française, 1969–. Continues *French VII* (1949–68). Published annually, not annotated.

Hughes, Griffith R., and Ruth Bury. *Eugène Ionesco: A Bibliography*. Cardiff: U of Wales P, 1974. Compiled to mark the occasion of the award to Ionesco of the International Writers' Prize by the Welsh Arts Council. Not annotated.

Klapp, Otto. *Bibliographie der französischen Literaturewissenschaft / Bibliographie d'histoire littéraire française*. Frankfurt am Main: V. Klostermann, 1960–. In French, not annotated, published annually.

Kyle, Linda Davis. "Eugène Ionesco: A Selective Bibliography, 1974–1978." *Bulletin of Bibliography* Vol. 37, no. 4 (1980): 167–84. Updates Hughes and Bury bibliography. Not annotated.

Leiner, Wolfgang. *Bibliographie et Index thématique des Etudes sur Eugène Ionesco*. Fribourg: Editions Universitaires Fribourg Suisse, 1980. Written in French; contains alphabetical listing of works on Ionesco, followed by two indexes to the works—an index of names and terms and an index of subjects and themes. Good source for interviews and for reviews of performances in the French and British press.

Modern Language Association of America. *MLA International Bibliography of Books and Articles on the Modern Languages and Literatures*. Vol. 2. General Romance, French. New York: MLA, 1921–. Annual, not annotated.

Rancoeur, René, ed. *Bibliographie de la littérature française du Moyen Age à nos jours*. Paris: A. Colin, 1967–. Comprehensive, not annotated, published annually.

See also the annual bibliography "Modern Drama Studies" published each year in the June issue (no. 2) of *Modern Drama* (Toronto: U of Toronto P). Not annotated.

C. Books: General and Comparative

Abel, Lionel. *Metatheatre: A New View of Dramatic Form*. New York: Hill and Wang, 1963. General treatment of the question of tragedy versus metatheater (reflexive, specular theater) in contemporary drama. No specific treatment of Ionesco, but useful for question of theater of the absurd.

Bradby, David. *Modern French Drama 1940–1980*. Cambridge: Cambridge UP, 1984. An excellent study that establishes historical, political, social, and literary background and context of postwar theater. Illustrated. Contains good bibliography and very useful chronology of production history of plays.

Cohn, Ruby. *From Desire to Godot: Pocket Theatre of Postwar Paris*. Berkeley and Los Angeles: U of California P, 1987. Excellent critical and historical study; good accounts of *The Bald Soprano, The Lesson,* and *The Chairs.*

Corvin, Michel. *Le Théâtre nouveau en France.* Paris: Presses universitaires de France, 1963. Rev. ed. 1987. In French. Concise but comprehensive study of playwrights and directors from 1950s to 1980s (in revised edition).

Dobrez, L. A. C. *The Existential and its Exits.* London: Athlone, 1986; New York: St. Martin's, 1986. Excellent study of philosophical aspects of Ionesco's theater in chapters 6, 7, 8 ("Ionesco and the Experience of Wonder" and two chapters on Ionesco and Heidegger). Many insightful examples taken from plays.

Duckworth, Colin. *Angels of Darkness: Dramatic Effect in Samuel Beckett with Special Reference to Eugène Ionesco.* London: Allen and Unwin, 1972; New York: Harper and Row, 1972. Comparative study.

Duvignaud, Jean, and Jean Lagoutte. *Le Théâtre contemporain: Culture et contre-culture.* Paris: Larousse, 1974. Emphasis on sociological analysis of major playwrights of 1950s and 1960s.

Esslin, Martin. *The Theatre of the Absurd.* New York: Doubleday, 1961 (London: Eyre and Spottiswoode, 1962); Rev. ed. London: Penguin, 1970, 1980; New York: Pelican, 1983. The seminal work that introduced the concept of theater of the absurd.

Gaensbauer, Deborah B. *The French Theater of the Absurd.* Twayne's World Authors Series 822. Boston: G. K. Hall, 1991. Very good follow-up and corrective to Esslin's *Theatre of the Absurd.* Contains very selective, briefly annotated bibliography.

Grossvogel, David. *Four Playwrights and a Postscript.* Ithaca: Cornell UP, 1962. Rev. ed. *The Blasphemers: The Theater of Brecht, Ionesco, Beckett and Genet.* Ithaca: Cornell UP, 1965. An early comparative work.

―――. *The Self-Conscious Stage in Modern French Drama.* New York: Columbia UP, 1958. With Abel, important early work on metatheater. Contains chapter on Ionesco.

Guicharnaud, Jacques, and June Beckelman. *Modern French Theatre from Giraudoux to Genet.* New Haven: Yale UP, 1961. Rev. ed. 1967. Brief chapter on Ionesco; contains useful list of first productions and revivals.

Hubert, Marie-Claude. *Langage et corps fantasmé dans le théâtre des années cinquante.* Paris: Jose Corti, 1987. In French. Sophisticated scholarly study of relation between language and body in Ionesco, Adamov, and Beckett. Includes interview with Ionesco.

Jacobsen, Josephine, and William R. Mueller. *Ionesco and Genet: Playwrights of Silence.* New York: Hill and Wang, 1968. Early comparative study.

Jacquart, Emmanuel. *Le Théâtre de dérision.* Paris: Gallimard, 1974. In French. Excellent, important studies of Ionesco, Beckett, and Adamov.

Norrish, Peter. *New Tragedy and Comedy in France, 1945–1970.* Totowa, N.J.: Barnes and Noble, 1988. Includes chapter on Ionesco.

Peter, John. *Vladimir's Carrot: Modern Drama and the Modern Imagination.* London: Deutsch, 1987; Chicago: Chicago UP, 1987. Solid study that reads plays (especially *Rhinoceros*) from a social rather than a metaphysical point of view.

Pronko, Leonard C. *Avant-garde: The Experimental Theater in France.* Berkeley and Los Angeles: U of California P, 1962. Influential early work.

Tynan, Kenneth. *Curtains: Selections from the Drama Criticism and Related Writings.* London: Longmans, 1961; New York: Atheneum, 1961. Reviews and essays. Includes pieces on *Amédée, The Bald Soprano, The New Tenant, The Chairs,* and *The Lesson.*

———. *Tynan Right & Left: Plays, Films, People, Places, and Events.* New York: Atheneum, 1967. Essays and reviews.

Vaïs, Michel. *L'Ecrivain scénique.* Montreal: Quebec UP, 1978. In French. Illustrated. Very useful analyses of collaboration between playwrights and directors. Contains interview with Ionesco.

Valency, Maurice. *The End of the World.* New York: Oxford UP, 1980. Sees Ionesco as a symbolist/surrealist; centers on Ionesco as a poet struggling with language. Contains some solid and some questionable readings of individual plays.

Wellwarth, George E. *The Theater of Protest and Paradox.* New York: New York UP, 1964. Rev. ed. 1966. Important early work with chapter on Ionesco.

Williams, Raymond. *Modern Tragedy.* London: Chatto and Windus, 1966; Stanford, Stanford UP, 1966. Rev. ed. Verso, 1979. Marxist-oriented analysis with some references to Ionesco compared to Chekhov, Pirandello, and Beckett.

Wulbern, Julian H. *Brecht and Ionesco: Commitment in Context.* Urbana, Chicago, and London: U of Illinois P, 1971. Solid, useful study of political aspect of Ionesco's theater.

D. Books: On Ionesco

Abastado, Claude. *Eugène Ionesco.* Paris: Bordas, 1971. In French. Good critical study. Includes interview with Ionesco, excerpts from reviews.

Benmussa, Simone. *Ionesco.* Paris: Editions Séghers, 1966. In French. Excellent study of early plays; often cited by other critics.

Coe, Richard. *Ionesco: A Study of His Plays.* Edinburgh and London: Oliver and Boyd, 1961. Rev. ed. London: Methuen, 1971. The best early study in English; bibliography and production data in revised edition.

Frickx, Robert. *Ionesco.* Paris: Fernand Nathan, 1974. In French. Excellent comprehensive study of works to 1974. Contains useful chronology, production data, bibliography. Preface by Ionesco.

Hayman, Ronald. *Eugène Ionesco.* London: Heinemann, 1972; New York: Ungar, 1972. Rev. ed. New York: Ungar, 1976. Contains some photographs, bibliography and some production data.

Hubert, Marie-Claude. *Eugène Ionesco.* Paris: Editions du seuil, 1990. In French. Excellent general study, written in close collaboration with Ionesco and his wife; contains many previously unpublished photographs and two interviews.

Lamont, Rosette C. *Ionesco's Imperatives.* Ann Arbor: University of Michigan Press, 1993. Excellent comprehensive study by the foremost scholar of Ionesco's work.

Lewis, Allan. *Ionesco.* Twayne's World Authors Series 239. New York: Twayne, 1972. Sketchy. Chronology contains some errors.

Saint-Tobi. *Eugène Ionesco, ou A la recherche du paradis perdu.* Paris: Gallimard, 1973. In French. Poetic, idiosyncratic reading.

Sénart, Philippe. *Ionesco.* Paris: Editions universitaires, 1964. In French. Early thematic study.

Tarrab, Gilbert. *Ionesco à coeur ouvert.* Montreal: Le Cercle du Livre de France, 1970. In French. Extended interviews with Ionesco.

Vernois, Paul. *La Dynamique théâtrale d'Ionesco.* Paris: Klincksieck, 1972. In French. Outstanding scholarly treatment of themes and style.

E. Collections

Ionesco, Marie-France, and Paul Vernois, eds. *Ionesco: Situation et perspectives.* Paris: Belfond, 1980. In French. These are the published proceedings of the international colloquium on Ionesco's works held at Cerisy-la-Salle in August 1978. Contains important essays by top scholars in the field (including Abastado, Eliade, Esslin, Jacquart, and Vernois).

Lamont, Rosette C., ed. *Ionesco: A Collection of Critical Essays.*
Twentieth Century Views 108. Englewood Cliffs, N.J.: Prentice-
Hall, 1973. Contains important essays by Doubrovsky, Schech-
ner, and Lamont, among others.
Lamont, Rosette C., and Melvin J. Friedman, eds. *The Two Faces of*
Ionesco. Troy, N.Y.: Whitston, 1978. A very valuable volume of
excellent essays, including those by Mircea Eliade and Robert
Champigny and two by Lamont. Includes an essay by Ionesco
and a good bibliography.
Lazar, Moshe, ed. *The Dream and the Play: Ionesco's Theatrical*
Quest. Malibu, Calif.: Undena, 1982. These are the published
proceedings of the symposium on Ionesco's works held at the
University of Southern California in the spring of 1980, while
Ionesco was artist in residence there. Contains important essays
by leading scholars (including Coe, Esslin, Wellwarth, Jacquart,
and Lamont) along with an essay by Ionesco ("Culture and
Politics") and three previously unpublished "dreams to be staged
eventually" which he had omitted from *Voyages chez les morts.*
Morris, Kelly, ed. *Genet/Ionesco: The Theatre of the Double. A*
Critical Anthology. New York: Bantam, 1969. Contains good
essays by Esslin, Schechner, and Jean Vannier.

F. Special Issues of Journals

L'Avant-Scène théâtre 373/74 (February 1967).
Cahiers Renaud-Barrault 29 (February 1960); 42 (February 1963);
53 (February 1966); 97 (January 1978)
Cahiers des Saisons 15 (Winter 1959).
Modern Drama 25 (December 1982).
Tulane Drama Review (TDR) 7 (Spring 1963).

G. General and Comparative Articles

Brée, Germaine. "Ionesco's Later Plays: Experiments in Dramatic
Form." In Lamont and Friedman, eds., *Two Faces* 101–18.
Coe, Richard. "Eugène Ionesco and the Tragic Farce." *Proceedings*
of the Leeds Philosophical and Literary Society 8 (1962): 219–35.
———. "On Being Very, *Very* Surprised . . . Eugène Ionesco and the
Vision of Childhood." In Lazar, ed., *The Dream and the Play*
1–19.
———. "Utopia and After." In Lamont, ed., *Ionesco* 135–53.
Cohn, Ruby. "Bérenger, protagonist of an Anti-Playwright." *Modern*
Drama 8 (1965): 127–33.

Corrigan, Robert W. "The Theatre of Ionesco: The Ghost and Primal Dialogue." In Lazar, ed., *The Dream and the Play* 49–61.

Craddock, George E. "Escape and Fulfillment in the Theatre of Ionesco." *Southern Quarterly* 10 (1971): 15–22.

DeFuria, Richard. "At the Intersection of Freud and Ionesco." *Modern Language Notes (MLN)* 87 (1972): 971–76.

Demaitre, Ann. "The Idea of Commitment in Brecht's and Ionesco's Theories of the Theatre." *Symposium* 22 (1968): 215–23.

Doubrovsky, J. S. "Ionesco and the Comic of Absurdity." *Yale French Studies* 23 (1959): 3–10. Rpt. in Lamont, ed., *Ionesco* 11–20.

Dukore, Bernard. "The Theatre of Ionesco: A Union of Form and Substance." *Educational Theater Journal* 13 (1961): 174–81.

Edney, David. "The Family and Society in the Plays of Ionesco." *Modern Drama* 28 (1985): 377–87.

Esslin, Martin. "Ionesco and the Fairytale Tradition." In Lazar, ed., *The Dream and the Play* 22–31.

Grossvogel, David. "Ionesco: Symptom and Victim." In Lazar, ed., *The Dream and the Play* 81–92.

Jacquart, Emmanuel. "Ionesco's Political Itinerary." In Lazar, ed., *The Dream and the Play* 63–80.

Karampetsos, E. D. "Ionesco and the Journey of the Shaman." *Journal of Evolutionary Psychology* 4 (1983): 64–77.

Kott, Jan. "Ionesco, or a Pregnant Death." In Lazar, ed., *The Dream and the Play* 121–34.

Lamont, Rosette C. "Eugène Ionesco and the Metaphysical Farce." In Lamont, ed., *Ionesco* 154–83.

———. "The Metaphysical Farce: Beckett and Ionesco." *French Review* 32 (1959): 319–28.

———. "The Proliferation of Matter in Ionesco's Plays." *L'Esprit créateur* 2 (1962): 189–97.

———. "The Topography of Ionescoland." *Modern Occasions* 1 (1971): 536–46.

———. "Yesterday's Avant-Garde, Today's Great Classics: Beckett, Ionesco, Tardieu." *Laurels* (American Society of the French Legion of Honor) 56 (1985): 37–56.

Lane, Nancy. "Expressing the Inexpressible: Ionesco and the Struggle with Language." *Postscript* 8 (1991): 1–7.

———. "Human/Non-human Relationships in Ionesco's Theatre: Conflict and Collaboration." *Kentucky Romance Quarterly* 30 (1983): 239–50.

Lazar, Moshe. "The Psychodramatic Stage: Ionesco and his Doubles." In Lazar, ed., *The Dream and the Play* 135–59.

Leyburn, Ellen Douglas. "Comedy and Tragedy Transposed." *Yale Review* 53 (1964): 553–62.

Martin, George. "Bérenger and his Counterpart in *La Photo du colonel.*" *Modern Drama* 17 (1974): 189–97.

Newberry, J. K. "The Evolution of the Dramatic Technique of Eugène Ionesco." *Nottingham French Studies* 14 (1975): 31–41.

Pronko, Leonard C. "The Anti-Spiritual Victory in the Theater of Ionesco." *Modern Drama* 2 (1959): 29–35.

Roberts, Patrick. "Ionesco: Paroxysm and Proliferation." In his *The Psychology of Tragic Drama.* London and Boston: Routledge and Kegan Paul, 1975: 102–26.

Schechner, Richard. "The Inner and the Outer Reality." *TDR* 7 (1963): 187–17.

Sontag, Susan. "Ionesco." In her *Against Interpretation and Other Essays.* New York: Farrar, Straus and Giroux, 1966: 115–23.

Straus, Todd. "Being-as-Actor in Ionesco and Genet: A Psycho-Theatrical Reading." *French Forum* 10 (1985): 97–108.

Strem, George G. "Ritual and Poetry in Eugène Ionesco's Theatre." *Texas Quarterly* 5 (1962): 149–58.

Swanson, Roy Arthur. "Ionesco's Classical Absurdity." In Lamont and Friedman, eds., *Two Faces* 119–53.

Tener, Robert L. "These Places. This Private Landscape. First Suggestions for a Topological Approach to Ionesco's Bérenger Plays." *Papers on Language and Literature* 13 (1977): 319–40.

———. "Scenic Metaphors: A Study of Ionesco's Geometrical Vision of Human Relationships in the Bérenger Plays." *Papers on Language and Literature* 23 (1987): 175–91.

Thomson, Peter. "Games and Plays: An Approach to Ionesco." *Educational Theater Journal* 22 (1970): 60–70.

Tookey, Mary D., Scott Woolridge, and Linda M. Tookey. "Pseudo-Psychotic Language in Experimental Theater." *Midwest Quarterly* 29 (1988): 171–93.

Vannier, Jean. "A Theatre of Language." Trans. Leonard C. Pronko. *Tulane Drama Review* 7 (1963): 180–86.

Wellwarth, George E. "Beyond Realism: Ionesco's Theory of the Drama." In Lazar, ed., *The Dream and the Play* 34–47.

Whitton, David. "*Ecriture Dramatique* and *Ecriture Scénique:* Two Playwrights' Points of View (Ionesco and Arrabal)." *Theatre Research International* 6 (1981): 124–37.

Witt, Mary Ann. "Ionesco and the Dialectic of Space." *Modern Language Quarterly* 33 (1972): 312–26.

H. Articles on Specific Works

THE BALD SOPRANO AND *THE LESSON*

Messenger, Theodore. "Who was that lady . . .? The Problem of Identity in *The Bald Soprano* of Eugène Ionesco." *North Dakota Quarterly* 36, no. 2 (1968): 5–20.

Schechner, Richard. "*The Bald Soprano* and *The Lesson:* An Inquiry into Play Structure." In Lamont, ed., *Ionesco* 21–37.

Takvorian, Richard, and Michael Spingler. "Sounding Ionesco: Problems in Translating *La Leçon* and *Jacques*." *Comparative Drama* 17 (1983): 40–54.

THE CHAIRS

Champigny, Robert. "Designation and Gesture in *The Chairs*." In Lamont and Freidman, eds., *Two Faces* 155–74.

Coleman, Ingrid. "Memory into 'Message': The Forgetting of the Myth of Origins in Ionesco's *Les Chaises*." *Perspectives on Contemporary Literature* 9 (1983): 60–68.

Harty, Kevin J. "Ionesco and Semiramis." *College Language Association Journal* 31 (1987): 170–77.

Klaver, Elizabeth. "The Play of Language in Ionesco's Play of Chairs." *Modern Drama* 32 (1989): 521–31.

Mendelson, David. "Science and Fiction in Ionesco's Experimental Theatre: An Interpretation of *The Chairs*." In Lamont, ed., *Ionesco* 94–98.

Schechner, Richard. "The Enactment of the 'Not' in Ionesco's *Les Chaises*." *Yale French Studies* 29 (1962): 65–72.

Tolpin, Marian. "Ionesco's *The Chairs* and the Theater of the Absurd." *American Image* 25 (1968): 119–39.

Williams, Edith W. "God's Share: A Mythic Interpretation of *The Chairs*." *Modern Drama* 12 (1969): 298–307.

VICTIMS OF DUTY

Chambers, Ross. "Detached Committal: Eugène Ionesco's *Victims of Duty*." *Meanjin Quarterly* 22 (1963): 22–33.

Dickinson, Hugh. "Eugène Ionesco: The Existential Oedipus." In his *Myth on the Modern Stage*. Urbana: U of Illinois P, 1969: 310–31. Rpt. in Lamont, ed., *Ionesco* 99–119.

Fletcher, John. "A Psychology Based on Antagonism: Ionesco, Pinter, Albee and Others." In Lamont and Friedman, eds., *Two Faces* 175–95.

Mast, Gerald. "The Logic of Illogic: Ionesco's *Victims of Duty.*" *Modern Drama* 13 (1970): 133–38.

AMÉDÉE

Donnard, Jean-Hervé. "*Amédée:* A Caricatural Ionesco." In Lamont, ed., *Ionesco* 38–54.

Kyle, Linda Davis. "The Grotesque in *Amédée, or How to Get Rid of it.*" *Modern Drama* 19 (1976): 281–89.

IMPROVISATION

Ronge, Peter. "Ionesco's *L'Impromptu de l'Alma:* A Satire of Parisian Theater Criticism." In Lamont, ed., *Ionesco* 120–34.

THE KILLER

Parish, Richard J. "Ionesco's *Tueur sans gages:* A Pascalian Reading." *Nottingham French Studies* 15, no. 2 (1976): 36–47.

Purdy, Strother B. "A Reading of Ionesco's *The Killer.*" *Modern Drama* 10 (1968): 416–23.

RHINOCEROS

Cryle, P. M. "Refusing to Go Down: *Rhinoceros* and *Le Piéton de l'air.*" In his *The Thematics of Commitment: The Tower and the Plain*. Princeton: Princeton UP, 1985: 295–331.

Lamont, Rosette C. "The Hero in Spite of Himself." *Yale French Studies* 29 (1962): 73–81.

EXIT THE KING

Barranger, M. S. "Death as Initiation in *Exit the King.*" *Educational Theater Journal* 27 (1975): 504–7.

Lamont, Rosette C. "The Double Apprenticeship: Life and the Process of Dying." In *The Phenomenon of Death*. Ed. Edith Wyschogrod. New York: Harper and Row, 1973: 198–224.

Tucker, Warren. "*Le Roi se meurt* et *Les Upanishads.*" *French Review* 49 (1976): 397–400. In French.

Wright, Elizabeth G. "The Vision of Death in Ionesco's *Exit the King.*" *Soundings* 54 (1971): 435–49.

A STROLL IN THE AIR

Gerrard, Charlotte. "Bergsonian Elements in Ionesco's *Le Piéton de l'air.*" *Papers on Language and Literature* 9 (1973): 302–22.
Guicharnaud, Jacques. "Ionesco Ex Machina." In Lamont, ed., *Ionesco* 55–61.
Lamont, Rosette C. "Air and Matter: Ionesco's *Le Piéton de l'air* and *Victimes du devoir.*" *French Review* 38 (1965): 349–61.

HUNGER AND THIRST

Ferlita, Ernest. *"Hunger and Thirst."* In his *The Theatre of Pilgrimage.* London: Sheed and Ward, 1971: 11–25.
Simches, Seymour. "The Mythic Quest in Ionesco's *Hunger and Thirst.*" *Journal of Evolutionary Psychology* 5 (1984): 237–43.

KILLING GAME

Michat-Dietrich. "The Massacre of Ionesco's *Jeux de massacre,* or Pitfalls in Translation." *Translation Review* 6 (1980): 20–24.
Sharp, Corona. "The Dance of Death in Modern Drama: Auden, Durrenmatt and Ionesco." *Modern Drama* 20 (1977): 107–16.

MACBETT

Benston, Alice. "From Ubu to Macbett: A Requiem for Theatre of the Absurd." *Genre* 16 (1983): 157–73.
Kamenish, Paula K. "Ionesco's Own *Ubu.*" *Postscript* 8 (1991): 9–16.
Kern, Edith. "Ionesco and Shakespeare. *Macbeth* on the Modern Stage." *South Atlantic Bulletin* 39 (1974): 3–16.
Lamont, Rosette C. "From *Macbeth* to *Macbett.*" *Modern Drama* 15 (1972): 231–53.

THE HERMIT AND *A HELL OF A MESS!*

Alvarez-Detrell, Tamara. *"Le Solitaire:* Ionesco's Ambiguous Answer to his Theatre." *Language Quarterly* 24 (Spring-Summer 1986): 51–53.

Suther, Judith D. "Ionesco's Symbiotic Pair: *Le Solitaire* and *Ce Formidable Bordel!.*" *French Review* 49 (1976): 689–702.

MAN WITH BAGS

Gaensbauer, Deborah B. "Dreams, Myth, and Politics in Ionesco's *L'Homme aux valises.*" *Modern Drama* 28 (1985): 388–96.

Lamont, Rosette C. *"L'Homme aux valises:* Ionesco's Absolute Stranger." *Performing Arts Journal* 2 (1976): 21–36. Rpt. in Lamont and Friedman, eds., *Two Faces* 247–67.

JOURNEYS AMONG THE DEAD

Lamont, Rosette C. *"Journey to the Kingdom of the Dead:* Ionesco's Gnostic Dream Play." In Lazar, ed., *The Dream and the Play* 93–119.

INDEX

842.914 Lane, Nancy.
LAN
        Understanding Eugene
        Ionesco.

                                        38388
$34.95